Mechanisms of
Motivation

A Text Workbook and Student's Manual

Georg Schulze
Michael-Roy Mariano

The University of British Columbia

National Library of Canada Cataloguing in Publication

Schulze, Georg

      Mechanisms of motivation / Georg Schulze, Michael Roy Tan Mariano.

Includes bibliographical references and index.

ISBN 1-4120-1230-9

      1. Motivation (Psychology) I. Mariano, Michael Roy Tan, 1978- II. Title.

BF503.S37 2004   153.8   C2003-904843-8

TRAFFORD

This book was published on-demand in cooperation with Trafford Publishing.
On-demand publishing is a unique process and service of making a book available for retail sale to the public taking advantage of on-demand manufacturing and Internet marketing. On-demand publishing includes promotions, retail sales, manufacturing, order fulfilment, accounting and collecting royalties on behalf of the author.

Suite 6E, 2333 Government St., Victoria, B.C. V8T 4P4, CANADA
Phone 250-383-6864   Toll-free 1-888-232-4444 (Canada & US)
Fax   250-383-6804   E-mail   sales@trafford.com
Web site www.trafford.com   TRAFFORD PUBLISHING IS A DIVISION OF TRAFFORD HOLDINGS LTD.
Trafford Catalogue #03-1608   www.trafford.com/robots/03-1608.html
10   9   8   7   6   5   4   3

Contents

Preface

PART I

ORGANISM, ENVIRONMENT, AND ADAPTATION

PART II

THE MECHANISMS THAT GENERATE DRIVES
Basic Mechanisms

PART II (continued)
THE MECHANISMS THAT GENERATE DRIVES
Advanced Mechanisms

PART III
The Mechanisms that Generate Goals

21 PROCESS CONTROL   21-1

PART IV
THE INTEGRATION OF TOPICS

22 A THEORY OF BEHAVIOR   22-1

Index

Student s manual

Preface

T his book is primarily for upper-division undergraduates and beginning graduate students in Psychology Departments and those with an interest in understanding the origin and nature of motivated behaviors and attending issues. We provide, along with an overview, explanations of our topic, our approach, and our ultimate objectives below.

THE TOPIC

In its most rudimentary form, a motivated behavior can be seen as an action that results from the presence of a "drive". Typically, the action taken is an attempt to reduce the drive. The drive is often associated with a goal. In particular, the external conditions and/or internal (e.g. physiological or psychological) states which obtain when the drive has been dissipated, constitute the goal of motivated behaviors. Achieving the goal thus reduces the drive. Motivational psychology, therefore, is the study of goals, drives, and the actions associated with these.

OUR APPROACH

In this book, we will look at factors that can account for the generation of drives, we will investigate the creation of "goals", and analyze the mechanisms that produce motivated behaviors. Throughout, we will closely examine the connection between an organism (cell, animal, human, or organization) and its environment, and how the interactions between these two agents influence the generation and execution of motivated behaviors. This analysis will highlight motivated behaviors as sophisticated behavioral attempts to achieve equilibrium between an organism and its environment. Throughout, we will approach motivational psychology from a mechanistic perspective - a perspective that will keep us focused on cause and effect. Our emphasis in this work is not so much on imparting *fact* to the reader, others have done so with great clarity and scope, but rather to encourage the development of *skills* that could be used for the interpretation of facts. In this respect perhaps, the approach is a unique one in motivational psychology.

AN OVERVIEW

Our study of motivation will proceed along the following path:

1. The relationship between an organism and its environment will be established. This would allow us to see the purpose and benefits of motivated behaviors in a larger context. All of the material in Part I of this book is intended to show the interplay between an organism in search of balance with its environment and that very environment, and the complexities that arise from these interactions, especially when the environment contains other organisms engaged in the same pursuits.

2. We shall then investigate the mechanisms producing drives and motivated behaviors and use control theory as a model. The fundamental concepts will be discussed in the lectures on homeostatic mechanisms. These concepts will then be applied to an understanding of hunger and thirst. An essential aspect of motivated behavior is the generation of hedonic states, and these advanced mechanisms will also be discussed in some detail in Part II of this book.

3. Following the discussion of the mechanisms generating drives and motivated behaviors, we will turn our attention to goals, the formation of goals, and the role of goals in executing motivated behaviors. This requires an understanding of neural networks and their computational abilities. We will therefore, in Part III, turn our attention to artificial neural networks, which are models of naturally occurring ones, their structures and operation, and the implications for goals, goal formation, and motivated behaviors that can be drawn from them.

4. Finally, in Part IV of the book, we will integrate the various topics covered in the preceding sections of the book to generate a General Theory of Motivated Behaviors, and discuss them with reference to Living Systems Theory. In particular, we will assemble the mechanisms discussed in previous chapters into an overall framework to explain and predict motivated behaviors. In essence, we will attempt to construct a conceptual 'robot' to see the extent to which it could mimic, in principle, real motivated behaviors. Although one can examine the various ways in which motivation could fail by investigating the consequences of systematically disabling the constituent components of every mechanism making up the system, and the reader is encouraged to do so, we conclude this book with a look at the failure of the motivational system as it relates to eating disorders.

A RECOMMENDATION

Readers are strongly encouraged to read the chapter where all the concepts are integrated soon and periodically after even though it may be rather unintelligible initially. Especially when the point of a chapter in Parts II or III of this text is unclear in the overall scheme of things, attempting to place it in the context of the integrative chapter would prove to be very helpful. It would also gradually enable the reader to tightly integrate all the information, concepts, and ideas communicated in this course, into a coherent entity.

OUR OBJECTIVES

The reader will frequently be introduced to basic principles and concepts and then be encouraged to engage in some *gedanken* experiments. The purpose of these hypothetical experiments or conceptual tasks is to gain an understanding of the possible ways in which the introduced concepts could be manipulated, to develop an understanding of what could be possible or likely given the data at hand, to hone skills of judicious selection between the possibilities, and, ultimately, so to understand the material and its implications. We hope, then, to exercise the reader's creative abilities in a reasoned and disciplined manner, and that the efforts will continue to bear fruits long after the tasks have been completed.

Georg Schulze and Michael-Roy Mariano

Vancouver, 2003

PART I
THE CONTEXT OF MOTIVATED BEHAVIORS

CHAPTER 1
Organism, environment, and adaptation

Some definitions of motivated behavior

It has been pointed out by many others that definitions of motivation abound and that they are linked to the particular point of view of the author. We wish to encourage the reader to formulate her/his own impromptu definition of motivated behavior to act as a partial safeguard against being biased by the views espoused here, and to record it for the benefit of later reference.

Definition of motivation/motivated behavior

Behaviour that is a means to an end which benefits the organism.

For the purposes of this treatment of motivated behavior, the following 2 definitions are given. They are important because we will attempt - among other things - to determine the role that goals play in the generation of motivated behaviors. *All motivated behaviors are considered to be goal-oriented behaviors. These are either: 1. Goal-directed behaviors, which include the explicit postulation of an internal representation of the goal to be achieved; or 2. Goal-seeking behaviors, which require no internal representation of the goal, but occurs because the organism is constituted such that its behavior is optimal given its environment. That is, a trade-off occurs between competing priorities* (see McFarland, 1989). Some obvious and interesting questions regarding these definitions now are: (a) whether all motivated behaviors can be exclusively accommodated under one of these definitions; and if not, (b) in what proportions are they accommodated.

A classification of behaviors

In order to orient ourselves, we need to establish the position of motivated behaviors relative to other behaviors. We shall loosely define "behavior" as the action (e.g. eating) or inaction (e.g. sleeping), mediated by the body and instigated by the mind, of a living organism. Under "body" we shall understand the interarticulated and interconnected physical units that comprise a self-replicating organism, and under "mind", a subunit of the body consisting of innate psychological mechanisms. It follows then that behaviors are produced by the operation of psychological mechanisms.

Let us now partition the set of all possible behaviors into the following categories:

1. Reflexes - these are simple, characteristic, involuntary motions performed upon interaction with stimuli. Reflexes generally occur in response to aspects held in common by stimuli. They are the most rigid of behaviors. It seems possible and necessary to define reflexes, a definition that could draw on the number of synaptic transmissions or the degree of parallel processing involved, but doing so falls outside of the scope of this introduction.

2. Fixed action patterns - these can be seen as a sequence of reflexes, a more complex behavior which occurs upon interaction with aspects specific to some stimuli. Stimuli that trigger fixed action patterns are recognized by hard wiring (that is, organisms are born with the ability to respond to them).

3. Imprinted behaviors - these can be seen as sequences of fixed action pattern-like behaviors occurring in response to various stimuli, the recognition of which is not hard-wired but learned. these behaviors are more plastic.

4. Goal-oriented behaviors - "imprinting" of actions that develop in response to interactions with varying stimuli. These actions are learned based on the 'punishment' and 'reward' experienced. They are the most plastic of behaviors.

The reader should be aware of the fact that psychologists could find the descriptions of the above categories very objectionable and he or she may wish to consider alternatives suitable for the same task. In particular, the categories would be considered "oversimplifications" of reality. We shall, however, for the present maintain our systematic approach and the categories as given above in order to establish a point of departure, while noting the following: (a) the categories consist of behaviors that become progressively more complex; (b) we assume that this complexity comes about due to the fact that modification or intervention could occur at the points where simple behaviors are linked to one another to form more complex ones. (Think of a behavior as a chain of reflexes - then modifications or interventions can occur at every link in the chain.); and (c) although motivated behaviors form the last category, it may be possible to identify one or more categories of behavior that are more plastic and complex than motivated behaviors. For the time being, all the behaviors more complex than imprinted behaviors shall be lumped under the heading of "motivated behaviors".

It is of further interest to note that the latter categories contain behaviors produced by domain general mechanisms while the former contain behaviors produced by domain specific mechanisms. Domain general mechanisms are those capable of addressing general conditions. For instance, a family doctor or general practitioner is a domain general physician capable of dealing with all sorts of afflictions and a 4x4 vehicle is a domain general vehicle, capable of motion across all sorts of terrain. Domain specific mechanisms are limited to a specific area but are often more efficient in that area than domain general mechanisms. A medical specialist is a domain specific physician trained to deal with very specific diseases and a formula 1 racing car is a domain specific vehicle, not capable of motion across rough terrain. Although a 4x4 is also capable of driving on a race track, a racing car is far more efficient at this task. Thus, domain general mechanisms are capable of performing a variety of tasks, while domain specific mechanisms are capable of performing only a specific task, but does so more efficiently than a domain general mechanism could on the same task.

Environmental determination of behavioral categories

Because an organism has to interact in an adaptive manner with its environment, the information in the environment has to be processed by the organism's psychological mechanisms. The amount and nature of information in the environment varies from niche (subenvironment) to niche. In a sense, we can view evolution via natural selection as defining information processing problems that an organism must be able to solve. Therefore, some authors argue (e.g. Tooby and Cosmides, 1989), organisms, especially humans, have developed in addition to whatever domain general mechanisms they may possess, also many domain specific or special-purpose psychological mechanisms to deal with these information processing problems. An understanding of behavior, including motivated behavior, thus requires analysis of these innate psychological mechanisms. Consequently, an understanding of these innate psychological domain-specific mechanisms is facilitated by an understanding of the environmental niche within which they arose. That is, understanding the adaptive problems the organismic mind was designed to solve is a great aid to discovering how it works. We would state things somewhat in reverse. Domain general mechanisms may be more complex than domain specific mechanisms. Then one could argue that domain specific mechanisms developed first and domain general mechanisms later. An organism with only domain specific mechanisms may be limited to a particular evolutionary niche, while one with some domain general mechanisms in addition may be much more capable of adaptation to many niches. Either way, an understanding of the environmental niche in which an organism developed would help in understanding the psychological mechanisms needed to produce adaptive behaviors in that niche.

Let us partition the information processing problems posed by a particular niche into categories as we did for behaviors earlier on. This partitioning is rather more arbitrary than that of behaviors, but should make qualitative sense. For this purpose, think of an environmental niche as consisting of an empty cage which may contain a number of stimuli. An organism is placed in this environmental niche and has to successfully interact with these stimuli in order to survive in this particular environment.

1. Very simple stimuli (VSS) - these are stimuli that occur in the same place and the same time, or, if they occur randomly, have the same (limited) properties on every occurrence.

2. Moderately simple stimuli (MSS) - these are stimuli that occur with slight variations in time and position, or in properties.

3. Moderately complex stimuli (MCS) - these are stimuli that occur with greater variation with regard to time, place and properties. They may also include clusters of stimuli that occur with some regularity and in fixed association.

4. Highly complex stimuli (HCS) - these include stimuli that exhibit complex patterns of occurrence and complex patterns of association with other stimuli.

We now argue that an organism which lives in an environment containing only VSS, needs only simple behaviors, that is reflexes, in order to cope with its environment. It could also cope in this environment if it had domain general psychological mechanisms, but these mechanisms are more costly in energy terms to produce and operate than domain specific mechanisms, hence such an organism would be less efficient than one that contains only the necessary domain specific mechanisms to cope with the stimuli in its environment. If the environment contains both VSS and MSS, the organism now requires simple and more complex psychological mechanisms to produce reflexes and fixed action patterns. Taken to its logical conclusion, we hold that an organism needs as many innate psychological mechanisms, but no more, of the required level of complexity to most efficiently produce adaptive behaviors in its given environment.

We can state this more quantitatively, but with some interpretative license. If 60% of the stimuli in the environment are VSS, 20% are MSS, 15% are MCS and 5% are HCS, then we would expect that 60% of innate psychological mechanisms produce reflexes, 20% produce fixed action patterns, 15% produce imprinted behaviors, and 5% produce motivated behaviors. Hence if an environment changes such that the proportions of the different categories of stimuli change, then the number of innate psychological mechanisms producing the required behaviors should also change *to the same proportions*. When the population does, its members are considered to be fully adapted to the new environment. Figure 1.01 illustrates this relationship.

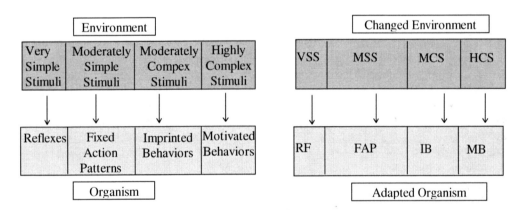

Figure 1.01

The relationship between a population of organisms and their environment. If the organisms are well-adapted to their environment, their collection of innate psychological mechanisms will reflect behaviors suitable for dealing with the subsets of stimuli in their environments. Should the environment then change in terms of the proportions of its stimulus subsets, the population will evolve to eventually reflect the new conditions.

It is important to note here that the environment could change suddenly to produce different proportions of stimuli of the various categories, but that an organism (more correctly, a population of organisms) may take time to acquire the necessary innate psychological mechanisms. If an organism is therefore studied and found to have mechanisms that do not conform to the dictates of the environment, it may simply reflect the fact that the (population of) organisms have not had enough time to adapt to the new circumstances. This, we shall hold, does not necessarily invalidate our view that the collection of innate psychological mechanisms must track and reflect environmental conditions.

Evolution of innate psychological mechanisms

Innate psychological mechanisms are changed through the process of evolution. This causes new mechanisms that produce adaptive behaviors to come into existence and old mechanisms that produce behaviors that are no longer relevant to be eliminated. Evolution proceeds via the following processes:

1. Genetic inheritance - this process produces the conservation of traits across generations, that is, the offspring inherit the characteristics of the parents.

2. Genetic mutation - this process produces the "random" emergence of new mechanisms and the "random" deletion of existing mechanisms in some individuals. Mutation may also "randomly" modify existing mechanisms. We have put "random" in quotation marks because we suspect that the number and nature of mutations that occur are to some degree actually determined by the changes that occur in the environment (Schulze and Mori, 1993).

3. Competition between individuals - this process causes the individual best "fitted" to its environment to be more likely to survive and leave offspring behind. The process of determining which organism is the best adapted to its environment is known as natural selection. We hold that the most fit organism would be the one that possesses the appropriate number and type of innate psychological mechanisms to produce the most efficient adaptive behaviors in its environment.

Aboitiz (1989) and others suggest that habits represent an adaptive way in which organisms behave in their environment. Those organisms with morphologies that enable the better execution of an adaptive habit will have the better chance of survival. This stabilizes the behavior or habit. In this view of evolution, behavior "drives" the morphological evolution because there would be selection for those bodies that facilitate the adaptive behaviors. Others think that developmental and genetic constraints are more important in directing morphological evolution.

According to Tooby and Cosmides (1989), the causal link between evolution and behavior is made through the psychological mechanism.

Evolution → Psychological Mechanism → Behavior

The evolutionary analysis of behavior therefore requires the evolutionary analysis of psychological mechanisms. This approach they termed "evolutionary psychology". Natural selection, they claim, cannot select for behavior directly, it can only select for mechanisms that produce behavior. Our approach here follows this general idea, but we note that organisms survive based on the behaviors that they exhibit in an environment. These behaviors are produced by psychological mechanisms. We hold then that natural selection acts directly at the level of behavior and indirectly at the level of mental mechanisms.

Tooby and Cosmides (1989) give the following guidelines for the method of evolutionary psychology:

1. Develop conceptions of adaptive problems the human psyche had to solve.

2. Determine the nature of these problems when humans first confronted them.

3. Develop a computational theory of the specific information processing problems posed by these adaptive problems.

4. Use the computational theory to develop competing candidate models of the psychological mechanisms that may have developed to solve these adaptive problems.

5. Eliminate alternative candidate models with experiments and field observations.

6. Test the best model with modern conditions: the results should agree with observed behavior.

We shall in the following chapters proceed to discuss a number of progressively more complex behaviors which emphasize the interactions between organisms and their environments.

References

Aboitiz, F. 1989. Behavior, archetypes and the irreversibility of evolution. Medical Hypotheses 30: 87-94.

McFarland, D. 1989. Problems of animal behavior. New York: Longman Scientific and Technical Publishers.

Schulze, G; Mori, S. 1993. Increases in environmental entropy demand evolution: a consequence of the entropic theory of perception. Acta Biotheoretica 41: 149-164.

Tooby, J; Cosmides, L. 1989. Evolutionary psychology and the generation of culture, part I: theoretical considerations. Ethology and Sociobiology 10: 29-49.

CHAPTER 2
Bacterial Chemotaxis

Introduction

Do you think a single cell can be motivated? Do you consider a cell as being basically inanimate because it is such a simple organism? Most people would probably answer "no" to the first and "yes" to the latter question. However, cellular behavior may provide important insights into some of the principles and mechanisms of behavior. Bacterial chemotaxis, a review of which is given in Eisenbach (1996), is an example of one such cellular behavior.

Chemotaxic mechanism structure

Bacteria such as *Eschericia Coli, Salmonella Typhimurium,* and *Vibrio Cholerae* possess one or more tails or flagella. These bacteria swim by rotation of their flagella. Each flagellum is driven by a tiny molecular motor at about 15,000 revolutions per minute which is powered by a proton flux of 1,000 protons per revolution. Each motor has a "gearbox" to switch the rotation of the flagellum from counter-clockwise to clockwise. The default setting for the switch is counter-clockwise. Every bacterium also contains receptors (specialized proteins) on its cell membrane to which noxious or food chemicals bind. In addition, the cell contains a number of other specialized proteins which also play a role in bacterial chemotaxis.

Chemotaxic mechanism operation

When a toxin in the bacterial environment binds to a methyl-accepting chemotaxis receptor (MCR) on the bacterium cell membrane itself, a protein (CheA) attached to the MCR on the inside of the cell phosphorylates certain other proteins (signaling proteins CheY) to produce phosphorylated signaling proteins (CheY-P). Phosphorylation involves the binding of a phosphorus-containing ion to a protein. The phosphorylated signaling proteins CheY-P then bind to the gearbox switch (another specialized protein) to change its rotation from counter-clockwise to clockwise. The binding of CheY-P to the gearbox is not permanent, but reversible, and the bound CheY-P becomes unstuck from the gearbox after some time. The gearbox then resumes its normal counter-clockwise rotation unless another CheY-P binds to it.

The build-up of CheY-P also activates a phosphatase protein (CheZ), which causes the dephosphorylation of free CheY-P. Dephosphorylation removes the phosphorous-containing ion from the protein, thus changing it from CheY-P back to CheY. CheY cannot bind to the gearbox, thus dephosphorylation deactivates it.

When a bacterium's flagella rotate in a counter-clockwise direction, the cell swims forward smoothly. When toxins or noxious substances bind to the MCRs, some of the flagella start to rotate in a clockwise direction, causing the cell to swim about in random directions. Figure 2.01 illustrates these events.

Bacterial behavior

Straight swimming or running occurs in the presence of food and the absence of toxins. Tumbling occurs in the presence of toxins, effectively causing swimming away from them. A moment's thought shows why. If a bacterium moves toward toxins, it is more likely to have toxins bind to its receptors, hence to have its flagellar rotation reversed, and so to change direction. If it keeps on changing direction at random in the presence of toxins, it will eventually and by accident find a direction which would move it away from the toxins. If the bacterium swims in a direction which takes it away from toxins, it is less likely to encounter toxins, thus less likely to have the direction of its flagellar rotation reversed, and hence less likely to change direction. The bacterial chemotaxis mechanism produces probabilistically correct motion over a long series of runs and tumbles. Consequently, these bacteria appear to be motivated since they exhibit goal-oriented behavior. Moreover, this is clearly an adaptive behavior.

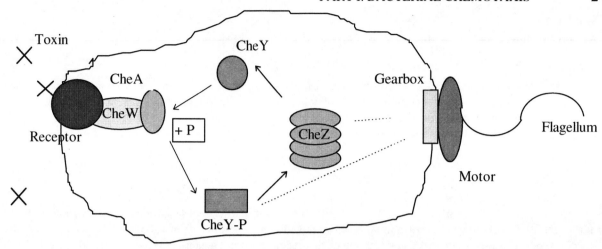

Figure 2.01

A much simplified schematic diagram of a bacterium showing some of the compounds involved in and the mechanism of operation of bacterial chemotaxis.

Parallels to perception in higher organisms and its implications

Pittenger and Dent (1988) discuss some of the parallels between bacterial chemotaxis and perception in higher animals as summarized below. These parallels may give us insights into some general principles of behavior which, in turn, may help us to explain human behavior. Cell psychology shows that even bacteria act in ways that parallel those of more complex organisms: they respond to spatiotemporal patterns and engage in behavior that optimizes their adjustment to the environment. It will be obvious to the reader that toxins or food can be considered to be stimuli to the bacterium and changing the direction of rotation as the behavior of a bacterium. Bacterial chemotaxis, therefore, is a stimulus-response relationship.

Motion provides access to information. Bacteria are too small to detect chemical gradients without motion (i.e. the length of the bacterial body is too short to detect meaningful changes in the surrounding chemical concentrations). The tumbling of bacteria is equivalent to searching - keep in mind that they do not initially know which direction to go into in order to escape the toxins or to find food. The straight swimming is somewhat like "homing in" on a source of food.

The importance of change and Weber's law. Information is contained in change. Higher organisms show increased neural firing rates in response to changes. Bacteria also respond to change. The bacterial response is proportional to the degree of change, rather than the absolute value of the change. That is, for the same percentage ratio, the same degree of tumbling would be observed. Mebisov et al. (1973) inserted pipettes with various concentrations of attractants into a dish of bacteria in a given concentration of attractants. By varying the given concentration of attractants in the dish and pipette, they could tell what percentage ratio between attractants in the pipette and that in the dish was necessary to get the bacteria to move into the pipette. They found that an approximately constant percentage ratio or more was necessary. For example, increasing the concentration of a sugar solution in the pipette from 5% to 10% would cause the bacteria to move from the dish where the concentration is 5% into the pipette. If the concentration in the dish is 10%, then that in the pipette has to be 20% before the bacteria would move from the dish into the pipette. In both cases, the concentration in the pipette has to be twice that in the dish, or 100% higher.

The effect of experience. Receptors for some chemical attractants such as glucose are constitutive ("inborn") while the receptors for others such as maltose 'develop' in response to exposing bacteria to these chemicals.

Attention. Like higher organisms, bacteria are faced with the problems of attending to the most important stimuli. This problem can be solved by having different receptors for different attractants and repellents. For instance, if the bacterium has receptors specific for sugars and others specific only for amino acids, it can still respond to changes in amino acid concentration even if the sugar concentration is very high and all the sugar receptors occupied. In this manner the bacterium can still 'attend' to different stimuli.

Direct and indirect processes of cognition. Indirect processes of cognition require internal representations. Does the bacterium have an internal representation of its environment (e.g. the image of something - like an apple - which you have in your head when you think of it, is an internal representation)? The next paragraph may provide an answer.

Memory and comparison. For comparison between past and present concentrations of chemicals, a bacterium needs to have a memory of the past and a memory of the present concentration in order to make a comparison. Pittenger and Dent (1988) claim that bacteria have no representation of the past and present and so cannot make comparisons. Is this true? Is it reasonable to attribute representation and comparison to organisms as simple as bacteria? If not, how do you decide at what level of organismic complexity it becomes reasonable to do so? Or can you attribute simple representations to simple organisms and more complex representations to more complex organisms? Let us consider these questions for a moment.

The phosphorylated internal cell protein CheY-P controls the amount of tumbling: large amounts of CheY-P imply frequent tumbling. Let the rate of activation of the CheY protein be V_f and the rate of deactivation be V_d. When V_f outstrips V_d, an excess of CheY builds up in the cell, causing frequent tumbling. Consequently, when a bacterium just encounters toxins, there is a build-up of CheY-P. The level of CheY-P can now be considered to be both an internal representation and a comparison of past and present concentrations of toxins. First, only if there are toxins in the environment is there CheY-P in the cell. CheY-P then internally represents the presence of toxins. Second, if the concentration of toxins increase, V_f will be larger than V_d, and if the concentration of toxins decrease, V_f will be smaller than V_d. Therefore, if the amount of CheY-P in the cell increases, it means that there are at present more toxins in the environment than there were in the past, and if it decreases, it means that there are at present fewer toxins than in the past. The rate of change of the CheY-P concentration, $V_f - V_d$, represents a "memory" of past and present toxin levels.

You may think that the presence of a certain chemical inside a cell does not constitute an internal representation of anything. Keep in mind, however, that an internal representation of an apple does not mean that you have an apple or a symbol in your head. The environment (e.g. the apple) is represented in your head also by chemicals and chemical changes.

The importance of mechanism in behavior and motivation. This chapter has shown that an organism's behavior can be understood in terms of *the operation of a mechanism*. In particular, because a mechanism relies on a chain of causal events for its operation, the benefits of a mechanistic understanding of some process is that it becomes easier to explain that process and also to predict how that process may be influenced by particular events. Different mechanisms then, could produce different behaviors. Looking at the mechanisms that produce behavior seem to make behavior more transparent. However, if the mechanism of behavior or motivation is understood, does it make the organism appear as being more inert and less alive? This question may surface again later, and perhaps with more urgency, when we consider mechanisms of behavior as they may apply to humans. We shall, in Part II of this book, specifically discuss possible mechanisms which could produce motivated behaviors in humans.

References

Eisenbach, M. 1996. Control of bacterial chemotaxis. Molecular Microbiology 20: 903-910.

Mebisov, R.; Ordal, G. W.; Adler, J. 1973. The range of attractant concentrations for bacterial chemotaxis and the threshold and size of response over this range. Journal of General Psychology 62: 203-223.

Pittenger, J. B.; Dent, C. H. 1988. A mechanism for the direct perception of change: the example of bacterial chemotaxis. Perception 17: 119-133.

Chapter 3
Social exploration, play, and play fighting

Introduction

Exploratory behavior is generally considered to involve the exploration of physical environments. However, we believe it can also be interpreted as the "exploration" of behaviors and the exploration of a social environment. You may readily recognize that the exploration of a social environment and the exploration of behaviors are as useful as the exploration of a physical environment. Because of the close interactions between behavior and environment, exploration of one would necessarily also have an effect on the other.

In the previous chapter, we saw how the environment affected the behavior of an organism. Play fighting will allow us now to introduce sex differences in behavior and consider their possible causes. Play fighting, or rough-and-tumble play, can be seen as the exploration of behavior which occurs in a social context or social environment. You should be aware though that certain drugs such as scopolamine reduce social behavior but not exploration of the physical environment. This dissociation can be used to argue for the exclusion of playing as an exploratory behavior.

Play and play fighting is common in many species of mammals and some birds. It has been well-documented in primates and rodents (Pellis and Iwaniuk, 2000). Play is mostly believed to involve species-typical behavior - often of precopulatory behavior and/or agonistic attack and defense. Some however, think that animals play because they are young while others think that animals play as a means of passing the time while they are growing up (see Pellis and Iwaniuk, 2000).

In both presexual and agonistic playing certain body parts serve as "targets" to be attained or defended. In play fighting, animals rarely hurt each other and these encounters rarely escalate into serious fights. Sexual differences exist in play fighting. Although these differences often seem to be quantitative in nature, there is also evidence that they are qualitatively different. The discussion and figures on play fighting in Long-Evans rats presented here are based on investigations by Pellis et al. (1996).

The structure of play-fighting in the rat

Experimental procedures. Long-Evans rats were housed in pairs in cages. There were 6 pairs of females and 6 pairs of males. Rats pups are normally weaned around day 21 and reach puberty around day 65. The rats were tested on days 31-40 after birth when play fighting is at a maximum. They were also tested at puberty and after. Periods of isolation of 1, 6, 12, and 24 h were used to determine if fighting changed when animals were not able to engage in the behavior. Rats were tested under a red light (rats are nocturnal animals), in a sound-attenuated room, and videotaped.

Observations: attack. The nape of the neck is the primary body target for attack and defense in the rat. The attacker attempts to rub the snout into the nape, while the defender tries to protect the area with the use of several defensive tactics, often followed by counterattack. About 90% of attacks are met by resistance, and where no resistance is encountered, the attacker briefly contacts the neck and then desists from further attack.

When rats were isolated, the frequency of play fighting increased as shown in Figure 3.01. The longer the isolation, the stronger the increase. This increase in play fighting was observed for both male and female rats. The frequency of defense did not change with isolation time. However, the type of defensive tactic used did change to comparatively less evasion and more rolling over. Keep in mind that isolation constitutes a change in the environment of the rats.

Males initiate 25%-30% more nape attacks than females. Attack occurs even if the partner's neck has been anesthetized, and anesthesia does not eliminate play defense. For both sexes, the frequency of nape attacks decrease with age, but the likelihood of defense remains the same. Neonatal testosterone treatment of females produces an increase in their frequency of nape attack.

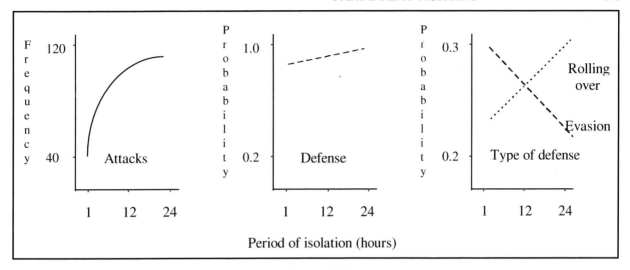

Figure 3.01
Qualitative changes in the subcomponents of play fighting as a function of isolation time.

Observations: defense. When attacked, a rat can adopt one of 3 major defensive tactics.

1. Evasion (see Figure 3.02). The defender rotates the head away from and the tail towards the attacker. In males the point of rotation is about mid-body, resulting in the male maintaining close proximity with the attacker. This makes a second attack or a counterattack more likely. In females, the point of rotation is near the tail resulting in the female increasing the distance between her and the attacker. A second attack can therefore be effectively met by another evasion. Evasion is gender-typical in Long-Evans rats, is used in other social contexts besides playing, and the difference is already manifest at birth.

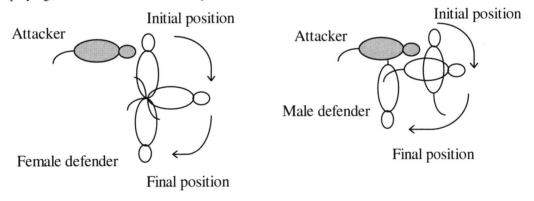

Figure 3.02
Evasion as performed by females and males in play fighting.

2. Rolling over (see Figure 3.03). The defender rolls over on his/her back and fends off the attacker with the front paws. Before puberty, evasion is the most prevalent form of defense amongst both sexes, but when they do not evade, rolling over is preferred by both. During puberty this pattern changes and males switch to staying put as a defense. When dominance relationships start to develop around 70 days of age, the subordinate male more frequently initiates play fighting and rolls over more in defense to play attack. Sexually mature females will continue to use the patterns of defense used as juveniles, whether interacting with males or females.

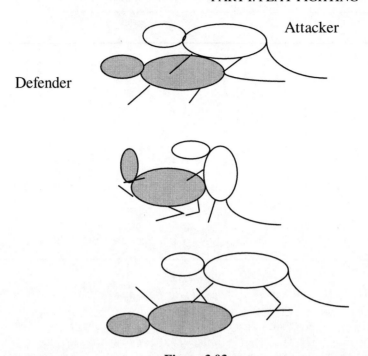

Figure 3.03
Rolling over as performed, from top to bottom, by males and females in play fighting.

3. Staying put (see Figure 3.04). The defender rears slightly on the hind-quarters while rotating the front-quarters towards the attacker and fending off with the front paws while keeping the rear paws put. With the onset of puberty, males, but not females, switch from more rolling over to more staying put. This change in defensive behavior of males is dependent on the action of sex hormones on the brain occurring perinatally, not at puberty. The behavior is only triggered at puberty. In other words, the staying put defense mechanism develops around the time of birth due to the presence of testosterone, but it is activated only at puberty.

Summary of sex differences in play fighting
Let us make a brief summary of the sex differences in play fighting before considering the causes of these sex differences. These differences are summarized in Table 3.01 below.

Table 3.01
The differences in play fighting between female and male rats.

Activity	Females	Males
Attacks	moderate declines with age increases with isolation	high declines with age increases with isolation
Defense	high	high
- evasion	female-typical	male-typical
- rolling over		decreases at puberty
- staying put		increases at puberty

Attacker   Defender

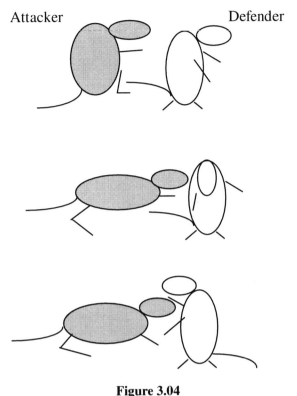

Figure 3.04

Staying put as performed, from top to bottom, by males and females in play fighting.

Possible causes of sex differences in play fighting

There are several possible sources for the sex differences observed in play fighting. They are discussed below and summarized in Table 3.02:

1. Motivation for play. Males engage in play attack more often than females, even when the opponent is injected with scopolamine to make them socially less responsive. This suggests that males have a higher motivation to engage in play fighting. The frequency of nape attacks for both sexes declines with age but the frequency of defenses does not. This implies naturally that the level of motivation declines with age. Other forms of play such as maternal play are more prevalent in the females of species exhibiting such play (e.g. monkeys). The motivational hypothesis receives also support from the previously mentioned increase in play fighting subsequent to various periods of social isolation (i.e., with isolation the drive or motivation for play increases).

2. Sensory sensitivity. Females tend to be more sensitive than males in many species. For instance, in humans, females have a better sense of smell. During play fighting, females respond to the approach of a partner sooner than males do, therefore the defensive action that they take is more successful than that of males. Pellis et al. (1996) found that females responded at a 50% greater distance than males. When tested with female partners, females responded less often to play attack than when tested with male partners. When treated neonatally with testosterone propionate, females tend to respond to and initiate attacks at about the same levels than males. Keep in mind that their normally greater sensory sensitivity may make play fighting unpleasant for females (e.g. by being too rough), but we don't know if this is so.

3. Motor organization. Some evidence indicates that differences in motor patterns, hence possible motor organization, produce sexually dimorphic play fighting. An example here is the differences in the evasion maneuver as executed by females and males. It has also been observed that females and males dodge robbers differently. When given a morsel of food, rats take hold of it with both front paws and consume it while sitting on their hind legs. When another rat tries to rob the eater of their food, rats dodge the robber by turning away from the robber. Males and females do this differently, in fact they do it in ways very similar to evasion play defense. Furthermore, when females dodge against male robbers, they modify their evasive action so that the rump of the

female opposes the head and shoulders of the male, rather than adopt the male method of evasion which accomplishes the same outcome. This modification of female dodging does not occur against a female robber. These findings support the view that differences in play fighting are possibly attributable to differences in motor organization between males and females.

Table 3.02

The effects of sex hormones on the differences in play fighting between female and male rats.

Source	Perinatal Hormones	Pubertal Hormones
Motivation		
- initiation	masculinize	no effect
- pubertal defense changes	masculinize	no effect
- dominance related	masculinize	activate
Sensory Sensitivity	defeminize	no effect
Motor Organization	defeminize/masculinize	no effect

Differences in motivation between males and females can account for the observed differences in attack frequency and differences in defense tactics, but not for the execution of behaviors. If females are less motivated to play fight, they could be expected to attack less often than males, and when attacked, to use evasion as a mode of defense more often than males. Differences in motivation may also account for the change in defense tactics that occurs in males around puberty. For example, staying put may reflect less willingness on the part of the male to engage in play fighting (compared to rolling over) and also an unwillingness to be displaced from his position (which would happen if he took evasive action).

If both females and males have the same degree of motivation, the more sensitive females may find play fighting more unpleasant, and engage less in the activity. This would not explain why they respond more often to attacks by males (who may be more rough in their playing) and less often to attacks by females, but could explain their propensity to choose evasion frequently as a type of defense.

Differences in motor organization could best explain the execution of female and male-typical evasive maneuvers, but not the differences in attack frequency between the sexes or the choice of defense type.

Of the 3 postulated possible causes of sex differences, differences in motivation and motor organization could explain most of the observed phenomena. On the other hand, sensory sensitivity seems to be a weaker explanation for behavioral dimorphism in play fighting.

Let us revisit bacterial chemotaxis momentarily. How could we adjust or modify the chemotaxis mechanism to effect a difference in "motivation" between 2 different bacteria? First we can consider straight swimming as "normal behavior" and tumbling as "play fighting attacks". Then, we can assume that the receptors do not detect food or toxins, but the presence of another bacterium. Since play fighting attacks are produced in this hypothetical situation by the phosphorylated signaling proteins CheY-P, an increase in the frequency of attacks could be brought about by an increase in the formation of CheY-P. To do this, it would suffice to suggest that the early presence of a sex hormone causes the development of a version of the phosphorylating protein, we shall call it CheAm, which converts CheY to CheY-P at a faster rate than the normal CheA does when the receptor becomes activated by a stimulus. Motivation, in this context then, appears to be the presence of CheY-P: the more CheY-P present, the stronger the motivation. The presence of CheY-P functions now as both a drive to provide the motivated behavior of the bacterium and as an internal representation indicating the presence of another rat. Comparing the 2 bacteria, one with normal CheA and one with modified CheA (i.e. CheAm), we may come to the following conclusion regarding the present mechanisms: a better or stronger internal representation of the stimulus is concomitant with a stronger motivation to engage in action. The reader may wish to ponder how bacterial chemotaxis mechanisms and behavior could be modified and recast to examine how differences in "sensory sensitivity" and "motor organization" could produce sexually dimorphic play fighting.

The function of play fighting

Many researchers consider play fighting to function as practice for adult skills. In the rat, play fighting does not involve the behavior patterns of aggression (where biting of the rear, flanks, and face is far more common than biting of the neck), but those of precopulation. Because nape contact is often a prelude to mounting, this type of playing would benefit males more. Hence one can reason that males should be more motivated to engage in play fighting. However, the authors (Pellis et al., 1996) argue that sex differences in play fighting do not support the hypothesis that it functions as practice for male copulatory behavior, but it may serve to develop dominance-subordinate relationships instead. This is why, they believe, pubertal changes in aspects of play fighting is seen in males and not females. Juvenile behaviors is often more appeasing, and play fighting in adults may function as "friendship". The authors fail to explain, however, why play fighting should occur at all in females where dominance relationships may not exist. Females have been observed to respond less often to attacks by other females than to attacks by males, which suggests that no dominance hierarchy exists among females, or that its establishment does not depend on play fighting.

The authors do point out that play fighting differs in species and between strains of the same species. In fact, there appears to be a correlation between the extent of prenatal growth and the degree of playing in animals. That is, animals that are born relatively mature play less than animals that are born very immature and need to grow a lot between birth and maturity. This raises the possibility that animals play in order to permit their bodies to develop properly - hence play is needed for growth (Pellis an Iwaniuk, 2000). But is this growth physical growth or the growth and refinement of skills? Would isolation with stimulating toys (that would permit some degree of physical and mental stimulation and growth) reduce subsequent play fighting or have no effect?

We started this chapter by suggesting that play may be a form of exploratory behavior of the environment - especially the social environment. However, we are ending this chapter finding ourselves confronted with several possibilities. Playing, including play fighting, could have as function the:

(i)   exploration of physical/social environments;
(ii)   development of physical/social skills;
(iii)   stimulation and coordination of muscle and nerve growth;
(iv)   establishment of social dominance hierarchies; and
(v)   passing of time while the body matures.

The reader is encouraged to try to explain the purpose of play, especially play fighting, based on the evidence discussed above and such information as may become available in later chapters. Note that none of the suggestions made above may account for the purpose of play or that all of them may do so. Be advised though that when claiming all of the above are reasons for play, the relative contribution of each to the phenomenon of play should be specified to render such an answer acceptable. We suggest therefore that the reader periodically refer back to this chapter and attempt to resolve the issue of play in animals.

References

Pellis, S. M.; Field, E. F.; Smith, L. K.; Pellis, V. C. 1996. Multiple differences in the play fighting of male and female rats. Implications for the causes and functions of play. Neuroscience and Biobehavioral Reviews 21: 105-120.

Pellis, S. M.; Iwaniuk, A. N. 2000. Comparative analyses of the role of postnatal development on the expression of play fighting. Developmental Psychobiology 36: 136-147.

Chapter 4
Aggression

Introduction

The relationship between the organism, especially its behavior, and the environment has been pointed out before. In particular, we have considered a classification of behaviors and how the environment influenced the relative sizes of each class of behaviors. It seems useful to follow a similar approach with aggression. What are the environmental factors that generate a *need* for aggression? The great biological imperatives are those of survival of the genes, survival of the individual, and survival of the species. Keep in mind that this list may be the middle portion of a larger list, the beginning and ends of which may not exist or which may not be evident given our present understanding. We can therefore expect that aggression may have some role in the support of these imperatives.

The purpose and types of aggression

Let us then take all aggressive behaviors, here defined as behaviors of real or implied physical violence directed by one organism at another, and classify them. Such a classification seem to indicate that 2 types of aggression could be identified. Here we distinguish between *primary* aggression and *secondary* aggression. We define primary aggression as aggression obligatory for individual survival. This is the type of aggression directed by predators at prey: the predator could not survive without this type of aggression. Primary aggression is normally directed at the individuals of another species. Clearly, the individuals in non-predatory species are not likely to exhibit primary aggression. This may seem odd, unless the definition is examined more closely, in which case one comes to the conclusion that herbivores are predators also, but in this case predators of plants. Plants, of course, cannot physically escape their predators and have evolved other mechanisms of defense.

Secondary aggression is defined as the use of real or implied violence to improve the standing of one individual relative to another of the same species (and often of the same sex). Secondary aggression is not obligatory: the non-aggressive individual would not necessarily perish, however, their chances of survival and procreation are diminished. Consider the case of 2 similar organisms that experience thirst and arrive at a source of water simultaneously. If the amount of water or access to the water is restricted, competition will most likely ensue. Here aggression comes into play, because it sequesters a scarce resource for the one organism which consequently stands a better chance of survival.

The above definitions of aggression types permit viewing primary aggression as being under the control of, or activated by, homeostatic mechanisms. Homeostatic mechanisms (HMs) will be discussed in some depth in Part II of this book. The secondary type of aggression seems to be directed at improving the chances that primary aggression will succeed. In this case, too, the behavior may be homeostatically activated, although at present we are uncertain about this. One could also call these types of aggression predatory and competitive aggression, respectively.

In humans, subtypes of aggression have been identified and investigated. It is believed that a simple extrapolation of the subtypes of animal aggression to humans is not possible because of the impact of complex cultural variables on behavior. However, a consistent dichotomy of aggression can be identified: an impulsive-reactive aggression (IRA) and a controlled-predatory aggression (CPA) (Vitiello and Stoff, 1997). This admits the temptation of mapping them onto competitive and predatory aggression as defined earlier. Other subtypes of aggression include maternal aggression, male-male aggression, sexual aggression, irritable aggression, fear-induced aggression, and instrumental aggression.

The control of aggression

Having reached some tentative conclusions about the roles of the different types of aggression, we can now look at some of the factors that control aggression. In this respect, we shall only consider secondary aggression, since the control of primary aggression will be investigated implicitly in discussions about HMs and hunger. As a concrete example, we will look at aggression in the wild house mouse (*Mus musculus domesticus* – after Sluyter et al., 1996) and the monkey (*Macaca mulatta* - after Wallen, 1996) and the relative effects of biological and environmental factors in the expression of aggression in these species.

The effects of aggression on the mouse's adaptation to its environment. The house mouse is a typical colonizing species where settled individuals live in reproductively isolated family groups called "demes" and successful reproduction occurs only within demes. Demes contain mostly more females than males, as well as juveniles born in the group. Migrating groups on the other hand consist mostly of young adult and subadult individuals that have left their parental demes. These 2 lifestyles, resident or colonizer, require different temperaments in order to be successful.

Male mice regularly patrol the borders of their territories where most agonistic encounters occur. In the laboratory, such territories and encounters can be controlled. Male mice from different experimental groups that have been allowed to "establish" a territory are confronted with another male mouse by the experimenter. In the standard opponent test, the opponent mouse has been bred to elicit offensive behaviors from the mouse being tested, but not to initiate aggression themselves. In this manner the behavior of the opponent can be controlled across all experimental groups.

Attack latency has been used as a means of measuring the degree of aggression in mice and has been found to be a robust indicator of aggression. Attack latency is the time it takes a mouse to attack an intruder measured from the moment that the intruder is first noticed by the attacker. Attack latencies for the wild house mouse shows a bimodal distribution: some individuals show a short attack latency (SAL) while others show a long attack latency (LAL). In practical terms this means that some rats attack readily while others attack only reluctantly. SAL mice perform better in a settled population while LAL mice are better able to gain territory when migrating. This may happen because SAL mice are more likely to aggressively protect their established territory, while LAL mice are less likely to activate animosity in resident populations in the area where they are traveling through.

These two behaviorally distinct groups are also genetically distinct. Consequently, different genotypes for aggression are of functional significance for the population dynamics of the wild house mouse. One must, however, assume that migrating groups of juveniles should contain both SAL and LAL individuals or at least LAL individuals that also carry SAL genes. This would allow a migrating group to establish new colonies that would then be protected by SAL individuals. Conversely, LAL individuals must be born also to some SAL mice in order to establish migratory groups. The dynamics of this process appears to need further elucidation.

The effects of environmental factors on aggression in the mouse. The effects of maternal factors on aggression in male mice can be of cytoplasmic, prenatal, or postnatal environmental origin. The prenatal environment can be changed by embryo transfer of SAL and LAL embryos to the same other pregnant mouse as shown in Figure 4.01. In this case, the mice, when born, would be of different genetic types, but would have shared the same prenatal maternal environment. This type of manipulation does not change the aggressiveness of SAL and LAL mice.

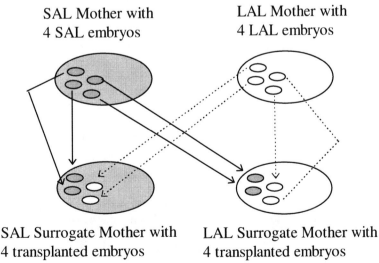

Figure 4.01

Changing of the prenatal environment of mouse embryos through embryo transfer to surrogate mothers.

The postnatal environment from birth to weaning lasts about 21 days. Lactating females will readily accept alien newborns, consequently it is easy to transfer SAL and LAL mouse pups to another mother. For these mice, the postnatal maternal environment is shared, but not the genetic makeup or prenatal and cytoplasmic environments. These manipulations have also failed to show an effect on levels of aggression. Cytoplasmic effects have not been studied, but the other 2 maternal factors show little effect. Here, rearing and social factors clearly do not influence aggression.

In many species, including rats and mice, aggression depends on the hormonal status of the animal. Testosterone, the male sex hormone, and its metabolites, affect behavior by virtue of its concentrations and timing of release. SAL mice show higher testosterone concentrations than LAL mice, but both types have the same capacity to produce the hormone since the administration of growth hormone produce identical levels in both types.

Differentiation may occur though, depending on the sensitivity of animals to testosterone during critical time periods occurring at puberty or perinatally (around the time of birth). Some effect of pubertal hormone replacement on castrated animals has been observed. Differences in perinatal circulating testosterone concentrations between SAL and LAL males have been found, suggesting that this period may also have an effect on the expression of aggression in adult mice.

Sex hormone modulation, especially during the critical perinatal and pubertal periods, have effects on neural development. Differences in brain dopaminergic activity between the SAL and LAL strains have been found. Furthermore, differences in the size of the pyramidal mossy fiber field terminals in the hippocampus are known to be correlated with aggression, and have been found to be smaller in SAL males. A direct involvement of the hippocampus in aggression, possibly via projections to the hypothalamus, is likely. Of the many neurotransmitters that have been found to play a role in aggression, the role of serotonin is the most pronounced and well-established. Increased levels of serotonin transmission reduce aggression either through a general sedative effect or through a direct inhibition of aggression or both (Miczek et al., 2001; Nelson and Chiavegatto, 2001).

The genetic effects, often operating via sites on the Y chromosome, exercise their influence on male aggression not only through the effects of sex hormone modulation, but perhaps also by affecting chemical signaling. Some investigators think that urine olfactory signals are almost exclusively responsible as offensive stimuli in mice. Urine odors can be discriminated by mice, and their production is not testosterone dependent. The genes may exert their influence on aggression in male mice by causing them to produce more offensive odors as well as causing them to find such odors more offensive. Some strains of mice have been specifically bred to be aggressive or non-aggressive. The genetic contributions to these traits have been confirmed with cross-fostering studies that showed these traits were not due to the postnatal maternal environment (Miczek et al., 2001). Some strains of mice have been bred to produce aggressive females and females of strains where the males were bred to be aggressive can also be aggressive. In the latter case though, it appears that social factors play a role in triggering latent aggression (Miczek et al., 2001).

The effects of environmental factors on aggression in the monkey. In the preceding discussion, the dominant role of genetic factors in the expression of aggression has been shown. From studies in the rhesus monkey, there have been indications that social factors may have a strong role in the determination of behavior.

Rhesus monkeys in nature live in complex social groups integrated around a matrilineal social structure. Adult patterns of behavior are strongly sexually differentiated and it appears that the social conditions under which rearing occurred, influence these behaviors.

When males and females are reared in peer-groups (i.e. no mother is present), males direct threats significantly more frequently at their peers than females during the 1st year of life. When infants are reared in peer groups with their mothers present, threatening between peers is infrequent, and there is no difference between the sexes.

When infants are raised by their mothers with limited or continuous access to peers, no difference in threat frequency is found in the 1st year of life between the sexes reared under these conditions. When the monkeys were weaned, however, those juveniles in the limited peer access group threatened significantly more than those in the continuous peer access group. Furthermore, males used threat 30 times more often than females and directed 75% of their threats at females.

Rough and tumble play is displayed more frequently by males than females and is virtually invariant under rearing condition except for a frequency increase of such play in males reared in peer-only groups. The presence or absence of neonatal androgens has not been found to have an effect on rough and tumble play in males. It did affect interactions between mother and infant. The presence of androgens in female monkeys during the same period, strongly alters their behavior to be more similar to those of males.

In general, it appears that the predisposition to engage in threats and rough and tumble play is largely determined by the prenatal hormonal environment. The actual expression of the behavior, however, is a consequence of the social environment of rearing. Thus, hormonal factors seem to establish the neural circuitry necessary for these behaviors; social conditions may only serve to elicit and shape them. A summary of social and biological effects on aggression is shown in Table 4.01.

Table 4.01
The effects of social and biological variables on juvenile aggressive behaviors.

Social and Humoral Context	*Threat*	*Rough Play*
Normal social group	No effect	No effect
Peer access < 0.5 h/day, no mother	+ Males	- Males
Peer access < 2 h/day, no mother	+ Males	+ Males
Peer access < 0.5 h/day, mother present	+ Males	Unknown
Peer access unlimited, mother present	No effect	No effect
Neonatal androgen suppression (males)	No effect	No effect
Neonatal androgen elevation (males)	No effect	No effect
Lengthy prenatal androgen elevation (females)	No effect	+ Females
Short, early prenatal androgen elevation (females)	Unknown	No effect
Short, late prenatal androgen elevation (females)	Unknown	+ Females

+ = increase; - = decrease

Analysis

However, before we accept things at face value, let us look at aggression and play fighting in the monkey more critically. For this purpose, we shall briefly revisit play fighting in the rat. You may recall that social isolation produced an increase in play fighting in rats. In the present context, one may suspect that social rearing conditions entailing limited peer access amounts to isolation. Upon increasing the opportunity for contact one may then expect an increase in play fighting. This interpretation is consistent with the data as discussed by Wallen (1996) although it differs from her interpretation. When monkeys are reared with their mothers with either continuous or limited peer access during the first year of life, those in the limited peer access group show increased levels of threat and play fighting compared to those in the continuous peer access group when tested after weaning. Furthermore, it appears that the levels of threats among males increase and the levels of play fighting decrease as access to peers is further restricted. Severely restricted access may have the effect of presenting a novel stimulus (another peer) generating fear and hence a threat response without allowing opportunity for play fighting to commence. This interpretation finds support in the observation that limiting peer access to 30 minutes per day caused infants to withdraw from peers significantly more often than those who had continuous access to peers. If play fighting, and perhaps threatening, serve to establish dominance hierarchies amongst males, it seems reasonable that limiting peer access will provide for limited opportunity to do so. When these limitations are removed, establishing a hierarchy can be resumed and increased levels of threat and play fighting will result.

The effects of social environmental factors on aggression in fish. The environment of an organism, on the other hand, also affects it by modifying its behavior and/or its physiology. This relationship is compactly illustrated by the behavior of salmonid fish (see Chew, 1995) and is recounted below.

After yolk-sac absorption, salmonid fry (e.g. salmon, trout, charr) need to feed incessantly. They usually strike at surface drift, but often at a variety of targets, learning what is edible. Random strikes at the same target sometimes occur, with accidental biting of the other fry. Within days, fry learn to modify feeding by using movements such as biting, chasing, tail beating, and body wagging to ward off or avoid others. These behaviors result in conflict resolution. The resolution proceeds in favor of the strongest or largest fry. This establishes a dominance hierarchy between fry and also establishes territory with dominant fry having the best, largest territory. Physiological changes accompany success or failure in competition. Dominant fish become lighter in color than non-dominant fish. Large light fish are the most aggressive and dominant. These physical characteristics signal competitive success without the need to determine relative standing anew: for both dominant and non-dominant individuals there is an advantage associated with this.

The reader should briefly recall the mechanism of bacterial chemotaxis and how environmental changes produce physiological (and consequently behavioral) changes in the bacterium. This may render the changes that occur in salmonid fish, at least in principle, plausible. For instance, if a color is associated with the phosphorylated signaling protein CheY-P, but not with the dephosphorylated CheY, the presence of a toxin in the environment would result in a change in color of the bacterium.

The function of aggression

The preceding discussions suggest that non-predatory aggression functions as a means of improving relative social standing, that is, it appears to be competitive in nature. Hence one should consider the possibility that all subtypes of aggression as currently identified may be variants of primary aggression (predatory or defensive-against-predators) or secondary aggression (competitive or defensive-against-competitors). Although this is in line with our classification of aggression into primary aggression and secondary aggression and the view that secondary aggression serves to improve the success rate of primary aggression, our view may nevertheless be at variance with reality. The reader is therefore urged to classify the subtypes of agression as mentioned earlier (and such other types of agression as s/he may be familiar with) into the class of either primary or secondary aggression in order to determine if any subtype falls outside of these classes. If so, we hope that the reader will then proceed to provide an improved explanation of the phenomenon of aggression.

References

Chew, L. 1995. Stable and chaotic patterns of fish agonistic activity. In R. Wong (ed.), Biological perspectives on motivated activities, pp. 379-396. Norwood, NJ: Ablex.

Miczek, K. A.; Maxson, S. C.; Fish, E. W.; Faccidomo, S. 2001. Aggressive behavioral phenotypes in mice. Behavioural Brain Research 125: 167-181.

Nelson, R. J.; Chiavegatto, S. 2001. Molecular basis of aggression. Trends in Neurosciences 24: 713-719.

Sluyter, F.; van Oortmerssen, G. A.; de Ruiter, A. J. H.; Koolhaas, J. M. 1996. Aggression in wild house mice: current state of affairs. Behavior Genetics 26: 489-496.

Vitiello, B.; Stoff, D. M. 1997. Subtypes of aggression and their relevance to child psychiatry. Journal of the American Academy of Child and Adolescent Psychiatry 36: 307-315.

Wallen, K. 1996. Nature needs nurture: the interaction of hormonal and social influences on the development of behavioral sex differences in rhesus monkeys. Hormones and Behavior 30: 364-378.

Chapter 5
Procreative Behaviors: Mating

Introduction

Evolutionary psychology (Tooby and Cosmides, 1989), the method of investigation of innate psychological mechanisms evolved to deal with specific information processing problems, has brought about recent advances in the understanding of procreative behaviors. Evolutionary psychology emphasizes that universal mental adaptations (innate psychological mechanisms) will sometimes be sex-specific because males and females faced sex-specific adaptational problems in their evolutionary history. This renewed interest in the evolution of sex has lead to the appearance of several theories attempting to explain the phenomenon of sex.

Background material

Genetics. (1) A chromosome is a large rod-shaped body (molecule) in the cell nucleus; (2) genes are sub-sections of chromosomes; (3) a genotype is the set of genes that an organism possesses; (4) a phenotype is the outward expression of genes as a trait (i.e. as a body or a behavior); (5) genes can be rearranged or replaced by others or a combination of the above - in general, this will provide a different genotype and phenotype; (6) genes direct the cell's functions and they can be replicated by the cell; (7) sometimes a "mistake" or mutation occurs in the replication process leading to a new genotype with its associated phenotype; and (8) all the different types of genes present in an entire *population* is the gene pool.

Reproduction. (1) Occurs asexually where a copy of the genes of the parent cell is made before the cell divides into 2 cells, each with a set of identical genes; and (2) occurs sexually, where half the genes of one (female) cell are copied to a (female) seed cell (e.g. egg) and half the genes of the other (male) cell are copied to the other (male) seed cell (e.g. sperm) before the seed cells merge to form a new cell.

Evolution. (1) Genes are inherited, thus genes and traits are conserved across generations; (2) genetic mutation produces the "random" emergence of new traits in some individuals; and (3) through the process of natural selection some individuals are allowed to reproduce and others not. Natural selection is a process which involves competition between individuals for resources (e.g. food, mates, etc.). The most successful individual in this competition is more likely to survive and leave offspring behind, and is termed the most "fit". In the case of the more fit, the mutation was advantageous and in the case of the less fit, the mutation was disadvantageous.

Theories of sex

All the theories about sex can be divided into 2 groups: theories of the first group generally claim that sex enables the creation and spread of advantageous genes through a population, while theories of the second group generally claim that sex enables the removal of disadvantageous genes from a population (see Hurst and Peck, 1996).

Simplification permits sex to be seen as a method of "artificially" increasing the mutation rate. This increases the rate at which new traits emerge, some of which would be advantageous, and some which would be disadvantageous. By so doing, it increases the process of selection, and speeds up the rate at which disadvantageous genes are eliminated from the gene pool. Both of these effects are likely to enhance the rate and degree of adaptation of a population.

The theories claiming the spread of advantageous genes do so on the basis of (1) that sex allows the creation of new genotypes; (2) that sexual populations have much more phenotypic space; and (3) that sex may allow beneficial genes to escape from deleterious ones. An increased rate of "mutation" may be necessary due to fast changes in the environment. Many researchers believe that parasites represent a particular fast-changing component of the environment. Parasites can produce strong pressures that favor a constant turnover of genotypes because they are thought to engage in "arms races" with host populations. Some support for this derives from molecular studies. A comparison of the rate of evolution of two classes of proteins (kinases and immunoglobulins), both with brain-specific and immune-specific members, show that in both classes the immune-specific system evolves faster. A comparison of the genetic differences between the related species of mouse and rat reveals that genes responsible for regulating aspects of the immune system differ more than genes responsible for regulating non-immune aspects of metabolism.

The theories claiming the elimination of disadvantageous genes do so on the basis that sex is a means to maintain a high variance in mutation number and hence ensures that one death can remove numerous deleterious genes. Selection reduces variance, but this can be restored in the next round of sexual reproduction. In asexual populations, the variance will be low unless a high rate of reproduction exists. Any mutation rate that leads to the emergence of novel genotypic individuals faster than the rate at which parasites can evolve to invade these individuals, is sufficient. However, a rate that is much faster than that at which parasites adapt is inefficient or wasteful ("overkill"). Consequently, in low mutation rate asexually reproducing species, many more individuals have to die to eliminate deleterious genes. This implies that sexual populations and asexual populations with high mutation rates adapt faster to environmental pressures and do so with the loss of fewer individuals, thus more efficiently. It is interesting to note that in some species, especially in mammals, the mutation rate in males is higher than that in females. If, for some reason, mutation rates in males are higher and asexual reproduction is not an option, it is more necessary to reproduce sexually frequently in order to keep on eliminating those deleterious genes that are generated rapidly in males.

Factors controlling sexual behavior

Genes. The cells of females contain two identical sex X chromosomes whiles males have one X and a smaller Y chromosome. Sexual reproduction results in the random combination of chromosomes from the female and the male, thus leading to equal likelihoods of XX (female) or XY (male) combinations occurring. All humans are by default females. The presence of the Y chromosome in humans determines the maleness of that human. The absence of the Y chromosome or the blocking of the effects of the Y chromosome results in the individual being phenotypically female.

Hormones. The genes of the Y chromosome cause some cells of the developing embryo to develop into testes instead of ovaries. The fetal testes already start to function by the end of the first trimester, producing the male sex hormone testosterone. The basic body and brain structures of humans are female. Testosterone and other hormones produced during fetal development cause the growth (by differentiation) of male body structures as well as brain structures. These are further enhanced or activated by hormones secreted at the time of puberty and after.

Brain dimorphism. Neural structures that develop in response to the presence or absence of specific sex hormones are often involved in sex-related behaviors. For instance, spinal nuclei controlling ejaculation in male mammals are larger in males than in females. The difference is much greater in the rat than in the human because rats face greater sperm competition. It is therefore to the advantage of the male rat to have large testicles in order to produce plenty of sperm. This improves a specific male's chances of fertilizing the egg of a female that has copulated with several other males. Consequently, it would also benefit from neural structures that can support such rates of sperm production and delivery.

Environment. The activation of brain and body reproductive structures by sex hormones are often cyclical in both males and females. In both sexes, environmental factors can modulate the levels of sex hormones which in turn allows the environment to exert an influence on the timing and rate of reproduction. For example, in songbirds the dimorphism of the structure and function of neural structures mediating song learning is greatest during the period of mate competition - usually the early spring.

Mating behavior

Advertising and selection. Sexually dimorphic brain structures produce sex-specific behaviors in males and females. Considerable empirical evidence now indicate that in humans men and women have different sexual psyches (see Thornhill and Gangestad, 1996).

Men are more eager and undiscriminating than women in mating decisions. Their fantasies have more explicit sexual content, partner variety, and sexual content alone. Women value resources and status of potential mates more than men do. They especially value traits in men which indicate a willingness on the side of men to invest in their offspring. Men become more discriminating when they intend to invest. Both women and men value intelligence in a long-term mate, but women apply far higher standards of intelligence than men in short-term sexual relations. Women's fantasies have more implicit sexual content, non-sexual content, affection, commitment, and emotionality.

Women's value judgment of men changes according to circumstances. In situations where investing males are available, female sexual psychology seems to produce sexual restraint, thus giving cues about paternity reliability and hence improved probability of male investment. In circumstances were investing males are not available, sexual access is exchanged for material benefits. For instance, it appears that father absence during a girl's development may speed her progress to sexual maturity and early sexual activity. In human evolutionary history, father absence may have been a reliable indicator of paternal investment, hence it may have been to women's advantage to use sex to profitably gain lost paternal resources and protection.

Given that women value some things more in men than others, and given that there may be some competition by males for the sexual favors of women, one might expect that men would tend to display those attributes which women value more. This display can be honest or dishonest. A dishonest display that tricks the female into copulation would serve the purpose as well from the male's point of view. The female therefore needs to be aware of the honesty of advertising signals. In humans, men display resources, status, and athleticism more than women do. Women display attractiveness and sexual restraint more than men do.

Testosterone appears to be an immunosuppressor and estrogen may be too at high levels. Sex-hormone dependent features may honestly advertise immunocompetence, because the high levels of sex hormones needed to produce attractive features would also make the individual more susceptible to diseases, except if they have uncommonly good immune systems.

Female facial attractiveness may display female genetic quality and male sensitivity to this attractiveness may display the male's ability to detect this genetic quality. Male facial attractiveness may likewise display male genetic quality and women's sensitivity to this attractiveness their ability to judge male genetic quality. The value of physical attractiveness in choice of a long-term mate increases with increased parasitic prevalence across human societies.

Fluctuating asymmetry may be a reliable indicator of and individual's genetic quality. It refers to the bilateral deviation from morphological symmetry. Because the same genes control development of the 2 sides of the body, asymmetry is thought to indicate developmental instability or disruption. Those with more robust genes will be less susceptible to developmental disruption and show greater bilateral symmetry. Fluctuating asymmetry increases with exposure to toxins and parasites. In a range of species, fluctuating asymmetry negatively predicts fecundity, growth rate, survival, and mating success. In men, low fluctuating asymmetry is found to be more attractive, produce more sex partners, more extra-pair copulations, and earlier onset of sexual activity. Partners of such men report more copulatory orgasms. This indicates that human females may have to deal with a possible dilemma: if they require a male willing to invest in the offspring, he should have high fluctuating asymmetry because those with low asymmetry are more likely to be unfaithful. Yet those with low asymmetry are also genetically of higher quality.

Mechanisms of selection. Sexual selection can occur through a variety of mechanisms. Some of the mechanisms of sexual selection are:
(1) choice;
(2) contests;
(3) scrambles;
(4) endurance rivalry;
(5) sperm competition;
(6) sperm retention;
(7) coercion; and
(8) infanticide.

Consequences of sexual selection. Among many species, male traits most often selected by females were song and display, body size, visual ornaments, and territory or other resources. Female choice is most prevalent among studies conducted so far, although male choice is also common. Mate choice has an effect on the characteristics that develop in the opposite sex (see Jacobs, 1996). In songbirds, those males with larger repertoires are more successful in competing for mates. A corresponding relationship has been found between repertoire size and size of the forebrain high vocal center (HVC). Because males compete for females on the basis of their songs, female selection of males would tend to favor those that can learn faster and retain a larger repertoire of songs. In this manner, females can exert a strong influence on the development of cognitive abilities in the male. Human females unhappy with the current state of the human male could ponder this issue.

The same effect appears in rodents. Female ground-squirrels, for instance, are sparsely distributed over some territory and females are receptive for only a few hours. Experiments indicate that males use their spatial memory of previous encounters to predict the daily distribution of estrous females. When more than one male arrive at the female's burrow, they queue for access to the female. Therefore, it is in a male's interest to get there first. The more females a male visits, the more territory he has to navigate and the higher his chances of predation. Consequently, some selection for memory and navigation occurs. In polygynous voles, males are better at navigating to food than females, but this difference does not occur in monogamous voles.

The strength of sexual selection can be determined from the Bateman gradient as shown in Figure 5.01 below (see Andersson and Iwasa, 1996). It relates fecundity to number of sexual mates. If the gradient is steeper in males, they are more subject to sexual selection and the mating system polygynous. If the gradient is steeper in females, they are more subject to selection and the mating system polyandrous. Monogamous species will tend to show flat gradients for both sexes.

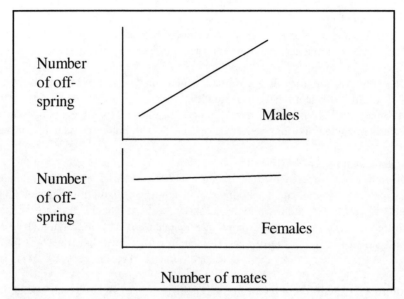

Figure 5.01

The Bateman gradient showing sexual selection pressure as the relationship between fecundity and mate number. Steeper gradients indicate stronger selection pressure.

Because sexual selection exaggerates the sex-specific traits of the opposite sex, and because these traits are often costly, it is unclear why females would make such choices. However, if males with the more pronounced traits are more often selected and hence leave more offspring behind, females that prefer such a male will also leave more offspring behind, especially if the trait is also a marker of genetic quality. The reliability of a signal of genetic quality generally increases with its cost. In this respect, selection for specific traits become self-limiting. For example, in the red-wing blackbird, females prefer large males. Large males, although able to compete well against others, have to spend more time foraging for food and have less time available to defend their territory and attract females.

References

Andersson, M.; Iwasa, Y. 1996. Trends in Ecology and Evolution 11: 53-58.

Hurst, L. D.; Peck, J. R. 1996. Recent advances in understanding of the evolution and maintenance of sex. Trends in Ecology and Evolution 11: 45-52.

Jacobs, L. F. 1996. Sexual selection and the brain. Trends in Ecology and Evolution 11: 82-86.

Thornhill, R.; Gangestad, S. W. 1996. The evolution of human sexuality. Trends in Ecology and Evolution 11: 98-102.

Tooby, J; Cosmides, L. 1989. Evolutionary psychology and the generation of culture, part I: theoretical considerations. Ethology and Sociobiology 10: 29-49.

Chapter 6
Procreative Behaviors: Parenting

The purpose of parenting

Parental care improves the survival rate of offspring and thereby increases the reproductive success, or fitness, of the parents. However, the great biological imperatives of survival of the genes, survival of the individual, and survival of the species, sometimes come into conflict with one another. Parenting provides one such an example where conflicts arise: here between the interests of the individual and those of the species (see Westneat and Sargent, 1996).

It does appear that aggression (predatory or competitive) has as its main objective the survival of the individual. Sex, on the other hand, seems to be entirely geared towards the survival of the species. Parenting also seems to have as objective the survival of the species but, due to its extended duration, conflicts arise with individual survival. These conflicts are often complicated by sexual conflicts.

Individual differences

It is known that in addition to the differences between the sexes, widespread differences occur between individuals of the same sex. It is important to consider the possible origins of these differences. They may reflect genetic differences and/or differences in environmental history. For genetically identical organisms, different environmental histories may produce different behavior patterns under identical conditions. In addition, such individuals may be genetically predisposed to show elaborate phenotypic alternatives. Genetically different individuals of the same species and the same sex could be expected to be phenotypically different.

It is now being realized that evolution has not given rise to a single best female and male phenotype for each species, but considerable phenotypic diversity. For instance, in the house mouse there is no single genotype for aggression, but at least 2 - the SAL and LAL genotypes - giving rise to 2 phenotypes of aggression (e.g. Miczek et al., 2001; Sluyter et al., 1996). This phenotypic diversity coupled with the capriciousness of environmental histories likely produce "individual differences". An important component of these environmental histories is social interactions, for example, as witnessed in the context of play fighting. As a result of individual differences, conflicts between individuals, sexes, and species will be varied.

Sexual conflict

Sexual conflicts can be pre-zygotic and occurs when one sex produces a larger seed cell (gamete) than the other. As soon as one sex produces a larger gamete, it becomes advantageous for the other to produce more but smaller gametes. This condition is called anisogamy. Sexual conflicts can also be post-zygotic if there are two caregivers. If one gives more care, the other benefits.

For example, in some birds, if the offspring within a brood differ in weight and age, the males tend to feed the older, heavier chicks and the females the younger, lighter ones. Experimental manipulation of hatching time produced increased mortality of females between seasons because of the greater demands made on them in caring for the more vulnerable offspring. Male survival, on the other hand, was lower when the offspring hatched at the same time. Because the males couldn't discriminate against younger offspring, they helped in the care of the entire brood and thus increased their overall contribution to care. Females can delay incubation until the last egg has been laid, thus reducing the difference in hatching times between first and last chick. This benefits the female by reducing demands made on her and increasing those made on the male.

Reproductive strategies

A strategy is a genetically-based decision rule to determine the allocation of developmental and reproductive effort among different tactics such as giving care to the offspring or searching for a sexual partner.

Alternative strategies are associated with genetic polymorphism such as in SAL and LAL mice. Or, in the example given above, caregivers (CG) are genetically different from searchers for sex partners (SP). This means an individual is capable of either one behavior or the other, but not both. The frequency of occurrence in the population may differ but the alternatives have equal fitness.

Mixed strategies: the same individual is capable of both care giving or searching for sex partners and each behavior has certain probabilities associated with it. The mixed strategy is associated with genetic monomorphism with differences in the frequency of occurrence of the tactics. The tactics provide equal fitness.

Conditional strategies: an individual is capable of both care giving or searching, but whichever happens will depend on (be conditional on) environmental circumstances. This is associated with genetic monomorphism and tactics with unequal fitness.

The selection of different strategies

Frequency-dependent selection. This type of selection occurs when the relative fitness of different phenotypes depends on their frequencies in the population as shown in Figure 6.01. Searching for sex may be more successful when SPs are rare, but less successful when SPs are common. If there are more SPs there will be more competition, and more time will have to be spent trying to attract a mate. This time could have been spent more profitably by caring for the young. If there are many SPs, care giving may thus be more effective. Consequently, when phenotype SP is present at low frequency in a population, its average fitness is greater than that of phenotype CG. If the phenotypes are expressed by different genotypes, the frequency of genotype SP will increase and that of CG decrease, until they are of equal fitness (not necessarily of equal frequency). With alternative strategies, it implies that a certain percentage of individuals will carry SP genes, and the remainder CG genes. The percentage of individuals with SP genes is *f* and that with CG genes is 1-*f* and is the evolutionary stable distribution. When a single genotype permits expression of both searching for a sex partner and care giving, but with probabilities SP and CG respectively, a mixed strategy results with SP behavior chosen a certain number of times and CG behavior chosen the rest of the time. The frequency of display of a behavior is *f* for phenotype SP and 1-*f* for CG and is the evolutionary stable frequency.

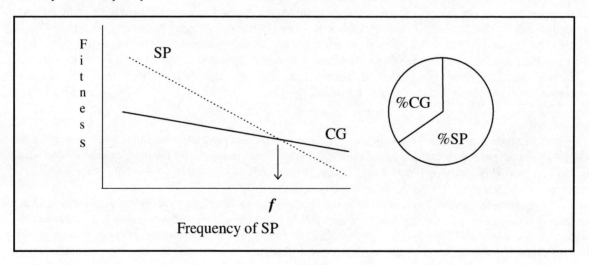

Figure 6.01
Phenotypic average fitness as a function of the frequency of phenotype SP. As the frequency of SP increases, its fitness decreases. At some frequency (f) both phenotypes have equal fitness; at higher frequencies of SP the fitness of CG overtakes that of SP.

Status-dependent selection. This type of selection is illustrated in Figure 6.02 and occurs when the relative fitness of alternative reproductive phenotypes depends on the status of the individual at that moment. The states of individuals always differ due to environmental influences (e.g. disease, accident, energy), genetic differences, and developmental stages (e.g. age). When through social interactions the state of an individual influences that individual's reproductive fitness, it is termed status (Gross, 1996).

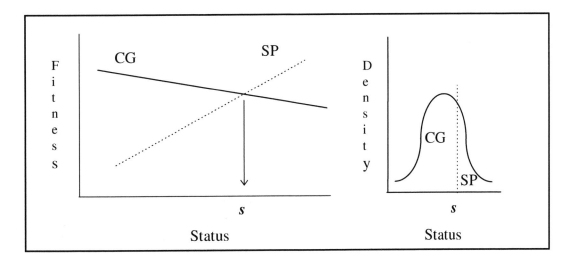

Figure 6.02

Phenotypic average fitness as a function of the status of an individual. An individual with status higher than the equilibrium status(s) benefits from behavior SP, while an individual with lower status benefits from behavior CG. The figure on the right shows that most individuals in the hypothetical population will exhibit behavior CG.

When individuals have a high status, they are benefited more by phenotype SP (e.g. searching) and when they have low status in a population they will benefit more from phenotype CG (e.g. care giving). This model (Gross, 1996) provides a framework for the conditional strategy of selection. The status at which the phenotypes provide equal fitness is **s**.

Parental investment

Because of the investment required in parenting, it is to the advantage of the heavier investor (often the female of the species) to be alert to signals and cues indicative of parental quality. As mentioned before, it may be in the interest of the other to deceive. In some species evidence have been found of honest signals of parental quality. The female house finch prefers males with brighter plumage. Such males have been found to provide more food to nestlings than more dull-feathered males. Plumage therefore is a reliable indicator of paternal quality.

It stands to reason then, that parental investment should be directed at the offspring of the parent. Since the female rarely has doubt about her offspring, the male is the one most often uncertain about paternity. Cues to paternity consequently are used to determine the amount of care that the male bestows on the offspring. For example, in the dunnock where 2 males may mate with the same female, the males provide care in relation to their paternity. Males use the extent of their mating access to the female during her fertilizable period as a cue to paternity and provide care accordingly. In house sparrows, a male may sometimes mate with two females. However, he will only attend one nest. Usually the second female mated with has to fend for herself and her offspring. Often the second female will raid the nest of the first female and commit infanticide which would then redirect the male s paternal care to her own offspring.

Parental strategy selection

Parental care adversely affects the survival of the caregiver, but increases the survival of the offspring. Consequently there is a trade-off between these concerns. The best route to follow is, from an evolutionary point of view, that which would maximize the total expectation of lifetime reproductive success. Because of the cost of parenting, one can expect some selection of strategies to occur: whether the parent should elect to engage in mating(i.e. benefit the survival of the genes), parenting (i.e. benefit the survival of the offspring), or in foraging (i.e. benefit the survival of the self). As an exercise, let us construct a formula to encapsulate these trade-offs. We shall limit the options to mating and parenting, but the reader is encouraged to expand the formula by adding foraging also.

Let the number of offspring that survive in any given day t be given by $O(t)$ and let this equal:
the success of an individual in mating $M(t)$; plus
the success of that individual in parenting $P(t)$; minus
deaths $D(t)$, unrelated to parenting (e.g. lightning), of the offspring of that individual. Thence we get the equation:
$O(t) = M(t) + P(t) - D(t)$ which we shall refer to as equation   (1).

Let now success in mating $M(t)$ be given by:
$M_m(t) = s_m(t)k_m(t)m_m(t)$ (2)
where $m_m(t)$ is the total number of matings possible during period t; $k_m(t)$ is the proportion of this time period spent in mating; and $s_m(t)$ is the proportion of successful matings over this period. The subscript m indicates that these variables pertain to the male.

Let further success in parenting for the male $P_m(t)$ be given by:
$P_m(t) = [p_m\{1-k_m(t)\} + p_f\{1-k_f(t)\}]O_m(t-1)$ (3)
where p_m and p_f are factors of success of parenting for male and female respectively (since both contribute to the survival of the offspring). These factors of success in parenting depends on the number of offspring that have to be cared for: the more offspring there are that need care, the more difficult parenting becomes, and the smaller the factor of success in parenting becomes. The term $1-k_m(t)$ means that an individual can only mate or parent, but not both. In practical terms this means that if one third of the day is spent mating, then only two-thirds of the day is available for parenting. If the proportion of the day spent mating is k_m, then the proportion of the day available for parenting is $1-k_m$. The index $(t-1)$ indicates the previous time period, e.g. the previous day.

Finally, let $D_m(t)$ be given by:
$D_m(t) = d_m(t)$ (4)
where $d_m(t)$ is the number of deaths of the male's offspring during the period t.

Substitution of equations (2), (3), and (4) into equation (1) yields the final equation:
$O_m(t) = s_m(t)k_m(t)m_m(t) + [p_m\{1-k_m(t)\} + p_f\{1-k_f(t)\}]O_m(t-1) - d_m(t)$ (5).

An inspection of the above formula reveals that if the male spends all his time mating, the survival of his offspring will depend only on the efforts of the female. If both male and female spend all their time mating, none of the offspring would survive. This is not true for all species, hence equation (5) should either be modified to a more general form or restricted in use to certain species. We shall assume here that equation (5) applies to a hypothetical species of bird. Inspection of equation (5) also reveals that if the male spends none of his time mating, there would be no offspring to parent. If only the first period is spent mating, and none thereafter, more time is available for parenting in later periods and success in parenting will increase.

Figure 6.03 shows how a change in the proportion of time spent parenting by our hypothetical bird species affects the number of offspring surviving parenting. It is clear from the figure that a bird is likely to leave more offspring behind if it spends between 80% and 90% of its time parenting and the remainder mating. If it spends more time mating, it may generate more offspring, but these will not receive adequate parental care and all may die. We have assumed the following values for the parameters: $s_m(t) = 0.8$; $k_m(t) = k_f(t)$; $m_m(t) = 10$; $p_m = p_f = -0.5(O_m(t-1))^2 + 2(O_m(t-1))$; and $d_m(t) = 0$. The precise values of these parameters have to be determined by field observation and/or by experiment.

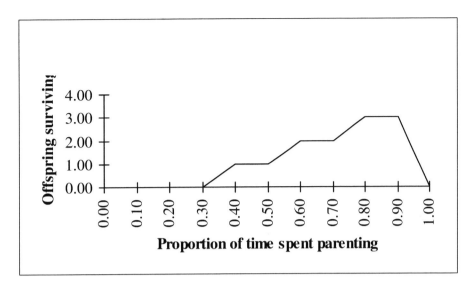

Figure 6.03
Survival outcome as a function of parental care

Parental care: Mother-infant interactions

In mammals, parental care generally involves interactions between the mother and young. Species inhabiting different environments can be expected to show different patterns of interaction. These interactions are often mediated by olfactory cues (e.g. Porter and Levy, 1995).

The rat mother (Rattus norvegicus) gives birth to large litters with about 7-14 pups after a gestation period of 21 days. Litters are born into a nest constructed by the mother. Rat pups are altricial (underdeveloped) at birth and are functionally deaf, blind, and not very mobile. However, they are not anosmic (without smell). During the first 2 weeks rat pups are helpless, but they begin to move around during the third week postpartum. Weaning is completed about 4 weeks after birth.

Odors of the mother's nest pacify rat pups and reduce locomotion. This may act to prevent helpless pups from straying from the nest. When made anosmic (with zinc sulfate perfusion) rat pups tend to become more active and emit ultrasonic distress calls more often. Older (intact) pups move toward home-cage rather than clean bedding.

Odors also facilitate nipple localization and attachment. Immediately after birth, the mother grooms herself, mostly the ventral area. Pups that are sensitive to and move towards salivary and amniotic odors deposited by the mother during grooming are more likely find the nipples and attach to them (it is interesting to contemplate whether the mechanism(s) responsible for such locomotion are in any way similar to those of bacterial chemotaxis). Olfactory bulbectomy (destruction of the olfactory bulbs of the brain) impairs nipple location and attachment. The alteration of olfactory nipple stimuli (e.g. by washing or scenting) also impair nipple location, but the alteration of other nipple properties such as temperature does not. Olfactory stimuli deposited by the pups themselves also play a role in nipple localization.

About 14 days postpartum, pups become sensitive to the odors of lactating females. This period of sensitivity lasts to the end of weaning. As one may expect, mothers start producing lactating odors during the period when pups are sensitive to these specific odors. This is also the period when pups become more mobile and explore around the nest.

Odor also plays a guiding role in determining the food choice of rats. Given that they are omnivorous, it seems essential to guide food selection as a means of protecting pups from ingesting possible poisons. This problem becomes more serious when the pups approach weaning. The flavor or odor of the mother's milk is generally altered by her diet. This provides guidance in the development of food preferences by the pups. Olfactory cues left by the mother and other adults at feeding sites where scraps of food often remain, further serve to indicate edible foods to the young.

The Egyptian spiny mouse (Acomys cahirinus) is a desert animal inhabiting rocky outcrops of northern Africa and southwest Asia. Spiny mice give birth to precocious (developed or mature) young. The litters tend to be small (about 2-3 pups) and, after a lengthy gestation period of about 39 days, the pups are rather large.

Shortly after birth, the eyes and ears of the pups are open and they are capable of locomotion. The mother does not construct a nest, presumably because the young can follow her around relatively early. The pups can be weaned at about a week of age, but when left with the mother, suckle for up to 4 weeks.

Like rat pups, spiny mouse pups move toward odors from the home cage. They also show a sensitive period to odors of lactating females at about the time when they become capable of independent locomotion. As one may expect, these stages occur much earlier in the mouse pups.

Spiny mice pups furthermore show a preference for chemical cues produced by conspecifics on the same diet as the mother. When a house mouse was used as a foster mother for spiny mouse pups, they learnt to prefer cues produced by the foster mother rather than those produced by conspecific females. This seems to indicate that "social" factors are more important than genetic ones in the development of spiny mouse food preferences.

Although early olfactory cues have a strong effect on mother-infant interactions, and determine food preferences, for example, such cues have not been found to have an effect on male rats in their choice of sexual partners. When male rat pups were reared with citral scented dams, they did not show a preference for citral scented females when mating (Moore et al., 1996).

In many species, odors affect also the mother: odors of the young stimulate or activate the mother to engage in certain behaviors. For instance, if the odors of the young are masked, the normal licking and cleaning of the young after birth is reduced.

Taken together, we can see that the rat and mouse mothers provide olfactory cues to their pups that are appropriate to each stage of their development, hence guiding their behaviors along adaptive avenues. In effect, one can say that the mothers manipulate the environments of the pups at each stage of their development. We shall see in a later chapter that pups, in turn, manipulate the environments of their mothers (to get the mothers to manipulate the environments of the pups appropriately). The environment, as we have already established, provides certain stimuli to an organism to which the organism should respond adaptively through the activation of the proper mechanisms.

References

Gross, M. R. 1996. Alternative reproductive strategies and tactics: diversity within sexes. Trends in Ecology and Evolution 11: 92-97.

Miczek, K. A.; Maxson, S. C.; Fish, E. W.; Faccidomo, S. 2001. Aggressive behavioral phenotypes in mice. Behavioural Brain Research 125: 167-181.

Moore, C. L.; Jordan, L. Wong, L. 1996. Early olfactory experience, novelty, and choice of sexual partner by male rats. Physiology and Behavior, 60: 1361-1367.

Porter, R. H.; Levy, F. Olfactory mediation of mother-infant interactions in selected mammalian species. In R. Wong (ed.), Biological perspectives on motivated activities, pp. 81-110. Norwood: Ablex.

Sluyter, F.; van Oortmerssen, G. A.; de Ruiter, A. J. H.; Koolhaas, J. M. 1996. Aggression in wild house mice: current state of affairs. Behavior Genetics, 26: 489-496.

Westneat, D. F.; Sargent, R. C. 1996. Sex and parenting: the effects of sexual conflict and parentage on parental strategies. Trends in Ecology and Evolution 11: 87-91.

CHAPTER 7
Hormones and hormonal cascades

Introduction

Hormones change the physiological states of organisms. These changed states make the organisms sensitive to particular stimuli from their environments. These stimuli, in turn, produce further hormone secretions in the organisms, thus producing cascades of hormonal release and physiological changes. In this chapter, we shall discuss the interactions that occur between physiological states, hormones, and environmental stimuli.

The role of hormonal cascades in the courtship and parenting behavior of the ring dove

Every stage of parental behavior in the ring dove is mediated by physiological (often hormonal) changes as illustrated in Figure 7.01 (see Leshner, 1978). Parental behavior in ring doves begins with courtship and nest building. In the female ring dove, this behavior is initiated by the sex hormones estrogen and progesterone. When ovariectomized females are given these hormones in that specific sequence, they stimulate nest building. Furthermore, when the female is treated with these hormones, nest building by the male is facilitated.

The same hormonal sequence is also necessary to start incubation. They cause the females to sit on eggs immediately upon presentation with eggs, whereas in their absence, this behavior takes 3-4 days. Once initiated, the hormone prolactin is necessary for the maintenance of incubation. When incubating females are removed from eggs for 10-12 days and then returned, they do not immediately resume incubation. However, if they were in the meantime treated with prolactin, they will do so immediately when presented with eggs.

The presence of a mate, nesting material, courtship, and eggs are all stimuli that trigger these hormonal changes. Presenting a female with a mate will initiate courtship, nest building, and mating, and trigger the secretion of estrogen and progesterone. This in turn leads to egg laying and the presence of the eggs induces incubation. The continued presence of the male helps to maintain incubation and is mediated in the female by an increase in prolactin levels.

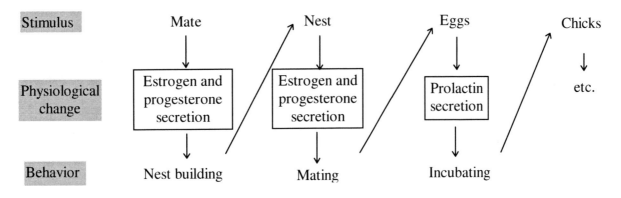

Figure 7.01
Schematic diagram of the mutual interactions between individuals as mediated by their physiologies and behaviors.

The mother-child interactions in mammals

Introduction. Maternal behaviors in mammals are highly motivated behaviors. Mothers work hard to provide for and protect their offspring. Maternal behaviors are selectively directed by a mother at her own offspring, consequently it is in her interests to learn to identify the young quickly. Mother-child interactions are usually thought of as psychological, especially in humans. However, it is becoming increasingly clear that these interactions are governed by neuroendocrinological factors (Uvnas-Moberg, 1996). It is our opinion that these hormonal factors serve to "synchronize" the mind or psychology of the organism with its (changing) physiological state and often also to initiate the next physiological stage by sensitizing the individual to particular stimuli. This makes the mother sensitive to stimuli from her young and the young sensitive to stimuli from the mother.

Pregnancy. During pregnancy, several hormones are secreted by both mother and child. Hormones secreted by the mother (including the placenta) generally serve to sustain pregnancy to term (e.g. progesterone).

Hormones , e.g. growth hormone (GH), secreted by the fetus generally serve to promote growth and development. Remember that some of this development is differential in order to provide the 2 genders (e.g. the secretion of the sex steroids estrogen and testosterone). Interactions may occur between the hormones of the mother and those of the fetus. For instance, if the (rat) mother is stressed, she secretes stress hormones (corticosteroids) which may inhibit the prenatal testosterone secretion patterns of male offspring, thus attenuating their effects on defeminization and masculinization of the developing brain.

The fetus swallows amniotic fluid which contains insulin-like growth factor. This facilitates growth of the fetus. Placental glucose transfer from mother to fetus regulates fetal insulin release. GH released by the mother stimulate fetal growth as well as maternal milk production (Gluckman and Harding, 1997). Fetal alcohol exposure interfere with the release of GH in the fetus, thus influencing the development of the fetus at least up to puberty (Conway and Swain, 19997), and so produces fetal alcohol syndrome. When fetuses start kicking at the end of the 2nd trimester, they start providing somatosensory stimuli to the mother, initiating the process of bonding.

Birth. When the pregnancy has proceeded to term, the mother gives birth. During parturition, both mother and young are subjected to intense reciprocal stimulation which triggers the release of a cascade of hormones. These hormones serve to prepare the mother for birth and nursing. In the child, the hormones prepare it for extrauterine life.

In rats, virgin females start to show maternal behavior after several days of cohabitation with pups. This process is called sensitization and occurs without the administration of exogenous (external) hormones. Somatosensory contact initially produced by sniffing, starts to induce maternal behavior in naive females. In the mother, the hormones of gestation and birth cause the area around the snout to become very sensitive to tactile stimuli. Olfactory structures of the brain also change causing odors associated with birth and pups to become more attractive to the mother. Because of the greater attractiveness of these odors, the mother is more inclined to sniff, lick, and handle the pups.

Cutaneous contact and compression of the newborn rat pup during vaginal birth has been shown to lead to the onset of rapid breathing. The absence of such cutaneous stimulation causes a pronounced reduction from 100% - 25% in the number of rat pups that breathe 1 hour after birth. Breathing is also facilitated by maternal licking (Ronca and Alberts, 1995). Licking furthermore ensures the close proximity of the female to her pups, enhancing the chances that the rooting pups will locate the nipples and start feeding. Licking by the mother of the anogenital region of the pups also stimulates urination and defecation (e.g. Suchecki et al., 1993). Keep in mind that the heart starts beating very early on in pregnancy, breathing however, becomes imperative only after birth. Cutaneous contact has a calming effect on human "pups": when babies are removed from their mothers, crying occurs in pulses but ceases abruptly on reunion with the mother.

During birth, the peptide hormone oxytocin is released in the mother. Oxytocin serves as a contractile agent facilitating the expulsion of the newborn (e.g. Gilbert et al., 1994). In humans, vaginal birth stimulates oxytocin secretion whereas cesarean section does not. Opioid receptors reach a maximum just prior to parturition, which heightens sensitivity to the opioids (the brain's natural painkillers) and reduces maternal pain perception (e.g. Dondi et al., 1991) while at the same time preventing the inhibition of oxytocin release by increased opioid release (which would otherwise be necessary to combat pain). Oxytocin itself also seems to elevate the pain threshold, thus further facilitating birth.

After birth, mothers rapidly learn to recognize their infants by smell, touch, vocalization, and eye-contact. Fathers can also learn these things, but they appear to be not as highly sensitive as the mothers. Mothers tend to touch their infants in a characteristic pattern following a normal birth: In the first 9 minutes, mothers spend more than 80% of their time touching, stroking, and massaging the baby. What does not work well for human babies is little and transient skin-to-skin contact and other forms of maternal interactions. In fact, such neglect leads to retardation of growth, resulting in psychosocial dwarfism and possible permanent impairment of health and mental abilities.

Lactation and suckling. After the newborn has started to breathe, the next concern is with feeding. Newborns, including human babies, instinctively search for the mother's nipple after birth. Their search for the nipple seems to be partly preprogrammed (rooting reflex) and guided by olfactory cues as evidenced by the fact that of two nipples, one of which was washed, babies seem to prefer the unwashed one. During the rooting reflex the baby's tongue is low in the mouth, thus facilitating attachment to the nipple. Interrupting the rooting reflex by forcing the baby to the nipple often means that the baby's tongue is against the palate which prevents it from feeding. Along with milk, warmth is also transmitted to the newborn. Suckling increases blood flow to the skin around the nipple, which makes suckling more pleasant, and soothes the baby. Nonnutritive sucking, such as on a pacifier, has been shown to increase growth rates in premature infants. It also increases the release of oxytocin in the brain of the baby and so reduces movement, sedates the baby, and elevates its pain threshold. Suckling is accompanied by increased digestive hormone release which may contribute to growth and development

In humans, there is at birth a greatly enhanced cutaneous sensitivity of the mother's breast. The mother thus is more sensitive to suckling by the baby. The more the baby suckles, the more systems of lactation and milk production are stimulated in the mother. During suckling, prolactin and oxytocin are secreted into the maternal blood. Prolactin stimulates milk production and oxytocin stimulates milk ejection. Oxytocin also causes increased blood flow to the area around the nipple. Oxytocin further stimulates transport of nutrients from maternal stores to the milk. In addition, suckling also increases the release of insulin. Because the number of insulin receptors in the mammary gland are increased, and decreased in maternal fat tissue during lactation, more nutrients will be trapped in the mammary gland and will be available for milk production. Suckling increases the release of digestive hormones in the mother, increasing the efficiency of food intake and growth (anabolism) in the mother and is mediated by oxytocin release. Lactating women also show a sedative effect in response to suckling, and exhibit a decrease in blood pressure and stress hormones.

Other maternal-child interactions. During suckling, mother and infant influence each other in various behavioral and hormonal ways. Separation of rat pups from their mothers produces distress calls from the pups, decreases pups' release of growth hormone and increases their levels of stress hormones. Cutaneous stimulation such as brushing (which mimics licking) will partly restore these changes. Oxytocin released in the brain during parturition and immediately after increases bonding between mother and offspring. Artificial bonding between ewes and lambs can be induced by the administration of oxytocin directly into the cerebral ventricles.

In humans, postnatal cutaneous contact between mother and baby (which appears to lead to the release of oxytocin in the brains of both) increases bonding between them and also increases short and long term interactions between them. Furthermore, the duration of breastfeeding is extended by immediate postnatal contact. Even a short separation of mother and child during the first day tends to shorten the duration of breastfeeding bouts. Plasma levels of oxytocin are elevated in mothers immediately following birth and breastfeeding. Like in animals, it also produces in humans a reduction in anxiety levels, increased patience, and reduced feelings of aggression.

As mentioned in the previous chapter, the behaviors of the offspring often induce or manipulate the mother to initiate appropriate parenting behaviors (e.g. Stern, 1997). Crying of the infant gets the mother's attention, inducing her to nurture the infant. This process of nurturing also facilitates mutual attachment and increases the sense of satisfaction of the mother (and presumably the baby). Infants that produce fewer releasing stimuli such as those that are deaf or blind or autistic often fail to evoke proper nursing responses in otherwise competent mothers. This is not true for infants with Down's syndrome who are capable of tactile, vocal, and visual interactions with the mother, and their mothers often report greater maternal satisfaction despite the knowledge that children with Down's syndrome may remain mentally underdeveloped and dependent on the parents, perhaps throughout life. Finally, it is interesting to note that rat mothers retrieve pups the age of their own litter and younger, but not older (place this in the context of Figure 7.01).

References

Conway, S.; Swain, R. 1997. Somatostatin-stimulated growth hormone-releasing factor secretion in vitro is modified by fetal ethanol exposure. Alcoholism, Clinical and Experimental Research 21: 703-709.

Dondi, D.; Maggi, R.; Panerai, A. E.; Piva, F.; Limonta, P. 1991. Hypothalamic opiatergic tone during pregnancy parturition and lactation in the rat. Neuroendocrinology 53: 460-466.

Gilbert, C. L.; Goode, J. A.; Mcgrath, T. J. 1994. Pulsatile secretion of oxytocin during parturition in the pig: Temporal relationship with fetal expulsion. Journal of Physiology 475: 129-137.

Gluckman, P.D.; Harding, J. E. 1997. The physiology and pathophysiology of intrauterine growth retardation. Hormone Research 48: 11-16.

Leshner, A. I. 1978. An introduction to behavioral endocrinology, p231. New York: Oxford University Press.

Ronca, A. E.; Albert, J. R. 1995. Cutaneous induction of breathing in perinatal rats. Psychobiology 23: 261-269.

Stern, J. M. 1997. Offspring-induced nurturance: animal-human parallels. Developmental Psychobiology 31: 19-31.

Suchecki, D.; Rosenfeld, P.; Levine, S. 1993. Maternal regulation of the hypothalamic-pituitary-adrenal axis in the infant rat: the roles of feeding and stroking. Brain Research 75: 185-192.

Uvnas-Moberg, K. 1996. Neuroendocrinology of the mother-child interaction. TEM 7: 126-131.

CHAPTER 8
Temperament in Primates

Introduction

Temperament is defined in the literature (see Clarke and Boinski, 1994) as a behavioral style that tends to be consistent over time and which reflects the individual's responsiveness to novel and stressful stimuli. Personality, on the other hand, refers to the individual's social style. Temperament is more easily studied in non-social situations and personality is more easily studied in social situations. When a novel situation is also a social situation, both temperament and personality may come into play.

Children and other young primates often exhibit temperament at a very early age. The extremes of temperament, found in about 15% of cases, namely very shy/reserved and very outgoing/active tend to remain stable over the life-span of the individual. For example, those infants that were temperamental at age 4 months of age were most likely to be temperamental at 14 and 21 months, as well as 4.5, 7.5 and 10.5 years of age (see Kagan et al., 2001). The majority of individuals, however, show a variation of temperament over their lifetimes.

Reserved individuals are classified as inhibited/reactive and outgoing individuals as uninhibited/non-reactive. This seemingly contradictory classification system makes more sense when viewed in terms of the behavioral/physiological components of temperament. Individuals that are behaviorally inhibited are also generally physiologically reactive: they show high heart rates, high blood norepinephrine (a neurotransmitter and hormone also known as noradrenaline) levels, and high blood cortisol (a stress hormone) levels in response to novelty. Their heightened and more volatile sympathetic nervous system responses to stimuli are also evident in cooler fingers (related to higher blood pressure and reduced blood flow to the extremities) and a temperature difference of 0.5 °C or more between the index fingers (Kagan et al., 2001). Individuals that are behaviorally uninhibited are generally physiologically non-reactive to novel stimuli. Temperament can thus be seen as a reflection of the relative arousability of the sympathetic nervous system (that part of the nervous system responsible for reacting to dangers - hence the "fight or flight" system). Now the reader may have a notion of why some people want to go bungee jumping while others find it difficult enough just to cross a busy street.

Given the reader's knowledge of the interactions between individuals and their environments, she or he may appreciate the fact that temperament and personality, at least to the extent that they modulate behaviors, will ultimately influence an individual's reproductive success. This relationship should become more clear when reading the rest of the chapter. The reader will also notice that each of an individual, a population, and a species can be seen as a being a single organism and that the concept of temperament will be applied to each of these.

Components of temperament

Statistical analyses of studies in various primate species have consistently identified 3 "dimensions" of temperament: confident/non-confident; active /hypoactive; and sociable/solitary (see Clarke and Boinski, 1994). Others prefer the terms novelty seeking (a tendency to thrive on excitement and novelty), harm avoidance (a tendency to respond strongly to adverse stimuli), and reward dependence (a tendency to respond strongly to rewards), based on hereditary traits, to describe aspects of temperament (see Bond, 2001). In general, reactive individuals tend to avoid excitement while non-reactive individuals tend to seek excitement. Note the difference between active (refers to the behavior) and reactive (refers to the nervous system).

The origins of temperament

<u>Genes.</u> The early display of temperament in some primates suggests that it is a constitutional, as opposed to an acquired, factor with a biological and thus possibly a genetic basis. The evidence from studies in humans suggest a moderate genetic influence on some aspects of temperament. In the rhesus monkey, temperament can already be detected in 30 day old infants and there is evidence for a genetic contribution to temperament. Personality traits, too, appear to be genetically influenced with a genetic component of about 40%; an environmental component of about 7%; and the remainder being due to other factors such as measurement uncertainty (Bouchard, 1994).

<u>Biology.</u> There is evidence to show that different aspects of temperament (as well as personality) have biological correlates (see Bond, 2001). High levels of serotonin transmission or serotonin receptor sensitivity seem to contribute to reduced anxiety and improved social functioning such as greater self-directedness and more self-discipline. Novelty-seeking and social attachment, in contrast, appears to involve the neurotransmitters dopamine

and norepinephrine. Reward-dependence appears to be mostly related to norepinephrine neurotransmission. The brain structures that appear to be involved in the generation of temperament (and possibly personality) are the nucleus of the solitary tract, the amygdala, and the prefrontal cortex (see Kagan et al., 2001). These structures and their neurotransmission will be examined in more depth in later chapters and then integrated in a further chapter. The reader is therefore urged to reread the present chapter and to provide an explanation of temperament in light of the integrated system at that stage.

Prenatal environment. In humans, a consistent association has been found between prenatal maternal anxiety and reactive temperaments in the infants of such mothers. This is possibly due to the high levels of stress hormones in the mothers impacting the fetuses. In both stressed rat and monkey mothers, the offspring have been shown to have heightened reactivity. When rhesus mothers are exposed to a 14 day treatment of ACTH during mid-gestation, which caused stress hormones to be released, their infants are irritable and very difficult to console. These findings should be seen in the context of the close interactions between mothers and children occurring on various physiological and behavioral levels that have been considered in some depth before.

Postnatal environment. Interactions between infant temperament and maternal style influence things such as mother-child bonding, confidence, and development. The children of excitable rhesus monkey mothers are found to be less confident than those of more placid mothers, especially noticeable in the male offspring. When low-reactive infants are given to foster mothers, they seem to be unaffected by mothering style. However, when high reactive infants are given to nurturing mothers, they develop behaviorally more rapidly. Monkey infants reared with early exposure to toys and peers are less fearful than those reared without. Macaque monkeys tend to be less social when they experienced brief maternal separation. Interaction styles in baboons have also been found to be related to physiological indicators of stress.

The social effects on temperament can be summarized in the following manner:

1. atypical rearing (in isolation, with inanimate surrogate mothers, in peer-only groups) increases negative responses to novelty;

2. more typical rearing produces less inhibition and more confidence toward novelty;

3. early experiences influence the development of the stress-sensitive sympathetic nervous system.

It is of interest to note that peer-only reared rhesus monkeys show reduced stress responses to moderately stressful stimuli while mother-reared ones show greater responses to moderately stressful stimuli. This could possibly indicate that the lower level of response of peer-reared monkeys may be inappropriately low. (Compare these findings with those of play-fighting and aggression in rhesus monkeys reared in similar groups).

In humans, parental style or genetics also appears to affect the temperament of offspring. Children with parents that have panic disorder are significantly more likely to be behaviorally inhibited than those of control ("normal") parents (Kagan et al., 2001).

Variations in temperament

Individuals It has been mentioned that in human individuals of Caucasian origin, about 15% exhibit one of the extremes of temperament. In rhesus monkeys, about 20% are easily stressed. The other 80% adapt rapidly to environmental changes such as social separation. In many primate species, it appears that a non-reactive temperament enables an individual to calibrate their responses to different intensities of stress, thus enabling them to deal with stress more effectively. Reactive individuals, on the other hand, tend to function near the top of the "reactiveness" scale under normal conditions. When unusually stressful situations prevail, they cannot increase their reactiveness much more, hence a ceiling-effect comes into play.

The reader should put this into the perspective established in the introductory chapter: if an individual is very non-reactive, that individual won't be able to respond to stress as much as may be necessary - this could be dangerous (e.g. they could be taken as prey). If an individual is over-reactive, they may respond too much to even small stressors, thus being inefficient (it costs energy to respond to stress). This approach should make the reader suspect that there must be an optimal level of "reactiveness" for a given environment. In other words, if someone talks about temperament, it may not be informative to mention only reactive vs. non-reactive. It is more informative to mention temperament in the context of the environment in which it occurs. If a population is well-adapted to its environment, then the "average" temperament would correspond with a suitable degree of reactiveness to an "average" environmental stressor.

Populations. Subpopulations of the squirrel monkey occur in Northern South America. The Gothic squirrel monkey originates from the eastern part and the Roman squirrel monkey from the western part. Roman squirrel monkeys have both male and female dominance hierarchies, live in segregated sex-groups in separate territories outside of the breeding season, and all females, who are generally aggressive, are dominant to all males. Gothic squirrel monkeys live in integrated groups year-round and have a single linear dominance hierarchy which includes both sexes.

In both populations, individual differences in temperament exist. However, the general temperaments of the two populations differ even more than those between individuals in the same population. Individuals of the Roman population have higher baseline stress-hormone (cortisol) levels than those of the Gothic population. The former individuals produce a greater increase in cortisol levels followed by a slower return to normal levels in response to stress. In Roman groups, dominant males have a stronger cortisol response to stress than subordinate males. In Gothic groups, subordinate males have a stronger cortisol response to stress than dominant males.

In the wild, Roman populations have to compete for food and defend against aggression more intensely than the Gothic populations. Consequently they appear to have a higher "set point" for the stress response system. In other species, such population differences in temperament have also been found. For instance, infant rhesus monkeys from a Chinese population were more irritable, reactive, and aggressive, than infants from an Indian population.

Species. It may not be surprising to discover that species-typical variations in temperament also occur in addition to population and individual differences in temperament. For distantly related species living in a similar tropical environment, the Titis and squirrel monkeys, different species-temperaments exist. Titis monkeys are mostly leave-eating (folivorous), territorial, and monogamous. Squirrel monkeys are mostly insectivorous, non-territorial, promiscuous and they live in large social groups. Titis monkeys are adapted to a more stable, less demanding ecological niche than squirrel monkeys. They have lower heart rates and plasma stress hormone levels in response to experimentally imposed stressors.

On the other hand, lion-tailed macaque monkeys have an omnivorous diet, and are bold, adaptive, and exploratory. Cynomolgus macaque monkeys are frugivores and are shy, diffident, and easily disturbed. In response to stressors they respond with high heart rates and stress-hormones. The findings for Titis, squirrel, lion-tailed, and cynomolgus macaque monkeys seem inconsistent, and it may interesting to consider why this is so. In particular, it appears that the folivorous Titis monkeys and frugivorous cynomolgus monkeys, which one would expect to inhabit similar, undemanding ecological niches, have opposite temperaments. This difficulty would disappear if the cynomolgus habitat is more unstable than that of the Titis monkey. On the other hand, it may be the case that the cynomolgus monkey has recently (in evolutionary terms) been displaced by another species or environmental change from its original habitat, is currently in a novel and unfamiliar environment, and has not had enough evolutionary time to adapt to its new environment. In the latter case, the more temperamental cynomolgus monkeys will gradually become less temperamental, provided they do not get displaced again. One should therefore keep in mind that a population put under stress may respond with a transient increase in temperament.

Consequences of temperament

Individuals. Macaque monkeys that rate highly in confidence and opportunism are more likely to be of higher rank, and those more insecure and dependent are more likely to be of lower rank. In rhesus monkeys also, less fearfulness is associated with greater sociability. In baboons, those rated lowest on fearfulness, are more often groomed and most likely to be of dominant rank. In chimpanzees, dominant individuals are more aggressive, more social, and more controlled, while those of lower rank are more timid and impulsive. These and other findings are tabulated below in Table 8.01. It is fairly clear from the primate evidence that the temperament of an individual can play an important role in that individual's social interactions. Recall, though, that personality is defined in terms of social style, but temperament not! Even so, temperament has clearly important social consequences.

Populations. The studies on the Roman and Gothic populations of squirrel monkeys suggest that the variation in the temperament of a population may reflect the degree of reactivity necessary to function in a particular environment. A more "unstable" environment demands a more reactive population.

Species. Why are there species-differences in temperament? The results from population studies suggest that rapidly changing environments favor reactive populations. Does this hold true for species? The degree of relatedness between species can be determined in a variety of ways. Because children inherit the genes of their parents, they will exhibit some of the physical and behavioral characteristics of the parents. Children tend to look like their parents. Species can be related to one another based on the similarities in their phenotypes. Species can also be related to one another based on the similarities between their blood proteins. The best way to determine species "family" trees would be to directly compare their genetic material (i.e. a DNA "fingerprinting" of species) which is currently only partially possible. However, based on the currently known evidence, humans are considered to be very closely related to chimpanzees and almost as closely related to gorillas. Together the 3 species are known as the great apes, which sometimes includes the orangutan. They are in turn related to baboons and Old World (African and Asian) monkeys, and less so to New World (North and South American) monkeys. Humans and monkeys are primates. Primates and animals giving birth to live young are mammals. Reptiles lay eggs (e.g. snakes and crocodiles) and are only extremely distantly related to mammals. Birds also lay eggs and are not closely related to mammals, but there is some evidence that they may be descended from dinosaurs, hence are distantly related to reptiles. Keep this in mind when you read the following.

When different species are confronted with novel objects, reptiles show the least reactiveness and primates show the most reactiveness. Among primates colobus monkeys (langurs) are least reactive, macaques and baboons are more reactive and great apes (to which humans belong) are the most reactive. Among great apes orangutans are withdrawn and brooding, gorillas tend to be diffident and shy, chimpanzees (most closely related to humans) outgoing and expressive, and humans are the most expressive.

Do not be under the impression that things stop there. As with different populations of squirrel monkeys, different populations of humans exist. It is, in our opinion, quite likely that the six different human races form such subpopulations of humans. Given the social sensitivity pertaining to issues of race, a further analysis may be problematic. However, the reader should still consider the implications of possible variation in temperament in human populations, and may ponder how, among humans, Africans, Europeans, and Asians are to be rated in terms of reactiveness.

Table 8.01

The relationships of temperament to various social and physiological factors across species.

Species	Individual Temper.	Status	Social	Aggres.	Heart Rate	StressS.	N.E.	Testos-terone	Sero-tonin
Monkey (vervet)		High	More						
Macaque (pigtail)	N.R.	High	More	-----	-----	-----	-----	-----	-----
Macaque (rhesus)	N.R.	High	Less	Low	Low	Low	Low	High	High
Baboon	N.R.	High	Less	More	-----	Low	-----	High	-----
Chimp	N.R.	High	More	More	-----	-----	-----	-----	-----

Temper. = temperament; Aggress. = aggressiveness; Stress S. = stress-related steroid hormones; N.E. = norepinephrine; N.R. = non-reactive.

References

Bond, A. J. 2001. Neurotransmitters, temperament, and social functioning. European Neuropsychopharmacology 11: 261-274.

Bouchard, T. J. 1994. Genes, environment, and personality. Science 264: 1700-1701.

Clarke, A. S.; Boinski, S. 1994. Temperament in nonhuman primates. American Journal of Primatology 37: 103-125.

Kagan, J.; Snidman, N.; McManis, M.; Woodward, S. 2001. Temperamental contributions to the affect family of anxiety. Psychiatric Clinics of North America 24: 677-688.

PART II
THE MECHANISMS THAT GENERATE DRIVES
Basic Mechanisms

CHAPTER 9
Homeostatic mechanisms

Introduction

In Part I of this text we have discussed the intimate relationship that exists between an organism and the environment in which it has to live. We saw that the environment produces stimuli to which the organism react. In the case of simple organisms like bacteria, these reactions are rather direct and relatively speedy. In the case of more complex organisms like mammals, these interactions can be very sophisticated and complex: some of the interactions already occur at the genetic level, some occur during pregnancy, others during childhood, and most perhaps, during the adult life of the animal. Consequently, the interactions between an organism and its environment can be of a short-term, medium-term, or long-term nature. Since the environment of an organism contains, as a rule, other organisms, interactions occur also between different organisms, thus adding to the complexity of organism-environment systems.

Although this complexity can easily overwhelm and confuse one, we believe that attempts at understanding these systems should still be made since we ultimately benefit from such knowledge in the form of improved health care, better education, improved conflict resolution, and a host of others benefits ultimately leading to a higher standard of living. To understand organism-environment interactions, we need to identify the systems and subsystems involved and their reciprocal effects. This would allow us to conceive of these interactions in mechanistic terms with their accompanying benefits of explanation and prediction. In Part II of this book, we shall then investigate some particular mechanisms, implemented by neural systems to form psychological mechanisms, that could explain motivated behaviors. We shall first look at basic mechanisms and their applications, and then at more advanced mechanisms.

A mechanism is a system or structure consisting of interacting parts, each of which performs a particular task, that, when operating together and in the proper sequence, produces some specific result. Machines were the classic implementations of mechanisms, however, the notion of a system consisting of subsystems that operate in concert to produce a desired outcome has been applied to other systems, including biological ones.

Homeostatic mechanisms

A homeostatic mechanism (HM) can be described as a mechanism which operates to keep a variable within a certain range of values (however small the range) by counteracting, in one or a variety of ways, perturbations which may move the variable out of this range. A HM consists of several key components and the character of its operation crucially depends on the arrangement of these components relative to one another.

Probably the most familiar type of HM is the thermostat or air conditioner used to regulate the internal temperature of a building. If the ambient temperature in the building as registered by the temperature sensor falls below a certain value (the set point) the switch controlling the heat source is switched on. This will result in an increase in the ambient temperature. When the temperature has risen to equal the set point temperature, the switch to the heat source is switched off. An air conditioner works on the same principle, except that the air is cooled instead of heated. This sequence of events will repeat itself over and over again and in the process the ambient temperature will stay relatively close to the set point temperature irrespective of the outside temperature.

Every HM has the following components:
1. an effector (the heating/cooling element);
2. a sensor (the temperature sensor);
3. a controller (the on/off switch);
4. a set point (the temperature dial - the 'desired' room temperature);
5. a regulated variable (the temperature of the room in general);
6. signal transmission lines (electrical wires); and
7. a current point (the present temperature of the room).

The arrangement of these components relative to one another can have very important consequences for the operation of the mechanism. Consider a HM consisting of a mixing tank that can hold a certain volume of water. The tank provides water to an end user (e.g. a shower) and proper regulation of the water temperature delivered to the end user is necessary. Water is pumped into the tank from outside and the incoming water temperature can fluctuate considerably depending on the season and the time of day. The tank is equipped with two effectors: a heating element and a cooling element. There is also a temperature sensor added to this arrangement.

Control Arrangements. Before this tank can be put into operation, the temperature sensor needs to be installed. This is not as trivial as it may seem. The sensor can be installed in the pipe that leads from the tank to the end user. From the sensor a connection leads to the controller which will switch the heating coil on when the temperature drops below the set point and off when the temperature rises above the set point. The controller will also switch the cooling coil on when the temperature rises above the set point and off when it drops below the set point.

If the water coming out of the tank is too cold, the temperature sensor will convey this information to the controller which will cause the heating coil to be switched on. This will lead to an increase in the water temperature coming from the tank. Such an arrangement forms a feedback control loop: the outcome of the heating or cooling process is fed back or used to control the ongoing activity of the process. However, if the water coming out of the tank is too cold, it doesn't matter whether the water will subsequently be heated, it is too late to affect the temperature of the water going to the end user. Therefore, installing the temperature sensor in the pipe leading from the tank to the aquarium may not be advisable.

The sensor can be installed in the pipe feeding water into the tank from outside. This would allow the mechanism to respond to changes in the temperature of the water before the water reaches the tank by switching the heating or cooling coils on and off. This arrangement constitutes a feedforward control loop and allows the system to anticipate the temperature of the water that will enter the tank: if cold water is headed for the tank, the heating element can be activated to heat the incoming cold water and vice versa for hot water entering the tank. However, since there is no temperature sensor monitoring the temperature of the water leaving the tank, it cannot be ascertained whether the temperature adjustments have been adequate: in response to cold water coming into the tank, the water in the tank could be overheated and thus the water fed to the end user would be too hot. A similar problem could result from hot water entering the tank. Consequently, installing the temperature sensor in the pipe feeding into the tank may also be ill-advised.

This leaves one more option: the temperature sensor could be installed in the tank itself. But such a solution may incorporate the worst elements of the previous two: the mechanism can now neither anticipate the temperature of incoming water, nor can it verify the temperature of the outgoing water. Finally, the arrangement of the heating and cooling coils would also affect the operation of the system and their placement should be taken into consideration.

The existence of control loops, i.e. feedback (Figure 9.01) and feedforward (Figure 9.02) loops, is an essential feature of homeostatic systems (Hardy, 1983; Smith, 1987; Colgan, 1989; Evans, 1989) and both may be incorporated into the same HM. There are two types of control loops: positive and negative. In the preceding examples, negative control loops have been discussed. These generally counteract disturbances to the system while positive control will tend to magnify disturbances. Depending now on the type of control and the relative positions of effectors and controllers, 4 basic arrangements could be obtained.

1. Negative control with feedback
2. Negative control with feedforward
3. Positive control with feedback
4. Positive control with feedforward

Table 9.01 is a summary of control arrangements and their relative benefits.

Table 9.01

The benefits and costs of different control methods

Control method	Advantage	Disadvantage
Feedback	Mistakes can be corrected	Mistakes are made
Feedforward	Problems can be anticipated	Mistakes cannot be corrected
Positive	Amplifies desired changes	Amplifies unwanted changes
Negative	Counters unwanted changes	Counters desired changes

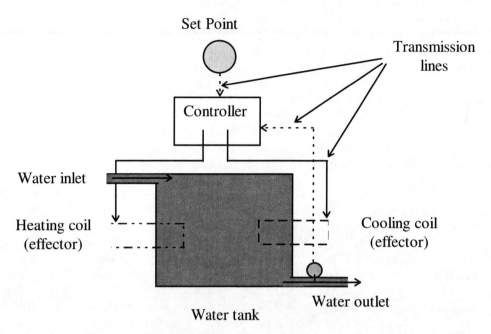

Figure 9.01

A water tank using a HM with feedback control to regulate the water temperature.

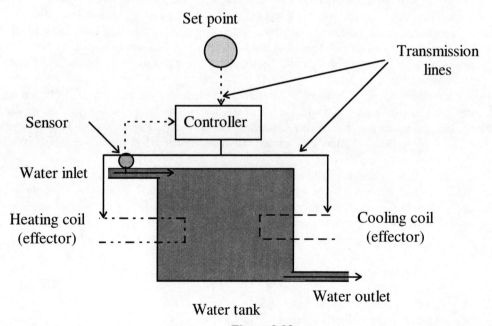

Figure 9.02

A water tank using a HM with feedforward control to regulate the water temperature.

Figure 9.03 shows the effects of negative feedback control on a regulated variable (temperature) of a system. When the temperature drops below the set point, a powerful heating mechanism is switched on. Because it takes a small amount of time for the heating mechanism to become fully operational, the temperature drops slightly below the set point. As the heating takes effect, the temperature increases above the set point. The heater is then switched off. However, due to the powerful heating that was triggered, the temperature will continue to rise for some time (think about the element of a stove, if the element is switched off, it does not cool down immediately, but takes some time to do so). Eventually, the heating stops completely and the system starts to cool down again.

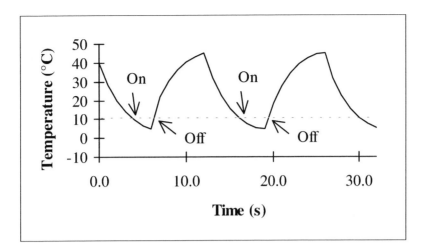

Figure 9.03

The effects of negative control on the regulated variable. The diagram shows the temperature fluctuations of a system with negative feedback control. The set point is at 10 °C.

Controller Types. In addition to the arrangements of the components of the HM, the nature of these components can dramatically affect the operation of the mechanism. This is perhaps especially true for the controller. There are four basic types of controller, each with a characteristic effect on variable regulation. This concerns the ways in which the controllers control the operation of the effectors. For instance, if the electrical current that flows through the heating coil can be regulated and control can be exerted over the amount of cooling fluid flowing through the cooling coil, a considerable amount of control can be exercised over the temperature of the water leaving the tank for the shower. The 4 controller types are the following:

1. The on/off controller.
2. The proportional controller.
3. The rate controller.
4. The integral controller.

The simplest way to regulate the temperature of the water in the tank is by merely switching the appropriate coil, say the heating coil, on or off as shown in Figure 9.04. That is, when the heating coil is switched on, the maximum amount of current flows through the coil to heat it.

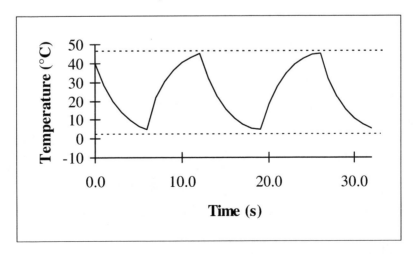

Figure 9.04

The effects of on/off control on the regulated variable. With on/off control, the value of the regulated variable (e.g. temperature) often oscillates markedly within a range.

On/off controllers are rather primitive, and often produce fluctuations in the regulated variable. For example, if there is a small drop in the tank temperature, just sufficient to let the water temperature fall below the set point (SP) and so trigger activation of the heating coil, there may be an overheating of the water in the tank which is likely to activate the cooling coil causing under-cooling of the water. This in turn will activate the heating coil and thus precipitate a ' temperature war' between the heating and cooling coil an event that is likely to be unnecessarily costly because in addition to temperature fluctuations from outside, the system now generates its own fluctuations. In other words, an on-off controller which works in an all-or-nothing manner causes by its very nature oscillations in the water temperature (Smith, 1987). A regular light switch which is either on or off, is an example of an of/off controller.

If, instead of the on-off controller, a proportional controller is used, then the temperature of the water in the tank can be much more smoothly regulated. For instance, if there is only a small drop in the temperature of the water, then a small current can be allowed to pass through the heating coil causing a small heating effect. On the other hand, a sudden large drop in the temperature of the water can be countered by maximal activation of the heating coil. Thus, the amount of heating or cooling effected is in proportion to the extent to which the temperature of the water deviates from the set point temperature (the error) as shown in Figure 9.05 below. A dimmer light switch is an example of proportional control.

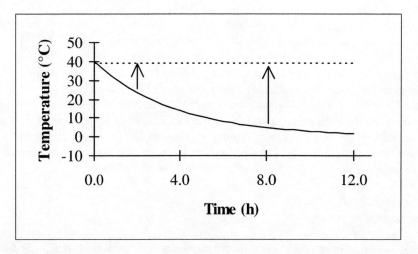

Figure 9.05
The effects of a decline in value of the regulated variable on the degree of activation of the effectors of a HM by a proportional controller. The size of the error determines the degree of activation of the effector. The arrows show errors of different size. At 8 hours the effector is more activated than at 2 hours because the error is larger at 8 compared to 2 hours. The set point is 40 °C.

Another way in which control can be exerted, is through rate control as illustrated in Figure 9.06. If the water in the tank is initially at the desired temperature and starts to change gradually, getting progressively colder, the heating coil needs to be activated in a manner that reflects the change in incoming water temperature and opposes it. A rate controller is sensitive to the rate at which the water temperature changes and will increase the flow of current through the heating coil at the same rate causing heating of the water in the tank at the same rate at which it is cooled by the incoming water. These opposing processes should then balance each other out. A rate controller allows the process to take corrective action at the rate at which it is needed: fast action results from fast occurring changes and slower action occurs in response to more gradual changes.

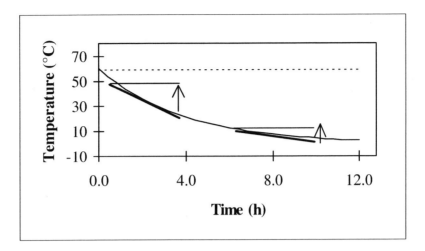

Figure 9.06
The effects of a decline in value of the regulated variable on the degree of activation of the effectors of a HM by a rate controller. The rate of change of the error determines the degree of activation of the effector. The gradients (steepness) of the heavy lines show the rate of change of the error at different times. Initially, around 2 hours, the temperature changes faster (the curve is steeper) and the effector is more activated than around 8 hours where the error is larger but doesn't change much anymore.

It is important to understand the difference between proportional and rate control: proportional control is based on how large the error is; rate control is based on how fast the error is changing. When comparing Figure 9.05 and Figure 9.06, the reader will notice that with proportional control, the effectors are more activated toward 8 hours and less toward 2 hours. The opposite is true for rate control *in the given examples* - not always.

There is one more type of control to consider, namely integral or reset control. Reset control causes heating or cooling for as long as an error exists. Controller action is based on the cumulative error as demonstrated in Figure 9.07 and thus even very small constant errors will eventually activate the controller enough to reduce the error to zero. In other words, if an error exists that is too small to activate the controller, it will eventually do so if the error is accumulated. The effector, then, is activated based on (e.g. proportional to) the sum of all the preceding errors. Thus, if the temperature in the tank is for some reason always constant and just slightly below the set point and it is imperative that the set point temperature be exactly maintained, integral control should be used.

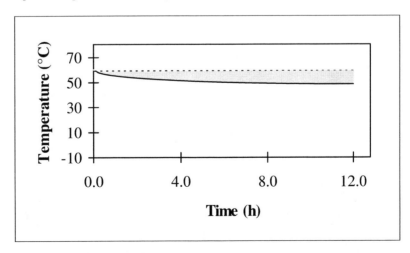

Figure 9.07
The effects of a small decline in value of the regulated variable on the degree of activation of the effectors of a HM by an integral controller. The cumulative error (shaded area) determines the degree of activation of the effector.

The proportional, integral and rate controllers can be used individually or in combination (in some form of hierarchy) to control a process. If one considers the fact that there are 4 different types of controller and 4 different control arrangements, each with its own implications for temperature regulation, it is clear that there are several control options available for regulating the temperature of the water in the mixing tank. In a later chapter we will discuss another type of controller that benefits from learning and is based on artificial neural networks - the adaptive controller. Nevertheless, this brief introduction should suggest to the reader that control systems can be highly sophisticated.

References

Colgan, P. 1989. Animal motivation. London: Chapman and Hall.

Evans, P. 1989. Motivation and emotion. London: Routledge.

Hardy, R. N. 1983. Homeostasis. London: Edward Arnold.

Smith, R. E. 1987. Mammalian homeostasis. In J. J. Head (series ed.) Carolina biology readers. Burlington, N. C.: Caroline Biological Supply Company.

CHAPTER 10
Homeostatic mechanisms and behavior

Introduction

An organism can be conceptualized as a collection of innate psychological mechanisms (Tooby and DeVore, 1987). Some of these mechanisms could be HMs. Behaviors are the consequences of the functioning of these mechanisms. That is, a particular behavior is only expressed if one of its associated HMs is operating. The primary function of HMs may be the preservation of the physical integrity of the organism. This implies that HMs will function by triggering behaviors to counteract environmental stimuli likely to compromise the organism's physical integrity. Figure 10.01 is a simplified mapping of the components of a HM onto an organism.

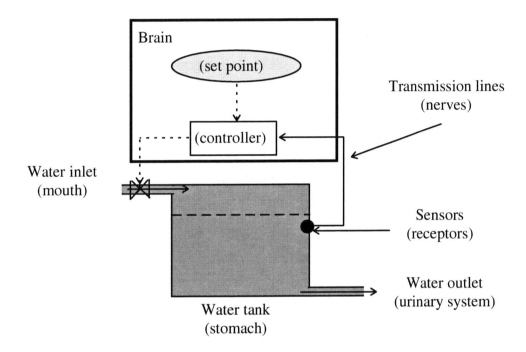

Figure 10.01
A HM controlling the water level in a tank mapped, in a very simplistic manner, onto an organism.

Although properly functioning mechanisms are always triggered into operation by factors external to the mechanism - stimuli provided by the environment or by other mechanisms in the same organism - they are ultimately prompted by factors external to the organism. The behaviors expressed by the operation of HMs are consequently all 'elicited' behaviors. If one HM is triggered by the operation of another, and the stimulus that triggered the first has not been noticed, the behavior expressed by the operation of the second HM may appear to be an 'emitted' behavior.

It should be noted that the activation of a HM can result in two types of 'behavior'. Both physiological processes and behavioral acts can contribute to regulation (Richter, 1927; Adolph, 1943). When a HM is activated as a result of the current value or current point (CP) of the regulated variable being moved away from the SP by some stimulus, it attempts to counteract this deviation from the SP through the activation of internal processes (e.g. sweating) or external processes (e.g. moving to a shady spot). For instance, there is some dissociation of physiological and behavioral thermoregulation (see Stellar and Stellar, 1985). It is possible that physiological and behavioral regulation are linked in a hierarchical order such that one is triggered when the other can no longer maintain homeostatic balance. Thus, homeostatically triggered behavior serves to control the relationship between organism and external environment and so helps to regulate the stability of the internal environment (Young, 1961; Koshtoyants, 1960; Richter, 1927; Adolph, 1943; Stellar and Stellar, 1985). The manner in which HMs control physiological processes and activate behavioral acts will be examined in more detail in later chapters.

HMs and hedonic states

As indicated in the previous section, HMs are ultimately triggered by environmental stimuli, that is, those stimuli that are likely to compromise the physical integrity of the organism. The impingement of such a stimulus causes the CP of a variable or variables regulated by a HM to be affected. Thus, every stimulus impinging on an organism serves to move the CP of at least one variable in a constant direction along the dimension on which that variable is being regulated for as long as this stimulus impinges on the organism. Although this movement of the CP of a variable by a stimulus is unidirectional, it may be either toward or away from that variable's set point depending on the original position of the CP of that variable relative to the SP when the stimulus first impinged. For instance, if an animal is initially hypothermic (say around 32 °C), its core body temperature is below some ideal value. If the animal now moves into the hot sun, its body temperature will increase until it reaches the ideal value. If the animal continues to remain in the sun, its body temperature will increase beyond the ideal value and it will start to experience heat stress. The conservation laws of physics are reflected in this unidirectionality of movement of the CP of the regulated variable.

A stimulus that serves to move a CP toward the relevant SP for that variable sets up a positive hedonic state in the organism (a state of pleasure). Similarly, a stimulus that moves a CP away from its relevant SP, causes a negative hedonic state (a state of displeasure). The intensity of the hedonic state set up by an impinging stimulus is assumed to depend on both the degree of displacement of the CP away from (or toward) the SP and the rate at which such displacement is occurring. When a stimulus sets up a positive hedonic state it is perceived as a 'pleasant' stimulus while it will be reacted to as an 'aversive' stimulus when it sets up a negative hedonic state. An organism will react to a stimulus that it receives in such a way that, if the stimulus is pleasant, it will continue to pursue that stimulus, while if the stimulus is aversive, it will not seek contact with that stimulus. The conjecture exposed in this paragraph is of crucial importance in linking HMs to behavior. These concepts are represented in Figure 10.02.

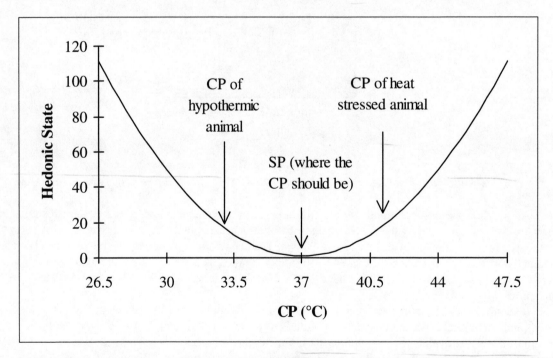

Figure 10.02

The relationship between current point (CP), set point (SP), and hedonic state. The hedonic state is negative when the CP is moving away (in either direction) from the SP, and positive when the CP moves toward (from either side) the SP.

It is important to realize that an organism reacts to a stimulus, not on the basis of the nature of the stimulus, but on the basis of the hedonic state set up by this stimulus. By way of illustration, let the CP of a variable regulated by a HM of an organism be such that for a given stimulus impinging on the organism, the CP is moved initially toward the SP. This sets up a positive hedonic state and the organism will continue to receive the stimulus. If this stimulus impinges on the organism long enough, the CP would eventually reach and then pass and move away from the SP. When the CP starts moving away from the SP, a negative hedonic state will be set up and the organism will avoid the stimulus. *Since the stimulus did not change, but the hedonic state did, it is clear that the organism responded to the stimulus on the basis of the hedonic state set up by that stimulus and not on the basis of the inherent qualities of the stimulus itself.*

One of the major consequences of this view is that stimuli cannot be considered to possess any intrinsic hedonic values, but that the organism, so to speak, assigns a hedonic value to a stimulus based on the internal state of the organism. If stimuli were given a consistent hedonic value, then responses to them should be consistent so that the resulting behavior is likely to be a reflex behavior (or perhaps a fixed action pattern) and not a motivated behavior. Under such conditions, hedonic states will essentially be superfluous.

Contrary to James' (1950/1890) view that pleasures and pains shape and modify behaviors but do not instigate them, hedonic states may serve to alert an organism and spur it into action - actions accompanied by feeling are actions accompanied by will (Spencer 1870). Hedonic states typically do not arise when action is automatic (Spencer 1870), but arise when the automatic or physiological regulatory mechanisms are not capable of counteracting a particular stimulus and the CP is being moved away from the SP by that stimulus.

Experimental evidence

There are several experimental findings to support the claim that an organism responds to the hedonic state set up by a stimulus as opposed to the qualities of the stimulus itself. It should be clear that the same stimulus can set up either a net positive or a net negative hedonic state, depending on the internal state(s) of the organism that are affected by a particular stimulus. This is characterized by the pleasantness ratings that subjects gave to temperature stimuli applied to the skin: their indication of the hedonic value of a stimulus depended greatly on their present body temperatures (Cabanac, 1979). The reader should be well aware of this phenomenon: when cold, a moderately warm stimulus is experienced as pleasant (e.g. hot soup on a cold winter's day), but when hot, the same stimulus is experienced as unpleasant (e.g. hot soup on a hot summer's day). This phenomenon has also been demonstrated in the rat (Cabanac and Lafrance, 1990). In this study glucose gastric preloads resulted in rats showing aversion to sweet stimuli but ingestive consummatory behavior to the same stimuli after water instead of glucose gastric preloads (see the chapter on applications of homeostatic mechanisms).

Other theories

The present homeostatically based view of motivated behaviors is also compatible with some theoretical positions, for instance the opponent-process model (Solomon and Corbit, 1974; Solomon, 1980). According to this theory, a stimulus causes a primary hedonic state to be established and in addition an opponent hedonic state as well, which is unmasked by withdrawal of the stimulus. At first, why the same stimulus should create two opponent processes may not make much sense, but once one interprets it in terms of homeostasis, these events become more intelligible. Consider the case where a stimulus impinges on an organism and moves the CP away from the SP. This stimulus immediately sets up a negative hedonic state. Furthermore, the HM affected by this stimulus will try to counter the movement of the CP away from the SP and so activates the opponent process (the physiological process associated with HMs, e.g. sweating). As this opponent process takes effect, it may slow down and even reverse the effects of the initial stimulus. Whether the HM manages to slow, stop or reverse the movement of the CP away from the SP will depend on the intensity of the stimulus and the robustness of the HM. At this stage, the CP has been displaced away from the SP and it may still be moving further away from the SP while a negative hedonic state has been established in the organism. If the original stimulus was now removed, the opponent process would come to dominate and succeed in moving the CP toward the SP. In so doing, it would establish a positive hedonic state. This sequence of events is consistent with the claim that primary affect closely tracks stimulus intensity and that the opponent process has greater inertia (Solomon, 1980). Repeated presentation of a stimulus will allow the hedonic effect of the stimulus to be anticipated and the opponent process can be activated earlier.

HMs and adaptive behaviors

It may now be possible to address the question of how an organism determines what is 'adaptive' in terms of its behaviors. In my opinion, the key to the answer lies in 'guiding hedonism' (Evans, 1989): the built-in hedonic states set up in response to stimulus impingement. A behavior that causes an organism to be subjected to a stimulus that sets up a negative hedonic state is inappropriate because such a stimulus is likely to cause the organism physical harm if it persists. The hedonic state that follows a behavior signals the 'appropriateness' of that behavior (Spencer 1870) and an organism that is readily reinforced by such events will acquire highly efficient behavior (Skinner, 1953). Therefore, behaviors that generate pleasure and avoid displeasure have useful homeostatic consequences and thus adaptive value.

The behavioral response to a stimulus is hypothesized to be proportional to the intensity of the hedonic state set up by that stimulus and should indicate the rate at and degree to which this behavioral response should occur. The term 'rate' may include both latency to activate a behavior and speed of execution of that behavior.

These considerations may allow some predictions to be made about an organism's behavior:

(i) The further the CP has been displaced from the SP, the more drastic or intense (greater in amplitude) the behavior will be; that is, the extent of behavior will be commensurate with the extent of displacement of the CP. For instance, an animal could be expected to consume a greater volume of water in response to a challenge of hypertonic saline of higher concentration than one of lower concentration given in equal volumes.

(ii) The faster the CP is moving away from the SP, the faster consequent behavior will be executed, that is, the speed (and perhaps latency) of behavior will reflect the speed at which the CP is being displaced - for example, the acute administration of hypertonic saline is likely to induce drinking behavior sooner and at a faster rate than the administration of exactly the same solution over a much longer period.

(iii) The behavior which reduces the intensity of a negative hedonic state or produces a positive hedonic state the fastest and to the greatest extent will be preferred, that is, an animal that received a challenge of hypertonic saline is likely to consume water rather than a strong sucrose solution provided that the HM regulating blood glucose level is not active.

A hedonic state is generated proportional to the displacement of the CP from the SP and the relative motion of the CP with regard to the SP. The intensity of a negative hedonic state may be correlated with the degree of physical stress induced in the organism and the intensity of a positive hedonic state correlated with the degree to which stress is relieved. It is not clear how the value of a set point is established by the organism, or what the precise physiological significance of a set point is. We suggest that they are not mental representations of goals that an organism wishes to achieve (see McFarland, 1989) but that they are ultimately linked to the physical properties of those materials that make up an organism under a certain set of environmental conditions. Set points may have been determined through evolution as a means of safeguarding the 'building materials' of the organism from undue and perhaps catastrophic stress and so allow an organism to maintain its physical integrity in a particular environment. It is therefore likely that set points reflect, directly or indirectly, some state of the environment when environment and system are in balance. As will be discussed in a later chapter, serotonin is most likely the neurotransmitter indicating set point values to the neural structures acting as controllers of HMs regulating physiological variables.

Hedonic states are mediated by nerve impulses and may be partially mediated by the peripheral nervous system (see Stellar and Stellar, 1985 for a discussion of neural mechanisms of reward). This can be expected to result in the automatic and rapid generation of hedonic states and frees the organism from cogitation about the inclusive fitness consequences of its behaviors. The manner of hedonic state generation and the types of hedonic states generated are likely to be the result of evolutionary processes. Natural selection selects for mechanisms (Cosmides and Tooby, 1987) which represent the manifestation of adaptive design at the psychological level (Symons, 1989) and HMs and their associated hedonic states may reflect such selection. The reasons why we believe that dopamine is the neurotransmitter generating hedonic states are discussed in a following chapter.

Hedonic states then, are set up when stimuli impinge on the organism and serve to activate and direct the organism's behavior in adaptive ways. In the most basic terms, the behavior of an organism causes changes in the stimuli that impinge on it (Manning, 1971) and so provides feedback in terms of hedonic states. These behaviors can be modified by learning, as will be shown in later chapters, hence greatly altering the apparent connection between physiological regulation and motivated behaviors.

References

Adolph, E. F. 1943. Physiological regulations. Lancaster, PA: Jacques Cottell Press.

Cabanac, M. 1979. Sensory Pleasure. Quarterly Review of Biology 54: 1-29.

Cabanac, M.; Lafrance, L. 1990. Postingestive alliesthesia: the rat tells the same story. Physiology and Behavior 47: 539-543.

Cosmides, L.; Tooby, J. 1987. From evolution to behavior: evolutionary psychology as the missing link. In J. Dupre (ed.), 'The latest on the best: essays on evolution and optimality', pp. 277-306. Cambridge MA: MIT Press.

Evans, P. 1989. Motivation and emotion. London: Routledge.

James, W. 1950/1890. The principles of psychology. New York: Dover.

Koshtoyants, C. S. 1960. Some facts and conclusions of comparative physiology as related to the problem of homeostasis. In A. E. Adolph (ed.), 'The development of homeostasis with special reference to factors of the environment', pp. 13-20. London: Academic Press.

Manning, A. 1971. Evolution and behavior. In J. L. McGaugh (ed.), 'Psychobiology: behavior from a biological perspective', pp. 1-52. New York: Academic Press.

McFarland, D. 1989. Problems of animal behavior. New York: Longman Scientific and Technical Publishers.

Richter, C. P. 1927. Animal behavior and internal drives. Quarterly Review of Biology 2: 307-343.

Skinner, B. F. 1953. Science and human behavior. New York: Macmillan.

Solomon, R. L. 1980. The opponent-process theory of acquired motivation. American Psychologist 35: 691-712.

Solomon, R. L.; Corbit, J. D. 1974. An opponent-process theory of motivation: I. Temporal dynamics of affect. Psychological Review 81: 119-145.

Spencer, H. 1870. The principles of psychology. London: Williams and Norgate.

Stellar, J. R.; Stellar, E. 1985. The neurobiology of motivation and reward. New York: Springer.

Symons, D. 1989. A critique of Darwinian anthropology. Ethology and Sociobiology 10: 131-144.

Tooby, J.; DeVore, I. 1987. The reconstruction of hominid behavioral evolution through strategic modeling. In W. Kinzey (ed.), 'Primate models of hominid behavior' pp. 183-237. New York: SUNY Press.

Young, P. T. 1961. Motivation and emotion: A survey of the determinants of human and animal activity. New York: Wiley.

CHAPTER 11
Multiple homeostatic mechanisms

Introduction

As we discussed in the introductory chapter, some authors argue (e.g. Cosmides and Tooby, 1987) that organisms, especially humans, have developed in addition to whatever domain general mechanisms they may possess, also many domain specific or special-purpose psychological mechanisms to deal with specific information processing problems posed by the organismic environment. Since we postulated in the chapter on HMs and behavior that some of these innate psychological mechanisms may be HMs, it follows that several HMs could exist in one organism. Furthermore, these HMs may work in isolation or they may interact. Such interactions, as we shall see in this chapter, can dramatically increase the complexity of the organism's behavior.

Examples of such systems and interactions are given in this chapter. Some of these examples serve merely to illustrate the concepts involved, rather than to illustrate particularly useful arrangements of HMs. Figure 11.01 is one such an example where the reader may have to assume that the outlet pipe from the tank is perhaps very narrow. This approach should generally not pose an obstacle to the understanding of the material in this and later chapters. It is not unlike one of the authors' experiences in undergraduate course work in engineering in South Africa: they had a North American text, and it posed the problem of how to mix large volumes of sand and salt, which, due to their different properties, is not as straight-forward as one might think. It was unclear why anybody wanted to mix sand and salt and they supposed it was to improve the taste of the sand... However, they proceeded to solve the problem, and learnt about mixing phenomena in the process.

Interacting and multi-component homeostatic mechanisms

It is possible that the operation of a particular HM can express or generate more than one type of behavior, for instance, when the HM has two or more different effectors. Different HMs may also be connected to one another. When HMs are connected, they may share components such as sensors and effectors. Figure 11.01 and Figure 11.02 show such examples.

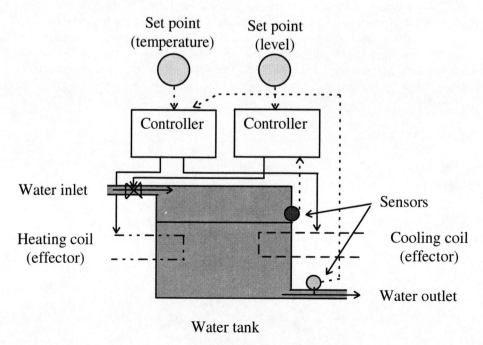

Figure 11.01

Two interconnected homeostatic mechanisms. The temperature regulating mechanism has 2 effectors and the level regulating mechanism only 1 effector.

In Figure 11.01 a water tank is shown of which both water level and water temperature are being regulated by 2 different HMs. The temperature regulating systems has 2 effectors, a heating element and a cooling element, while the water level regulating mechanism has only one effector, an inlet valve. When water enters the tank, it would affect both the water level and the water temperature. For example, if the water level in the tank is too low, the water level regulating mechanism would open the valve to let more water in. If the incoming water is too cold, the temperature regulating system would be activated to heat the water in the tank. In this case, the operation of one mechanism triggered another.

In Figure 11.02 HMs that have a common effector are shown. Both the HMs control the inlet valve to the tank. If the incoming water is too cold, the temperature regulating system heats it up. If the incoming water is too hot, the temperature regulating system closes the inlet valve. If the water level in the tank is too low, the level regulating system opens the inlet valve. It may therefore happen that the temperature system needs to close the valve, while the level regulating system needs to open it.

Note that action taken by either system would influence the other. When water is let into the tank to adjust the water level in the tank, the water would also affect the temperature in the tank. When water is prevented from entering the tank, the level of water in the tank may drop too low.

If a conflict arises between the two systems, how could it be resolved? The reader should consider 2 possible alternatives: (i) that the mechanisms are connected in a hierarchy such that either one or the other always has precedence in case of a conflict; or (ii) that the system experiencing the largest error gets precedence.

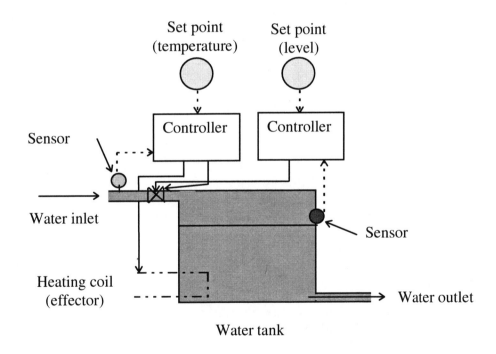

Figure 11.02
Two interconnected homeostatic mechanisms. The temperature regulating mechanism and the water level regulating mechanism share the same effector.

If more than one variable is influenced by the same stimulus, such as in the above examples where both water temperature and water level are influenced by the stimulus of water entering the tank, it must not be assumed that all of those variables are moved in the same direction relative to their set points. Some can be moved toward and some away from their set points. It should also make intuitive sense that a stimulus causing the current value of a variable to move away from its relevant SP is likely to cause the organism distress, while movement toward the SP will not. Since more than one variable can be affected by the same stimulus, or more than one stimulus can impinge on the organism, several variables are likely to be influenced at the same time and not necessarily in the same direction. We suggest then, that there may be a summation of hedonic states to yield a single positive or negative state. The stimulus that changes this net hedonic state to the greatest degree will be the one that the organism reacts to.

Application

The operation of HMs with multiple effectors and HMs connected to other HMs can lead to confusion when interpreting homeostatically driven behaviors. Some investigators (e.g. Falk, 1977) have claimed that certain behaviors, such as adjunctive behaviors (e.g. schedule-induced polydipsia), are not under homeostatic control. This conclusion is likely to be drawn if two different behaviors are under control of the same HM, but not to the same extent or in the same ratio. Let us briefly examine how HMs could be applied to explain adjunctive behaviors.

Under some conditions, a mechanism which normally expresses one behavior, may express another. Because such behavior is unlikely to make sense when viewed in terms of the mechanism which is normally responsible for its expression, it may be considered not to be due to the functioning of that mechanism. However, to conclude that it is then not the consequence of the functioning of any HM is inappropriate. For example, let us assume that the temperature of the water in the tank in Figure 11.02 can be elevated by letting hot water into the tank (the preferred method) or by heating the water with the heating element. If the water temperature is too low, hot water is let into the tank. However, if there is no hot water available, the heating element is used. In behavioral terms, if the ingestion of fluids can affect the regulation of energy level, water balance, salt balance and perhaps other systems, then it is to be expected that drinking behavior, the only normal way through which fluids are ingested, may be expressed by (i.e. under the control of) several different HMs. Normally, the mechanism responsible for the regulation of energy levels may express eating behavior when it is triggered, but in the absence of 'edibles', drinking behavior may be expressed in spite of the fact that water balance does not need to be adjusted.

An adjunct behavior, such as polydipsia, occurs when an animal is prevented from taking optimal action given its internal state. For instance, when rats have been food deprived for a few hours and they are then given access to small food pellets under intermittent schedules of delivery while having water freely available, they drink regularly and almost continuously after each pellet (Falk, 1977). This drinking occurs even in the manifest absence of a water deficit and even though water intake is clearly in excess of that required to maintain homeostatic balance. Therefore polydipsic behavior is considered to be anomalous. Roper (1983) considers the problems of potentiation (degree or extent of behavior) and selection (type of behavior) to be the most prominent problems of schedule-induced behavior. Both these problems may be tractable given the homeostatic approach.

A food-deprived animal experiences a negative hedonic state as a result of the displacement of the CP away from the SP of the relevant HM. The consumption of a small food pellet generates a positive hedonic state because the CP is now moved toward the SP. The animal consequently wants to continue with this behavior, but cannot since no more food is available. Given that nourishment can be obtained by either eating or drinking and that eating is thwarted, the animal now switches to drinking. This switch occurs in an attempt to maintain the positive hedonic state experienced during eating. This solves the problem of selection: it is most likely that another behavior will be selected that is controlled by the same HM as the thwarted behavior.

The consumption of water will affect the HM regulating water balance. It is to be expected that the hedonic states set up by this mechanism will also influence the amount of water consumed. This may solve the problem of potentiation: water is consumed until the negative hedonic state generated by overconsumption of water exceeds the negative hedonic state caused by food deprivation. Figure 11.03 shows a homeostatic interpretation of polydipsia..

Adjunctive behaviors exhibit additional complexities, and the reader may wish to revisit this phenomenon at a later stage to apply an increased arsenal of skills to its analysis.

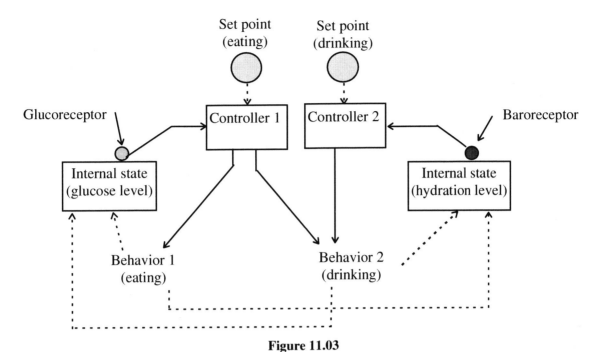

Figure 11.03

Interconnected homeostatic mechanisms and polydipsia. Food deprivation causes mechanism 1 to activate eating. When food is not available, it switches to drinking. Drinking persists until the negative hedonic state created by overconsumption of water exceeds the negative hedonic state created by food deprivation.

HMs and complex behaviors

An organism typically has more than one HM incorporated into its set of innate psychological mechanisms. This coexistence of HMs may have several implications. Conflicts may arise due to the simultaneous activation of some of these mechanisms. If the behavior or part of the behavior expressed by the operation of one mechanism is incompatible with the behavior or part of the behavior of another mechanism, both the mechanisms generally should not be activated concurrently. This logic suggests the existence of a hierarchy of HMs or a protocol for their activation as alluded to before. For instance, if incompatible HMs are neurally integrated to ensure lateral inhibition, the activation of one HM will inhibit the simultaneous activation of other incompatible HMs. If a stimulus or several stimuli displace several regulated variables from their set points, the HM associated with the regulated variable producing the most intense hedonic state will be activated.

The sequential activation of HMs due to such a hierarchy or protocol may give rise to specific behavior patterns. The HMs contributing to a stable behavior pattern (foraging, day journey) can be investigated by some form of multivariate analysis analogous to the determination of factors influencing body weight in baboons (Dunbar, 1989). Since the activation of two different HMs may result in the same behavior, the latency, speed and intensity with which this behavior will be executed may be very complex. This could complicate the analysis of behavior patterns and it may necessitate an investigation to identify those HMs contributing to a single behavior first.

Figure 11.04 shows that eating affects the glucose as well as hydration levels of an organism. Eating will cause the glucose CP to move towards its SP and the water balance CP to move away from its SP. This will cause a cessation of eating and initiation of drinking. This suggests that under normal conditions some stable behavioral patterns would be observed, such as that drinking often follows eating.

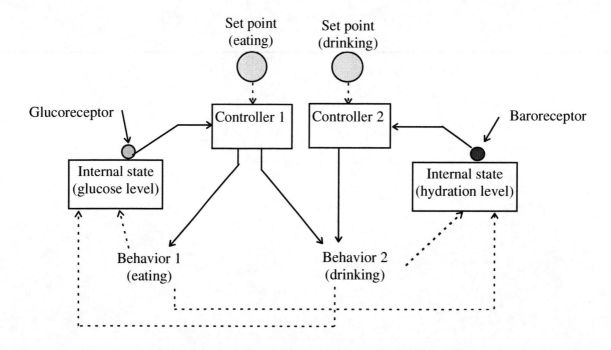

Figure 11.04

HMs and complex behaviors. The activation of one behavior (e.g. eating) affects both glucose level and hydration state. In particular, eating is likely to move the glucose CP towards its SP and the hydration level CP away from its SP. Therefore, eating is likely to be followed by drinking.

HMs and learning and memory

     Learning is a ubiquitous and important phenomenon (Toates and Evans, 1987) and may also be manifest in biological homeostatic systems, especially in the controller. It may be hypothesized that some memory is incorporated in the controller of every HM as shown in Figure 11.05.

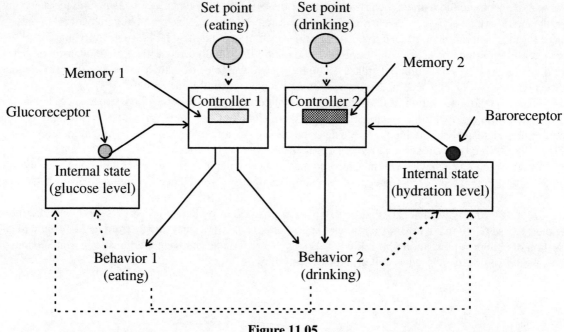

Figure 11.05
HMs that incorporate memory.

Learning may cause the controller function to be modified in ways that would optimize regulation and so improve the efficiency of the system. A more efficient operation of a particular HM will result in fewer deviations from the set point and consequently fewer and less intense hedonic states will be experienced. It implies that as learning progresses, behaviors triggered by a HM are more likely to be anticipatory behaviors although ultimately they are still hedonically driven: learned behaviors are responses to expected hedonic states rather than presently experienced hedonic states. This interpretation of the relationship between HMs and learning may bear on the debate regarding the control of feeding behavior. Learning is likely to play a more important role in the feeding strategies of more experienced animals, while inexperienced animals are more likely to feed based on their level of energy depletion.

The physiological correlates of hedonic states evoked by stimuli acting on an organism may have a twofold function: they set up hedonic states that direct the responses of the organism in adaptive ways and they may simultaneously facilitate the association of stimuli, responses and hedonic states. This facilitation of learning by (the physiological consequences of) hedonic states is supported by two lines of evidence. First, some hormones play a role in memory formation (Kupfermann, 1985a) and endocrine levels may be sensitive indices of emotional responses to social and physical stimuli (Mason and Brady, 1964). Second, there are experimental findings indicating that recall may be state dependent (Singer and Salovey, 1988), that attention may be biased by emotional stimuli (Williams et al., 1988), and that hormones activate certain behaviors (Kupfermann, 1985b). These considerations may bring a different perspective to the study of attention. Attention is frequently considered to facilitate sensory pathways and to play a role in directing an organism to appropriate stimuli. However, it is not clear how an organism would know what to pay attention to. From a homeostatic perspective, this problem would not arise. A deviation of a variable from its set point would set up a negative hedonic state. This hedonic state will in turn have several physiological (e.g. biochemical) effects, some of which may involve the modulation of the animal's hormone levels. As pointed out above, hormones can activate certain behavioral pathways and memory processes and presumably sensory pathways as well. In other words, a specific deficit may result, via hormone adjustments, in the activation of sensory pathways needed for the registration of stimuli pertinent to the generated deficit. Attention is thus much more likely to be seen as an effect or consequence of homeostatic regulation than as a cause of sensory activation or stimulus selection. Keep in mind that a direct effect most likely exists between attention and hedonic states: the most intense hedonic state compels attention. This has been pointed out before in the context of the selection of behaviors.

If one postulates that ease of learning depends on the intensity of the hedonic state evoked, it can be concluded that salient stimuli, i.e. those that have pertinent survival consequences, will be learned rather more rapidly than other stimuli because they are more likely to produce strong hedonic states. Furthermore, if recall is state dependent, *the hedonic state set up by a stimulus may not only facilitate learning, but also recall*. The hedonic state functions here as a 'cue' in memory retrieval. A combination of endocrine response to and neural activation by a stimulus could cause the sensitization of the relevant behavioral circuitry.

The use of the HM concept as a research tool
It is one thing to claim that biological organisms incorporate HMs but quite another to investigate whether this is so. Here we wish to discuss ways in which hypotheses regarding biological HMs can be empirically tested. In order to fully demonstrate that a certain behavior results from the operation of a HM, it has to be shown that the essential complement of homeostatic components is present. These components are: sensors, effectors, a variable being regulated around a set point and also a controller.

It should be kept in mind that various HMs can interact with each other (Davis, 1979; Smith, 1987; Toates and Evans, 1987; Haussinger et al., 1988; Colgan, 1989). Raible (1994) discusses the control of feeding behavior by three interacting regulatory systems: the emergency system, the short-term system and the long-term system. The interaction between various HMs can be direct in the sense that components are shared between two systems in a manner analogous to the interaction between motor systems and speech (Kimura, 1982; Watson and Kimura, 1989) and may occur at the level of the hypothalamus, brain stem or spinal cord (Stellar and Stellar, 1985), or it can be indirect in the sense that the operation of one mechanism may activate another (e.g. the ingestion of cold water in the process of water balance regulation may have an effect on the thermoregulatory mechanism). Interactions or competition between different systems (Stellar and Stellar, 1985) are frequently used to induce behavioral 'cost', such as foraging in a hostile environment (Cabanac, 1985) or crossing an electrified grid to gain some reward. It is therefore rather important to isolate systems through appropriate experimental manipulation to avoid ambiguity in interpretation.

The Regulated Variable. The most salient aspect of a homeostatic system is that a certain value of a variable will be defended. This suggests ways in which such a regulated variable can be investigated. For instance, body weight may be directly regulated or may be the result of the regulation of other factors, e.g. fat levels (Mrosovsky and Powley, 1977). If body weight was directly regulated by a HM, then an experimental manipulation of body weight, in ways that did not affect other HMs, should result in a change in the organism's behaviors responsible for effecting changes in body weight. This can perhaps be accomplished by the implantation of silicon pads under the skin of an experimental animal. Since the body weight of the animal has now been increased relative to its baseline value, it is to be expected that the animal's food intake may be reduced until the baseline value is reached. In this case, the body weight baseline value serves as a first approximation of the set point value for body weight. If, given that the increased energy expenditures due to increased body weight are corrected for, there is no effect on food intake of such manipulation of body weight, then one has to conclude that body weight per se is not regulated by any HM.

It should be kept in mind that not every stable or defended physiological factor is necessarily under direct control of a HM. For instance, although body weight may appear to be regulated, *it may also be the product of the combined action of other homeostatically regulated variables such as water balance and fat level.* If a variable (e.g. body weight) is not directly regulated, but its stability is the result of contributing factors that are being regulated (e.g. water balance and fat level), it is not useful to talk about a set point for that variable. In other words, body weight may be stable, not because it is being regulated, but because other factors contributing to body weight are. If body weight per se is not regulated, there will be no sensors and effectors and thus no HM associated with body weight. However, it may not be correct to claim that body weight is non-homeostatically regulated. Therefore, care should be exercised before discarding the notion of homeostasis altogether if experimental data do not conform to a simple interpretation of homeostasis.

The Set Point. Stimuli, hedonic states and set points have been related in previous sections. These relations should provide ways in which the values of set points can be determined. If a stimulus is experimentally provided that moves a regulated variable away from its set point, the organism experiencing this manipulation will perceive the stimulus as being hedonically negative and is likely to express aversion to it. If, on the other hand, a stimulus is experimentally provided and serves to move the variable toward the set point value, it would set up a positive hedonic state and an organism is likely to express pleasure in response to this stimulus. This is borne out well by the phenomenon of alliesthesia (e.g. Cabanac and Lafrance, 1990). *The point at which an organism fails to express affect in response to a stimulus, is likely that value which represents the set point.* Experimental procedures such as that used by Cabanac and co-workers (e.g. Cabanac, 1979; Cabanac and Lafrance, 1990) are well suited to the determination of set point values. Furthermore, since an organism regulates the variable in question around the set point for that particular variable, the baseline value for that variable in an unstressed organism can be taken as a good first approximation of the set point value.

The Sensors. A HM cannot function without appropriate sensors. It may rely on only one type of sensor, but it is far more likely that several different types of sensors at one or various locations are involved. For instance, opioids may exert their effects on food intake through κ and σ receptors while glucoreceptors in the tongue, liver and ventromedial hypothalamus may play a role in the regulation of glucose levels (see the review by Raible, 1994). It is also possible that a single type of sensor may feed information to two or more different HMs. An example here is provided by Raible's discussion (1994) of the effects of cholecystokinin (presumably acting on its receptors) on both carbohydrate and fat ingestion. It is therefore necessary to establish (i) how many different sensor types are associated with a specific HM and (ii) which other HMs are being subserved by a particular sensor type. Experimental stimulation or inhibition of sensor function should have an effect on the HM(s) that this sensor type is associated with. Disabling or inhibition of a sensor type should render the mechanism less sensitive to particular stimuli while artificial stimulation of a sensor type should result in a hypersensitivity to specific stimuli.

The Effectors. Considerations applying to sensors are equally likely to apply to effectors. That is, one HM may exert control over several different effector types or several different HMs may exert control over a single effector type. For instance, the operation of the same HM may express several different behaviors: the operation of the mechanism regulating blood glucose level may express behavior that results in the ingestion of solid sources of glucose (eating behavior) or liquid sources of glucose (drinking behavior). Another example may be provided by the activation of both feeding and hoarding behaviors in food-deprived rodents (Raible, 1994). Likewise, the same behavior may be expressed upon the activation of different HMs: the ingestion of liquid sources of glucose may affect both water balance and glucose balance, thus drinking behavior can be expressed by the glucose level regulating mechanism as well as by the water balance regulating mechanism.

If a particular effector (type) is associated with a particular HM, experimental activation or inactivation of the effector should have an effect on the level of the variable being regulated by that mechanism. It is therefore necessary to establish for effectors too (i) how many different effector types are associated with a specific HM and (ii) which other HMs are being subserved by a particular effector type.

The Controller. The final and potentially the most complex component of a HM that has to be investigated is the controller. The various types of controllers have been discussed in a previous section and it is suggested that they be investigated in the order mentioned, that is, from the more simple to the more complex. If a HM incorporates an on-off controller, then the behavior expressed when this mechanism is in operation is likely to be fairly constant: it is either present at a certain level or it is not. For instance, if the controller controlling drinking behavior is of the on-off type, then the rate of drinking, once the behavior is initiated, will be the same irrespective of how long the animal has been water deprived. If the rate of drinking is proportional to the length of water deprivation, then drinking behavior is likely to be controlled by either a proportional or a rate controller. Methods to differentiate between these two types of controller as well as for investigating combinations such as proportional and reset (PI) control can be obtained from texts on process control (e.g. Balchen and Mumme, 1988). Manipulating 'signals' to biological controllers or perturbing biological processes in a tightly controlled manner may not be as easy as doing the same in engineering type processes, but psychologists can in a variety of ways still perform analyses on biological control systems (see Fitzsimons, 1987 for a discussion of some techniques).

In summary then, the following questions should be answered:

(i)   is the variable of interest being regulated?

(ii)   what is the set point of the variable?

(iii)   are there detectors for that variable? Where are they? Are there different types of detectors?

(iv)   are there mechanisms (effectors) to manipulate the level of that variable? Are there different types of effectors?

(v)   what type of control is exerted over the regulated variable - on/off, proportional, derivative, integral, a combination of these or a more complex type of control?

(vi)   are there transmission lines converging from sensors and effectors on a specific brain area?

The characterization of the components mentioned should satisfy even the most dubious that a HM is involved in the expression of a certain behavior. However, for a complete description of the mechanism in question, the nature of its neural circuitry has to be elucidated: whether feedforward or feedback or a combination is used by the process and, perhaps the most daunting, how the neural circuits of one HM may interface or connect to the neural circuits of other HMs.

References

Balchen, J. G.; Mumme, K. I. 1988. Process control. New York: Van Nostrand Reinhold.

Cabanac, M.; Lafrance, L. 1990. Postingestive alliesthesia: the rat tells the same story. Physiology and Behavior 47: 539-543.

Cabanac, M. 1985. Influence of food and water deprivation on the behavior of the white rat foraging in a hostile environment. Physiology and Behavior 35: 701-709.

Cabanac, M. 1979. Sensory pleasure. Quarterly Review of Biology 54: 1-29.

Colgan, P. 1989. Animal motivation. London: Chapman and Hall.

Cosmides, L.; Tooby, J. 1987. From evolution to behavior: evolutionary psychology as the missing link. In J. Dupre (ed.), The latest on the best: Essays on evolution and optimality, pp. 277-306. Cambridge, MA: MIT.

Davis, J. D. 1979. Homeostasis, feedback and motivation. In F. M. Toates; T. R. Halliday (eds.), Analysis of motivational processes, pp. 23-37. London: Academic Press.

Dunbar, R. I. M. 1989. Ecological modeling in an evolutionary context. Folia Primatologica 53: 235-246.

Falk, J. L. 1977. The origin and functions of adjunctive behavior. Animal Learning and Behavior 5: 325-335.

Fitzsimons, J. T. 1987. Some methods for investigating thirst and sodium appetite. In F. M. Toates; N. E. Rowland (eds.), Feeding and drinking, pp. 393-428. Amsterdam: Elsevier.

Haussinger, D.; Meijer, A. J.; Gerok, W.; Sies, H. 1988. Hepatic nitrogen metabolism and acid-base homeostasis. In D. Haussinger (ed.), pH Homeostasis: mechanisms and control, pp. 337-377 . London: Academic Press.

Kimura, D. 1982. Left-hemisphere control of oral and brachial movements and their relation to communication. Philosophical Transactions of the Royal Society of London B298: 135-149.

Kupfermann, I. 1985a. Hypothalamus and limbic system I: peptidergic neurons, homeostasis, and emotional behavior. In E. R. Kandel; J. H. Schwartz (eds.), Principles of neural science, pp. 611-625. New York: Elsevier.

Kupfermann, I. 1985b. Hypothalamus and limbic system II: motivation. In E. R. Kandel, J. H. Schwartz (eds.), Principles of neural science, pp. 626-635. New York: Elsevier.

Mason, J. W.; Brady, J. V. 1964. The sensitivity of psychoendocrine systems to social and physical environment. In P. H. Leiderman; D. Shapiro (eds.), Psychobiological approaches to social behavior, pp. 4-23. Stanford, CA: Stanford University Press.

Mrosovsky, N.; Powley, T. L. 1977. Set points for body weight and fat. Behavioral Biology 20: 205-223.

Roper, T. J. 1983. Schedule-induced behavior. In R. L. Mellgren (ed.), Animal cognition and behavior, pp. 127-164. Amsterdam: North-Holland.

Singer, A. J.; Salovey, P. 1988. Mood and memory: evaluating the network theory of affect. Clinical Psychology Review 8: 211-251.

Smith, R. E. 1987. Mammalian homeostasis. In J. J. Head (series ed.) , Carolina biology readers. Burlington, NC: Carolina Biological Supply Company scientific publications department.

Stellar, J. R.; Stellar, E. 1985. The neurobiology of motivation and reward. New York: Springer.

Toates, F. M., Evans, R. A. S. 1987. The application of theory, modeling and simulation to feeding and drinking. In F. M. Toates; N. E. Rowland (eds.), Feeding and drinking, pp. 531-562. Amsterdam: Elsevier.

Watson, N. V.; Kimura, D. 1989. Right-hand superiority for throwing but not for intercepting. Neuropsychologia 27: 1399-1414.

Williams, J. M.; Watts, F. V.; MacLeod, L.; Matthews, A. 1988. Cognitive psychology and emotional disorders. New York: Wiley.

CHAPTER 12
Applications of homeostatic mechanisms

Introduction

This chapter is meant to consolidate some of the concepts and ideas introduced in the previous chapters. To this end, we will discuss a number of experiments and apply the "homeostatic theory of behavior" to their analysis. This may simultaneously reveal the usefulness of the theory and some of its shortcomings.

A short introduction will be given to explain the experimental procedures used and report the general findings obtained. Some of the interpretations of these results by the original authors will be given as well as possible homeostatic interpretations. The figures are redrawn from the originals, often simplified, and are quantitatively approximate only. We should emphasize that the representation of the 2 studies given here largely reflects our perspective on them. You, the reader, are strongly encouraged to consult the originals to formulate your own opinion.

Study #1: "Postingestive alliesthesia: the rat *tells the same story." M. Cabanac and L. Lafrance. Physiology and Behavior 47: 539-543, 1990.*

Specific question: Would a glucose gastric preload in rats render unpleasant a sweet stimulus that was pleasant prior to the load and vice versa with a water preload? If so, it would replicate results obtained in humans.

Animals and surgery. The experimenters used 6 male Sprague-Dawley white rats. When under anesthesia, 3 polyethylene catheters or tubes were chronically implanted in each animal. One catheter was implanted through the nose and throat, ending in the stomach. Solutions could therefore be infused directly into the stomach, bypassing the taste sensors on the tongue. Two other catheters were implanted through the nose, ending one on each side of the tongue. Two different solutions could therefore be infused directly onto the tongue to activate its taste receptors. The animals were housed in individual cages, with food and water freely available, for 8 days to recover from surgery.

Variables. Different taste stimuli constituted the independent or manipulated variable. Quinine sulfate in concentrations that were weak (0.4 g/l) and strong (1.2 g/l) were used as bitter taste stimuli. Sucrose in concentrations that were weak (67 g/l) and strong (200 g/l) were used as sweet stimuli. Pure water was used as neutral control taste. When taste stimuli were given, they were spaced 5 minutes apart to allow salivary rinsing of the preceding stimulus to occur.

The facial response of the rat was used as the dependent or measured variable. The number of positive and negative responses were counted after presenting every taste stimulus. Positive responses were: moving upper lip; tongue protrusion; paws to mouth; head nodding. Each type of response was counted as + 1. Negative responses were: mouth gaping; chin rubbing, forepaw stamping; dribbling. Each type of response was counted as -1.

Procedure. Two experimenters, blind to the experimental conditions, rated the responses of the same rat to the same taste stimuli. The rat was placed into an observation chamber and the tubes were connected to deliver solutions when needed. Taste stimuli (2) were given at 5 minute intervals before the gastric load and the responses recorded. The gastric load was then injected and taste stimuli were administered every 5 minutes for the next 60 minutes and the responses recorded after every administration. The administration of gastric loads and taste stimuli were given in counterbalanced sequences.

Experiment 1
Experimental conditions

Taste stimuli but no gastric loads were given. The rats were not deprived of food beforehand. The responses of the animals to the different taste stimuli were recorded.

Results

Rats showed facial and body responses reflecting the nature and strength of the taste stimuli as shown in Figure 12.01. This proved that using facial responses were reliable indicators of the pleasantness/unpleasantness of the taste stimuli.

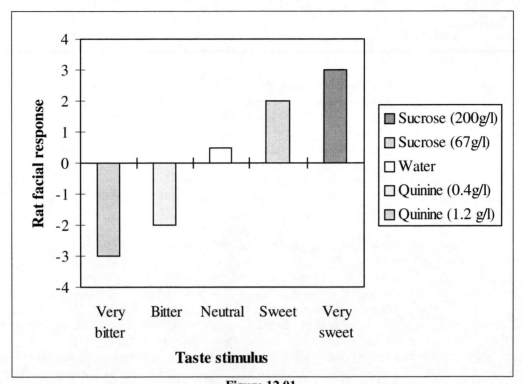

Figure 12.01

Median ratings of rat facial responses to different taste stimuli.

<u>Experiment 2</u>

Experimental conditions

The rats were deprived of food for the 24 h preceding testing. A gastric load of either 5 ml water (the control group) or 1 g of glucose in 5 ml of water was given to the rats, followed at 5 minute intervals by very sweet taste stimuli as described above. The responses of the rats were recorded.

Results

Rats showed positive responses to sweet tastes after water gastric loads and no or negative responses after glucose solution gastric loads (Figure 12.02).

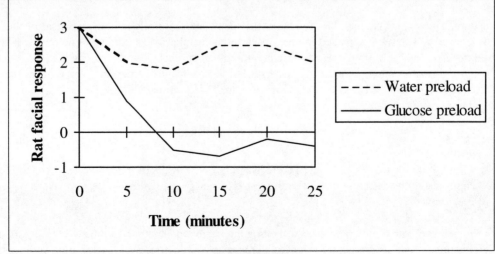

Figure 12.02

Median ratings of rat facial responses to a very sweet stimulus at different intervals after a water gastric preload (broken line) and a glucose gastric preload (solid line).

Experiment 3

Experimental conditions

The rats were not deprived of food before testing. Each of the following gastric preloads was given to every rat, but on different days and in a counterbalanced order : (i) 5 ml water (large volume); (ii) 1 g of glucose in 5 ml of water (glucose, large volume); (iii) 1 g of glucose in 1.7 ml of water (concentrated glucose, small volume); or (iv) 3 g of glucose in 5 ml of water (concentrated glucose, large volume). Gastric preloads were followed after 5 minutes by a very sweet stimulus and the responses of the rats were recorded. The effects of glucose concentration and load volume could therefore be compared.

Results

The differences between scores taken before and after gastric loads show that responses to sweet taste stimuli were suppressed by glucose gastric loads, but not by water. The greatest effect was shown in response to the concentration of glucose, rather than the mass of glucose or the volume of the gastric preload - see Figure 12.03.

Discussion. Rats exhibit certain facial responses to bitter taste stimuli indicating displeasure and in response to sweet taste stimuli they exhibit responses indicative of pleasure. These responses are as consistent and reliable as verbal responses in humans.

Rats found sweet stimuli increasingly aversive with time elapsed after glucose gastric loads. A demonstration of alliesthesia.

Gastric distention did not contribute much to this change in the pleasure evoked by sweet stimuli, but glucose concentration did. Identical results were obtained in humans in other studies.

After loads of 1 g glucose in 5 ml water, satiated rats showed a smaller response than fasted rats to sweet stimuli. Even the concentrated glucose loads were unable to produce in satiated rats the same strong responses that the weaker concentrations did in fasted rats. The authors suggest that this happened because the satiated rats had food in their intestines which effectively "diluted" the glucose gastric loads to the extent where glucose receptors in the intestine only detected a weak concentration of glucose. However, the authors fail to explain why the small volume of concentrated glucose solution was not diluted more than the larger volume of concentrated glucose solution. In other words, dilution would lead one to expect that the small volume of concentrated glucose would have less of an effect than the larger volume of concentrated glucose. In Experiment 3 both were found to have a similar effect.

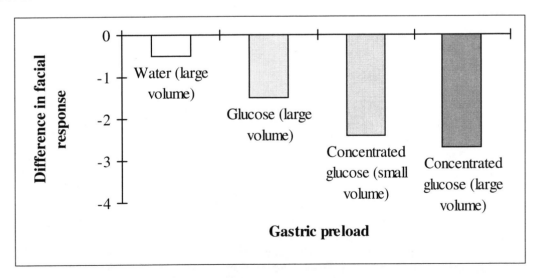

Figure 12.03
The effects of different gastric preloads on the perception of sweet taste stimuli in fed rats. The graph shows the largest differences in ratings of rat facial responses to sweet stimuli before and after the preloads. The concentrated glucose solutions had a significantly greater effect than water (p<0.05).

Homeostatic analysis: The homeostatic theory of behavior indicates that the hedonic properties of a stimulus would change depending on whether the error is being increased or decreased by the stimulus. By a combination of fasting and giving gastric loads, the direction in which the error changes can be manipulated. Fasting moves the glucose CP away from the glucose SP. In a fasted rat, the consumption of glucose would move the glucose CP towards the glucose SP and the stimulus would have a positive hedonic value. The consumption of water would not move the CP towards the SP and would have no hedonic value. When a rat has been given a (sufficient) gastric load of glucose, the CP would be driven away from the SP (i.e. from CP past the SP to CP' in Figure 12.04). Sweet stimuli would tend to move the CP even further away from the SP and hence attain a negative hedonic value. Gastric distention can be expected to be hedonically neutral because it has no effect on the size of the error. The findings reported in this paper are in good agreement with these predictions.

How could the homeostatic theory explain the effect of the stimulus itself since the small amount of solution infused into the mouth is presumably not enough to affect the animal's homeostatic balance? The reader is invited to supply a plausible answer to this question and may wish to employ the concept of feedforward control.

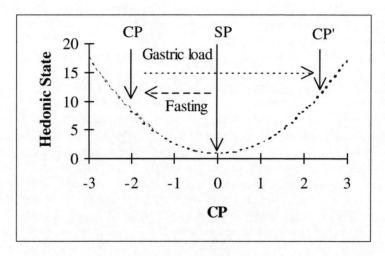

Figure 12.04
The effects of fasting and gastric loads on hedonic states.

Study #2: "Influence of food and water deprivation on the behavior of the white rat foraging in a hostile environment." M. Cabanac. Physiology and Behavior 35: 701-709, 1985.

Specific question: How does the motivation to eat compare to the motivation to drink after equal periods of deprivation when the same cost (foraging in a cold environment) is incurred in both cases?

Animals. The experimenters used 6 female white rats as subjects.

Variables. The independent variable was the length of food or water deprivation. Animals were deprived of food for periods of 0, 12, 22, 46, 70, or 94 hours. Animals were deprived of water for 0, 12, 22, 46, or 70 hours. A number of dependent variables were measured. These were: the speed of the rats running to food/water; the meal/drinking bout duration; the speed of eating; the amount eaten/drunk; and the number of meals/drinking trips.

Procedure. The experimenters used 6 adult female rats of the Charles River strain. The rats were trained that either food or water was available only during a specific 2 hours every day. To find the food or water, they had to run from their home cage down a 16 m long zigzag alley. During training sessions, the cage and alley were kept at room temperature. During experimental sessions, the alley was kept at -15 °C, but the cage was at room temperature.

If the rats were deprived of food beforehand, food was available at the end of the alley for 2 hours, while water was freely available in the cage. Regular rat food was powdered to avoid hoarding. If the rats were deprived of water beforehand, then water was available at the end of the alley and food in the cage. The water was warmed to 40 °C and placed in a Dewar bottle to prevent freezing.

The movements of the rats were registered by micro-switches at various points in the alley, the feeder, and the entrance to the home cage, thus permitting the recording of the rats' feeding and drinking behaviors. Food/water deprivation sessions of different lengths were given in a random order.

Experiment 1

Experimental conditions

Rats were deprived of food during 6 sessions for 0, 12, 22, 46, 70, or 96 h. Food was then made available for 2 h at the end of the cold alley to the fasted rats. After each session the rats were allowed free access to food/water until their body weight was recovered.

Results

Food deprivation caused a decrease in body weight as shown in Table 12.01. The longer rats were food deprived, the more often they ventured into the cold to eat. Speed of eating and meal duration varied little with length of food deprivation. The total amount of food consumed per 2 h session is shown in Figure 12.05.

Table 12.01
The influence of the length of food deprivation on body weight.

Deprivation period (h)	0	12	22	46	70	94
Body weight (g)	302±18	295±19	263±14	254±9	239±11	241±15
Change in body weight from baseline (g)	18±1	19±5	3±1	-15±2	-24±4	-38±3

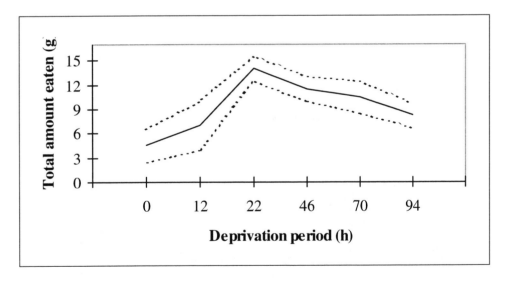

Figure 12.05
The influence of the length of food deprivation on the total amount of food eaten per 2 h session. The dotted lines show the margin of standard error.

Experiment 2

Experimental conditions

Rats were deprived of water during 5 sessions for 0, 12, 22, 46, or 70 h. Water was then made available for 2 h at the end of the cold alley to the rats. After each session the rats were allowed free access to water until their body weight was recovered.

Results

Water deprivation caused a loss of body weight in rats as shown in Table 12.02. The longer rats were water deprived, the more often they ventured into the cold to drink. The speed of drinking varied little with length of water deprivation, but the total amount drunk per session did as shown in Figure 12.06.

Table 12.02
The influence of the length of water deprivation on body weight.

Deprivation period (h)	0	12	22	46	70
Body weight (g)	320±22	326±21	306±21	293±19	279±20
Change in body weight from baseline (g)	1±9	8±6	-17±1	-31±1	-43±3

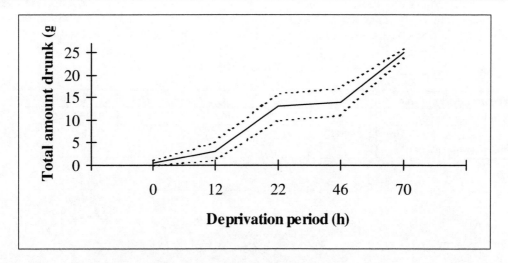

Figure 12.06
The influence of the length of water deprivation on the total amount of water consumed per 2 h session. The dotted lines show the margin of standard error.

Discussion. Rats have a mechanism for storing food (in the form of fat) but not for storing water. One would expect food deprivation to be less taxing to the animal than water deprivation. The main purpose of the author of this paper was to establish whether the urge to eat or the urge to drink was strongest after equal periods of deprivation. These urges were pitted against the cost of foraging in the same cold environment.

The author compared food deprivation against water deprivation based on the speed of running down the alley, the number of rats out foraging at one time, and eating or drinking bout duration. These criteria were believed to reflect the rats' motivation better than the amount consumed or the speed of ingestion which could be dependent on the composition of the food, the nature of the drinking tube and other such factors. The author believed that the speed of running toward the feeding site, the mean meal or drinking bout duration, and the number of rats out foraging could be indices of the strength of motivation.

The speed of running was faster for food deprivation than water deprivation. This indicated that the urge to eat was stronger than the urge to drink. A ratio of 1 implies equal urges to eat and drink. The mean bout duration was longer for eating than drinking. This also indicated that the urge to eat was stronger than the urge to drink. The ratio declined with deprivation time. The number of rats foraging for food was higher than the number of rats looking for water at every deprivation length. This further confirmed that the urge to eat was stronger than the urge to drink.

Homeostatic analysis: The meal/bout duration declined with deprivation time. This implies that the urge to drink became stronger with deprivation time, although the urge to eat was still the strongest. However, the ratio of running speed for food to running speed for water remained relatively constant for the longer deprivation periods, suggesting that the urges to eat and drink remained steady! From the number of rats foraging one would conclude that the urge to eat was stronger than the urge to drink, but that both increased at the same rate with deprivation time (at least until a ceiling effect for eating was reached). Although all 3 measures indicated that the motivation to eat was stronger than the motivation to drink, further analysis leads to conflicting interpretations.

How can we interpret the results reported in this study using the homeostatic theory of behavior? According to the homeostatic theory, a difference between CP and SP (the error) produces a hedonic state that instigates the appropriate behavior. The periods of food and water deprivation used in this study can be seen as *implicit* attempts (because the authors did not use this theory as a framework for interpretation) to manipulate the size of the error. In particular, it appears that the author implicitly assumed that equal lengths of food and water deprivation produced equal degrees of deprivation, that is in homeostatic terms, equal errors. From the point of view of homeostatic theory, this is a point of criticism, since it has not been shown that equal periods of deprivation under these conditions produced equal sizes of error.

Furthermore, according to the homeostatic theory, it is possible for equal errors to produce different intensities of hedonic states. If equal degrees of error were in fact achieved with the deprivation regimen, then the strength of the response or the frequency of choice would indicate which system (food or water control) produced the strongest hedonic state. In the homeostatic theory of behavior, we can define the strength of motivation as being directly related to the strength of the hedonic state. We recommend that the reader produce a small graph to illustrate this point.

The homeostatic theory of behavior also suggests that we can predict how much a rat would eat/drink to regain homeostatic balance. If a rat is food deprived for 22 h, then it will no longer have food in the gut and one can assume that it would eat enough food in the following 2 h when food is available to restore its homeostatic balance. This can be inferred from Table 12.01 where there is only a small change shown from the body weight baseline for 22 h of deprivation suggesting that no food remains in the digestive tract. The changes in body weight from the baseline are given for each deprivation period and an average baseline body weight of 272 g can be calculated. Food deprivation also causes the body weights of rats to fall, consequently, one would expect them to eat less as their body weight declines (assuming here that all the components of body weight such as fat, fluid, bone, and muscle decline to the same extent). We can now say that the amount eaten after 22 h, which was 14 g, was sufficient when digested to restore the rat's homeostatic balance given a baseline body weight of 272 g. This gives a food to body weight ratio of 5.1%. That means that a rat has to eat an amount of chow equal to about 5% of its body weight to restore (glucose) homeostatic balance. We can then use the body weights of the rats at periods of deprivation greater than 22 h to predict the amount of food that they should eat. These predictions, along with the observed amounts eaten, are shown in Figure 12.07. The results show that the amount eaten can generally be predicted within experimental error, save for the very last value. Figure 12.07 shows, however, that the total amount of food eaten per period declines faster than what we would predict.

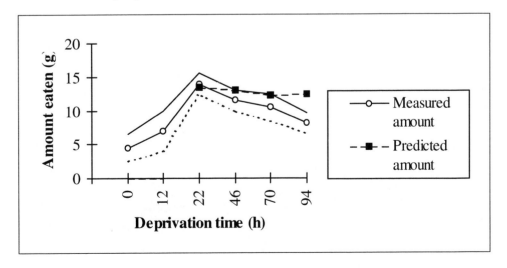

Figure 12.07
The predicted (based on homeostatic considerations) and measured amounts of food consumption for various lengths of food deprivation.

A similar calculation can be done based on water consumption. The average baseline weight of the rats is calculated from Table 12.02 to be 321 g. Table 12.02 also suggests that there is no water in the gut the same way that there could be food in the gut for up to 22 h. We can then estimate that after 12 h of deprivation a rat needs to drink about 3 ml (3 g) of water. This gives a ratio of water consumed to baseline body weight of 0.93% or about 1%. The amounts of water consumed and predicted to be consumed are shown in Figure 12.08.

The results show that the amount of water drunk cannot be predicted. The question here is: why not? One suggestion is that the change in body weight that occurs with water deprivation is entirely due to water loss from the body. The decrease in body weight is then not due to "shrinkage" of the body, but only to water loss from the body. This implies that the water loss would simply generate a larger error in the water balance mechanism, thus requiring greater water intake to restore the water balance. If a rat of 321 g requires 3 ml of water after 12 h of deprivation, it would require 6 ml of water after 24 h, and so on. This revised interpretation is shown in Figure 12.09.

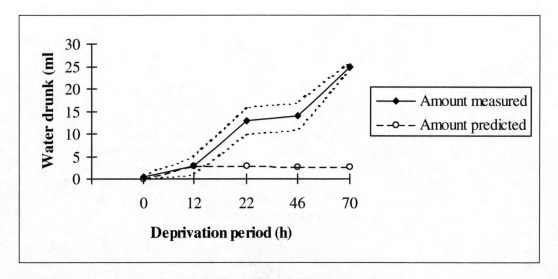

Figure 12.08
The predicted (based on declining body weight) and measured amounts of water consumption for various lengths of water deprivation.

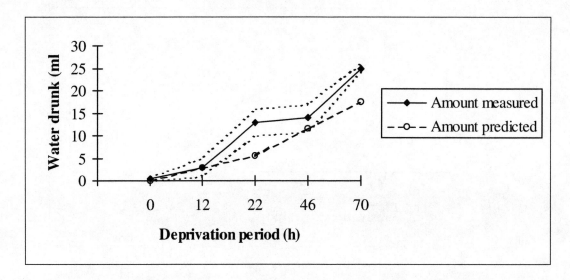

Figure 12.09
The predicted (based on increased water loss) and measured amounts of water consumption for various lengths of water deprivation.

Based on this homeostatic analysis, one may come to the opposite conclusions than those arrived at by Cabanac because it appears that rats drink more than they eat. In fact, the homeostatic analysis suggests that food deprivation can be compensated for by requiring a reduced intake of food, but that water deprivation cannot be compensated for and simply leads to a greater water loss that has to be overcome. This brings us right back to the suggestion of the author that rats have a mechanism for storing energy, but none for storing water, and that the drive to obtain water could be expected to be stronger than the drive to obtain food. This view is more readily supported by the homeostatic analysis, but not by the author's interpretation of his findings The reader is once again encouraged to consult the original articles and to independently assess them.

References
Cabanac, M; Lafrance, L. 1990. Postingestive alliesthesia: the rat tells the same story. Physiology and Behavior 47: 539-543.
Cabanac, M. 1985. Influence of food and water deprivation on the behavior of the white rat foraging in a hostile environment. Physiology and Behavior 35: 701-709.

CHAPTER 13
Hunger

Introduction

Hunger is often used as a major example of a motivated behavior. Therefore, researchers frequently investigate the various psychological and physiological aspects of hunger. This chapter provides a brief review (with an engineering bias) of the physiology and psychology of hunger. Then we proceed to a discussion of different theories of hunger and compare them to an application of the homeostatic theory to hunger. The objective is not to provide the reader with a comprehensive analysis of hunger, but rather to provide a further demonstration of the application of homeostatic mechanisms. In the following chapter on thirst, we will repeat this approach, but the application will be rather more detailed.

Physiology of the digestive system

Food generally consists of carbohydrates, proteins, and fats. The purpose of food digestion is to break these constituents up into components that the body can use. Carbohydrates are complex sugars and are broken down into simple sugars such as glucose. Fats are somewhat similar to sugars and can be stored directly or be broken down into simple sugars. Proteins are complex chains of amino acids and are broken down into their constituent amino acids. Glucose is used for energy by the cells of the body and amino acids are reconnected into specific chains to produce proteins (e.g. enzymes, receptors, muscles). The digestive process takes 4 to 8 hours in humans.

The mouth serves as intake and primary milling and mixing mechanism for food. Food is crushed by the teeth and mixed with saliva to facilitate swallowing. Saliva contains enzymes which starts the digestion of food. In addition, saliva brings food particles into solution to enable taste receptors to detect them. Saliva is also the first line of defense against foreign organisms (e.g. bacteria, viruses, fungi) and contains antibodies. Swallowing moves the food down the esophagus to the stomach.

The stomach secretes gastric acid and more enzymes and furthers the milling and mixing process by churning its contents. The acid facilitates the dissolution of food and acts as a further line of defense against foreign organisms. The stomach enzymes break proteins up into the different amino acids that they consist of. The stomach contents are emptied into the duodenum (a part of the gut). The stomach also contains receptors for various components of food.

The duodenum is the last milling and mixing digestive stage and controls the rate at which the stomach contents are accepted. If fat is present, bile is secreted by the gall bladder into the duodenum to help with the fat absorption. The digestion and absorption of carbohydrates and proteins are easier than that of fats and result in faster emptying of the stomach. The duodenum contains its own set of receptors. More enzymes are secreted into the duodenum by the pancreas. The pancreas also produces the hormones insulin and glucagon and secretes bicarbonate to neutralize the stomach acids. The duodenum passes its contents on to the small intestine.

The small intestine absorbs the glucose, amino acids, and fats in the neutralized slurry received from the duodenum. The small intestine is the first major absorption stage of digestion. The absorbed food chemicals are transported by a vein (the hepatic portal vein) directly to the liver where most toxins are neutralized before the food chemicals are allowed into the body. The small intestine also has receptors. Symbiotic intestinal bacteria live mainly on the undigested cellulose taken in through the diet and produce some essential nutrients such as vitamin K.

The large intestine recovers water and minerals from the food-depleted slurry, resulting in compaction before subsequent elimination. It is the final major absorption stage of the digestive system. The large intestine also has receptors.

The digestive mechanisms can be seen as performing one or more of 5 major functions as shown in Figure 13.01:

1. Milling and mixing functions (physical breakdown);
2. Dissolution functions (chemical breakdown);
3. Filtration functions (removal/neutralization of harmful organisms and chemicals);
4. Nutrient and moisture recovery functions (food and water absorption); and
5. Nutrient synthesis functions (by friendly bacteria).

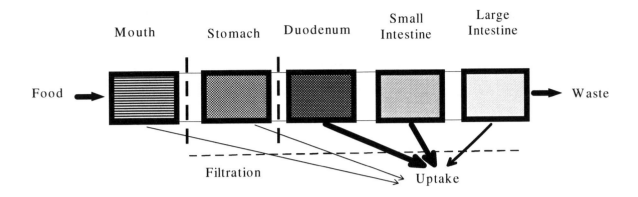

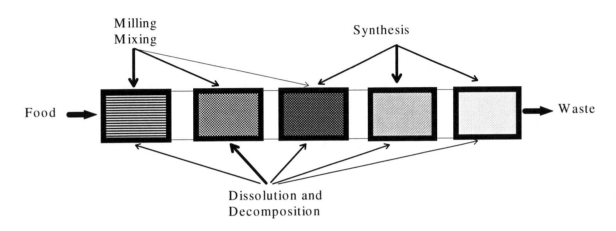

Figure 13.01

A schematic diagram of the digestive system. The top section identifies the major components of the alimentary tract and where filtration (dashed lines) occurs, while the bottom section indicates primary and secondary stages (corresponding to arrow size) of mixing, dissolution, and synthesis.

The preceding discussion of the digestive system should make it clear that several factors could effect changes in body weight as shown in Table 13.01 below: The table is evidently not exhaustive, but serves to illustrate the point that weight gains could occur for reasons other than the increased consumption of food.

Table 13.01

The table shows how body weight can be influenced, not only by a change in the consumption of food, but also by changes in the other processes of digestion.

Mixing	Dissolution	Absorption	Consumption	Weight
0	0	0	+	+
0	0	+	0	+
0	+	0	0	+
+	0	0	0	+

0 = no change
+ = increase

Functioning of the digestive process

The digestive process occurs in 2 phases. The absorptive phase occurs when food is being absorbed after a meal. Because more nutrients are then available than required by the body at that time, excess is converted to fat and glycogen and stored. The fasting phase occurs when a meal has been absorbed and an abundance of nutrients are no longer available. When the blood glucose level starts to fall, insulin secretion is stopped and glucagon is produced by the pancreas. Glucagon reverses the actions of insulin and plays a role in the conversion of fats and glycogen into glucose.

Given the complexity of the digestive system, it is to be expected that many chemical signals may be involved in the different stages and sub-processes of the system. Of these, some related to the digestion of the 3 macronutrients are mentioned here: glucose (involved in carbohydrate digestion), leptin (involved in fat digestion), and amino acids (involved in protein digestion.

The presence of hyperglycemia (high blood glucose) stimulates the secretion of insulin and the cessation of feeding. Insulin in turn activates both glucose transport into cells and the enzyme glycogen synthase in skeletal muscle and liver. This enzyme then converts glucose into glycogen which is stored. Glycogen conversion to glucose occurs when blood glucose levels become too low.

The peptide leptin is derived from fat cells and circulates as a satiety factor. Receptors for leptin have been found in the hypothalamus. Injecting leptin into the cerebral ventricles causes a dose-dependent reduction in eating and body weight. Infusion of leptin directly into the arcuate nucleus of the hypothalamus produces the strongest reduction in feeding, while infusion into the VMH and LH reduce eating also (Satoh et al., 1997).

Amino acids are also regulated. Some amino acids can be synthesized by the body, but some, the essential amino acids, must be obtained from the diet. It has been shown (Fromentin and Nicolaides, 1996) that rats have the ability to balance their intake of amino acids. When a diet deficient in one amino acid is given, rats consume less of that diet and eventually come to dislike it. When a diet deficient in another amino acid is given, the same happens. However, when both diets, each deficient in a different essential amino acid, are separately available to the rats, they will consume both of the aversive diets in a proportion that supplies the correct bodily requirements of these amino acids. It appears that their intakes of the correct proportions of amino acids are mediated by specific amino acid hungers.

Central regulation and control

Hepatic hyperglycemia is mediated by 3 distinct pathways: the direct action of epinephrine on the liver, the action of glucagon on the liver, and through direct innervation of the liver. The neurotransmitters acetylcholine, histamine, and serotonin increase hypothalamic norepinephrine activity which is associated with hyperglycemia, while γ-amino butyric acid (GABA) inhibits hepatic glucose metabolism (see review by Nonogaki and Iguchi, 1997). Thus, central neurotransmitters appear to act in concert to play a role in the homeostatic regulation of hepatic glucose metabolism.

The hypothalamus, and especially 3 of its nuclei(the arcuate, ventromedial and lateral nuclei), have been shown to have a strong influence on eating behaviors. Lesioning (destruction) of the ventromedial hypothalamus (VMH) produces the VMH syndrome which consists of overeating, obesity, and finickiness. Rats with VMH syndrome will become obese even if forced to take small meals or prevented from overeating altogether. Electrical stimulation of the VMH produces decreased eating, increased sympathetic nervous stimulation, lowered insulin and increased blood glucose levels. Lesioning of the lateral hypothalamus (LH) decreases eating, while electrical stimulation increases eating, parasympathetic nervous activity, and decreases blood glucose levels (see Nonogaki and Iguchi, 1997; also Powley, 1977).

Theories of hunger

The hunger and satiety centers hypothesis. Because of the effects of electrical stimulation and lesioning on the brain, the VMH has been considered a "satiety" center and the LH a "hunger" center. This view is known as "the hunger and satiety centers hypothesis".

The cephalic phase hypothesis. Another explanation of these effects is that of the cephalic phase hypothesis. The cephalic responses of digestion are autonomic and hormonal reflexes triggered by sensory contact with the food (e.g. salivation, insulin secretion, gastric acid secretion). The cephalic responses ready the digestive tract to move, digest, and absorb food, to prepare for the storage of excess food, and to provide feedback to the organism about the consequences of food intake (it resembles homeostatic feedforward control). When the VMH is lesioned, the cephalic phase responses are exaggerated and body fat metabolism disrupted. Specifically, more insulin is secreted and more glucose is converted to fat and stored. This means less glucose is available in the blood for immediate use, consequently the animal increases food intake. These cephalic responses are organized in the LH. The VMH modulates (mostly dampens) the cephalic responses from the LH (Powley, 1977). Therefore, destruction of the VMH would result in undamped or stronger cephalic phase responses to food which would amplify normal food preferences and aversions to produce finickiness. For instance, let us assume that the preference for fat was 3, and that for glucose was 2 (a difference of 1 unit) on some "rat food preference scale" before VMH lesioning. After lesioning, amplification of preferences (e.g. doubling) resulted in a fat preference of 6 and a glucose preference of 4 (a difference of 2 units). This implies that fat would now be more preferred than before. The cephalic phase hypothesis appears to explain many of the behavioral changes following VMH lesions.

It has also been suggested that it is not the VMH itself that is important, but nerve fibers passing through the VMH that are involved. Destruction of the VMH would therefore also destroy these fibers which originate elsewhere. Lesions of the posterodorsal amygdala produce hyperphagia and obesity. When the amygdala is lesioned, heavy degeneration of nerve fibers that it sends to the VMH occur. However, unlike VMH lesions, amygdaloid lesions produce no finickiness (King et al., 1997). This suggests that the VMH itself may play a role in the generation of finickiness.

The homeostatic view. If the control of feeding is interpreted in terms of HMs, which we believe can be done, one possible simplified mapping that could be effected is shown below in Figure 13.02:

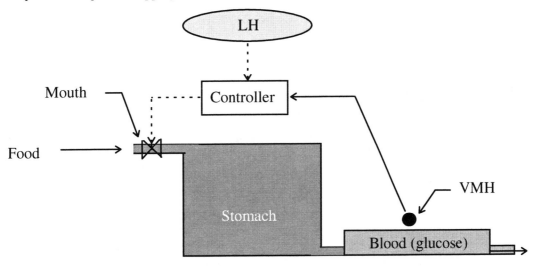

Figure 13.02
A schematic diagram of the HM of feeding.

As before, the tank is mapped onto the stomach, the VMH (which contains glucose receptors) is mapped onto the sensor, and the LH is mapped onto the set point. Blood glucose is the regulated variable. If the blood glucose signal from the VMH drops below the set point signal from the LH, a negative hedonic state arises and the controller activates the feeding mechanism. If the blood glucose signal from the VMH increases above the set point signal from the LH, a negative hedonic state also arises and the controller deactivates the feeding mechanism. If the VMH is lesioned, the signal from the blood glucose detector could be 0. Because the set point will always remain higher, the animal will experience perpetual hunger and overeat.

The hunger and satiety centers hypothesis can account for (1) satiety, (2) hunger, (3) obesity (with VMH lesioned), but not for (4) neurotransmitters, (5) finickiness, (6) small meal weight gain, and (7) no overeating weight gain. The HM of feeding can account for (1) satiety, (2) hunger, (3) obesity (with VMH lesioned), and (4) neurotransmitters, but not for (5) finickiness, (6) small meal weight gain, and (7) no overeating weight gain. However, a modification of the system to account for the regulation of fat levels (e.g. via leptin) can be made as shown in Figure 13.03. Let the set point for fat be provided by brain structure Y and the sensor provided by receptor(s) X (most likely in the arcuate nucleus of the hypothalamus).

If the blood glucose signal from the VMH drops below the set point signal from the LH, a negative hedonic state arises and the controller activates the feeding mechanism. If the blood glucose signal from the VMH increases above the set point signal from the LH, a negative hedonic state also arises and the controller deactivates the feeding mechanism. Likewise, if the blood leptin signal from the brain area X drops below the set point signal from the area Y, a negative hedonic state arises and the controller activates the feeding mechanism. If the blood leptin signal from X increases above the set point signal from Y, a negative hedonic state also arises and the controller deactivates the feeding mechanism. If the VMH is lesioned, blood glucose levels cannot be detected and the signal from the blood glucose detector could be 0. Because the glucose set point will always remain higher than the glucose current point, the animal will experience perpetual hunger and overeat. More specifically, the animal will eat until the leptin current point is so far above the leptin set point that the negative hedonic effect produced by the fat regulation system, caused by additional eating, would exceed the negative hedonic effect form the glucose regulation mechanism caused by lesioning. Consequently, the animal would stop eating. However, the animal could not be expected to be very happy: it would experience 2 about equally negative hedonic states. One of these would be a state of glucose hunger, and the other would be a state of fat oversatiation.

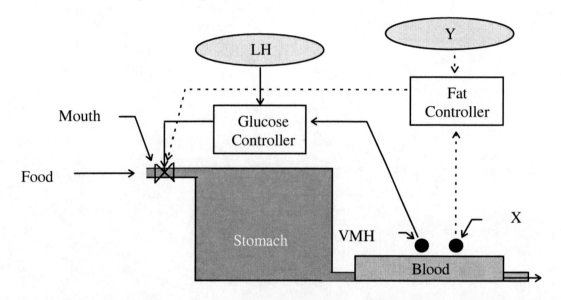

Figure 13.03
A schematic diagram of the augmented HM of feeding. It now accounts for both glucose and fat regulation.

You may realize that we can now also account for finickiness - the VMH-lesioned animals could be expected to show a glucose preference. This augmented HM can now account for(1) satiety, (2) hunger, (3) obesity (with VMH lesioned), (4) neurotransmitters, and (5) finickiness, but not for (6) small meal weight gain, and (7) no overeating weight gain. Although we have demonstrated here how one can account for finickiness, the reader is cautioned that the real picture is rather more complex, especially since rats seem to prefer fatty rather than sweet foods and since they become fat relative to controls even if they are prevented from eating more than the controls (see Powley, 1977). Nevertheless, the potential of the mechanistic approach can clearly be discerned.

References
Fromentin, G; Nicolaidis, S. 1996. Rebalancing essential amino acids intake by self-selection in the rat. British Journal of Nutrition 75: 669-682.
King, B. M; Rossiter, K. N.; Cook, J. T.; Sam H. M. 1997. Amygdaloid lesion-induced obesity in rats in absence of finickiness. Physiology and Behavior 62: 935-938.
Nonogaki, K.; Iguchi, A. 1997. Role of central neural mechanisms in the regulation of hepatic glucose metabolism. Life Sciences 60: 797-807.
Powley, T. L. 1977. The ventromedial hypothalamic syndrome, satiety, and a cephalic phase hypothesis. Psychological Review 84: 89-126.
Satoh, N.; Ogawa, Y.; Katsuura, G.; Hayase, M.; Tsuji, T.; Imagawa, K.; Yoshimasa, Y.; Nishi, S.; Hosoda, K.; Nakao, K. 1997. The arcuate nucleus as a primary site of satiety effect of leptin in rats. Neuroscience Letters 224: 149-152.

CHAPTER 14
Thirst

Introduction

Thirst, like hunger, is often used as a major example of a motivated behavior. This chapter provides a brief review of the physiology and psychology of thirst. Then we proceed as in the previous chapter to an application of homeostatic systems to thirst, but in rather more detail.

Physiology of the water balance system

All the fluid in the body can be considered as belonging to either the intracellular compartment (fluid inside the cells) or the extracellular compartment (fluid outside the cells). The extracellular fluid is either blood plasma or interstitial fluid (fluid in the spaces between cells). Intracellular fluid accounts for 67%, interstitial fluid for 26%, and blood plasma for 7% of the total body fluid.

Many of the organic and inorganic chemicals in the body are water soluble, hence the different fluid compartments contain solutions of many chemicals. Furthermore, the cell membrane forms a barrier between intracellular fluid compartment and interstitial fluid. Likewise, blood capillary vessels form a barrier between blood plasma and interstitial fluid. These membranes are only semi-permeable, meaning that only certain compounds can move across the barrier. In general, proteins cannot diffuse across the barriers, but water and some salts can.

Blood plasma is more concentrated than interstitial fluid, because it carries nutrients absorbed from the digestive system and waste products transported to points of elimination (e.g. kidneys). Consequently, water would tend to move out of the interstitial fluid to the plasma to equal the concentrations in both compartments. This tendency produces osmotic pressure. The osmotic pressure is countered by the pressure set up in the blood vessels by the pumping heart. The blood pressure tends to force water back into the interstitial compartment.

It should be clear therefore, that changes in the composition of one compartment would affect changes in the other. Furthermore, the total volume of water inside cells must be regulated closely. Too much can cause lysis (rupture) of the cells. Similarly, too much blood volume can lead to dangerously high blood pressure and too little to dangerously low blood pressure.

Water and salts are normally ingested by mouth and lost in urine (due to filtration by the kidneys), in perspiration (sweating), respiration (breathing), and possibly saliva and tears. Significant amounts of water are also lost in gastric secretions (during the digestive phase) and recovered by the large intestine. Keep in mind that the contents of the digestive tract is not, strictly speaking, inside the body, but outside. Significant amounts of water are also lost and recovered by the kidneys.

Drinking in order to maintain homeostatic balance is termed primary drinking, and drinking for all other reasons is termed secondary drinking. Furthermore, primary drinking due to a deficit of water in the extracellular compartment is called extracellular or hypovolemic thirst. Drinking due to a water deficit in the intracellular compartment is called intracellular or osmotic thirst.

Given the nature of the fluid compartments system, it is to be expected that both the fluid volume of and the concentration of nutrients, metabolites, and wastes in the fluid compartments should be measured. The total body volume is fixed, within limits, by the skin, thus any change in the volume of a fluid compartment must result in a change in pressure. Under these conditions then, the detection of pressure is tantamount to the detection of fluid compartment volume. Baroreceptors (e.g. in the heart) detect changes in pressure while osmoreceptors detect changes in concentration (e.g. in the stomach, liver, brain).

Drinking behavior therefore can result from the activation of different regulatory systems: e.g. hydration level; salt balance; blood volume; and arterial pressure amongst possible others. Drinking may also be closely linked to other regulating systems such as feeding, thermoregulation, and respiration. For reviews on thirst see McKinley et al., 1996; Schwartz, 2000; Stricker and Sved, 2000; Weisinger et al., 1996.

Homeostatic mechanisms involved in the generation of drinking behavior

We discuss a number of homeostatic mechanisms in brief here that contribute to the generation of thirst and the ingestion of fluids. Once again, the emphasis is not to provide a definitive analysis of the phenomenon, but rather to demonstrate how homeostatic mechanisms could be applied to accommodate greater detail. Specifically, we will discuss 8 regulated variables: gut distention (D_{gut}); arterial blood pressure (BP_{art}); heart rate (HR); blood volume (BV); gut Na$^+$ content (Na$^+_{gut}$); CSF Na$^+$ levels (Na$^+_{CSF}$); plasma osmolality (Osm$_{plasma}$); and plasma Na$^+$ levels (Na$^+_{plasma}$).

Visceral distention. Mechanosensitive vagal afferents provide sensory information, arising from the stomach, pylorus, duodenum, and apparently also from the jejunum and ileum to the nucleus of the solitary tract or NTS (see Schwartz, 2000) in the caudal brainstem where load-sensitive neurons have been identified (see Schwartz, 2000; Stricker and Sved, 2000 and their references). These afferents respond in a manner that reduce meal size according to gastrointestinal loads and irrespective of nutrient content in the stomach although coordinated with nutrient content in the small intestine (see Schwartz, 2000). Hence stretch receptors in the gut function as sensors of a systems regulating gut distention and their afferents (transmission lines) employ cholecystokinin (CCK) as neurotransmitter (e.g. Schwartz, 2000).

Motor neurons from the dorsal motor nucleus (DMN) of the vagus project to gastric and duodenal sites (gastric branch efferents), distal stomach and proximal duodenum (hepatic branch efferents), duodenum, jejunum, cecum, and colon (celiac branch efferents) and are involved in its contractile responses (Schwartz, 2000 and references). The DMN is adjacent to the NTS and receives input from the NTS (e.g. Taylor et al., 1999 and references). Hence these efferents appear to serve as the effectors of a gut distention regulating system.

The NTS itself, in addition to receiving input from sensors and sending output to the DMN effector nucleus, also receives a dense serotonergic input from the B1 and B2 serotonergic groups as well as the nodose ganglion (see Lawrence and Jarrott, 1996 and references). This serotonergic input to the NTS is regarded as providing a SP for the regulation of gastric distention (we will discuss the role of serotonin as set point indicator in a later chapter). The NTS therefore meets all the requirements of connectivity to be considered a controller in a HM that regulates visceral distention.

Arterial blood pressure. Myelinated and unmyelinated projections from baroreceptors in the carotid sinus, myelinated projections from baroreceptors in the aortic arch, and possibly elsewhere in the vascular system, project mainly to the ipsilateral NTS. The ventral medulla oblongata seems to possess separate populations of neurons that affect the adrenal medulla, different vascular beds, cardiac rates, and so on, and receive afferent input probably from the NTS via denritic overlap. Selective bilateral lesions of the ventral medulla abolish the vasomotor component of the baroreceptor reflex but not cardiac acceleration (see Taylor et al., 1999 and references). It is thus reasonable to view a subset of NTS neurons as the controller for an arterial blood pressure regulating system with cardiac and vascular baroreceptors (and possibly chemoreceptors) being the sensors and the ventral medulla and its innervation of vascular beds the effector of the system.

Heart rate. The major cardiac innervation in mammals originates in the nucleus ambiguus (nA) adjacent to the NTS and it provides a vagal tone to the heart reflecting input from arterial baroreceptors to the NTS (see Taylor et al., 1999 and references). It is therefore likely that another subset of neurons in the NTS also perform the function of a controller in a homeostatic system that regulates heart rate (HR). As with BP_{art}, baroreceptors (and possibly chemoreceptors), are the sensors of the system while the nA and the heart itself constitute the effector. However, it may be plasma flow rate or plasma volume turnover that is the actual regulated variable as opposed to HR per se, but for the present we shall conceive of it as a HR regulating system for the sake of simplicity.

Blood volume. Volume receptors in low-pressure capacitance areas and high-pressure resistance areas as well as intrarenal baroreceptors detect volume contraction (Marquez-Julio and Whiteside, 1985). This information is possibly relayed to the NTS via an afferent innervation from the kidney (Fitch et al., 2000). Furthermore, hypovolemia gives rise to renin secretion from the kidney (Stricker and Sved, 2000 and their references; Robertson et al., 1997; Marquez-Julio and Whiteside, 1985) and subsequent conversion to ATII occurs. We suggest therefore that once again a (distinct) subpopulation of NTS neurons act as the controller of a homeostatic system with intra- and extrarenal baroreceptors as its sensors and a ventral medullary site along with kidney as its effector. For the sake of simplicity, this system is denoted a blood volume (BV) regulating system although it may be that renal perfusion pressure, glomerular filtration rate, or another variable is the proper regulated variable instead.

Visceral sodium levels. Many studies indicate that sections of the gastrointestinal tract are sensitive to various nutrients and digestive products, that some of these do so in combination with visceral distention, and that visceral content information affect intestinal contraction and motility (see Schwartz, 2000). Nutrients include glucose, lipids, fatty acids, and others. The infusion of glucose and linoleic acid leads to cFos expression in the medial NTS caudal to the AP, while amino acids do so in the AP and its rostral neighborhood (see Schwartz, 2000). Stricker and Sved (2000) discuss evidence pointing also to the existence of gut (termed "hepatic") Na^+ receptors that appear to project to the NTS. Thus we assume a HM exists that regulates gut Na^+ content that also has the NTS as controller. Although it is understood that discrete systems most likely exist to regulate these putative nutrient-related variables individually and possibly within circumscribed regions or specific organs, we collapse them here into a gut Na^+ system, except where otherwise noted, for the sake of simplicity.

Cerebrospinal fluid composition. The nature of the AP as a circumventricular organ and the increase in Na^+ intake after AP lesions (Curtis et.; 1999) suggests that AP neurons are sensors of a central Na^+ regulation system. Selective destruction of the AP with sparing of the NTS produced large increases in Na^+ intake, while collateral damage to the NTS blunted or eliminated this increase (Curtis et al.; 1999). The AP also projects prominently to the NTS (Cunningham et al.; 1994; Shapiro and Miselis, 1985). The NTS itself, as pointed out above, receives serotonergic input and utilizes the kidney, pituitary, and visceral smooth muscles as effectors. Whether just one or more of these or even other effectors are involved in this case is not presently clear. Furthermore, the AP is sensitive to components of cerebrospinal fluid (CSF). Taken together, this system may regulate aspects of CSF composition including Na^+ content.

Plasma osmolality. Likewise, a subset of neurons in the subfornical organ (SFO) respond to changes in extracellular osmolality in the presence of constant electrolyte concentrations (Anderson et al., 2000) and others respond to ATII. The SFO projects to the, PVN and SON. These hypothalamic nuclei also receive serotonergic input and they project to the pituitary where they mediate vasopressin (VP), an antidiuretic hormone, release (e.g. Huang et al., 2000a, b; Stricker and Sved, 2000). Blood-borne VP in turn affects the retention of water by the kidney and stimulates vasoconstriction (e.g. Schimmer and Sellers, 1985). We conclude therefore that the SFO, PVN/SON, and the pituitary along with oxytocinergic targets, function as the sensors, controller, and effector(s) of a homeostatic system regulating extracellular osmolality.

Plasma sodium concentration. Cells sensitive to plasma Na^+ levels are present in the organum vasculosum of the lamina terminalis (OVLT) and their projections to the anterior hypothalamic nucleus (AHN) use norepinephrine for signaling this information (Peng et al., 2000). Hypertonic intravenous saline infusions stimulate secretion of oxytocin (OT), a natriuretic hormone, into the general circulation by the posterior pituitary (e.g. Huang et al., 2000a; Stricker and Sved, 2000). Blood-borne OT in turn affects the retention of Na^+ by the kidney and stimulates vasodilation (e.g. Schimmer and Sellers, 1985). Furthermore, the AHN receives serotonergic input from the midbrain raphe nuclei which we deem to convey SP information as discussed above. Hence the AHN fulfills the connective requirements of a controller, the OVLT those of a sensing system, and PVN/SON, along with their humoral targets, those of an effector and together they form a homeostatic system regulating plasma Na^+ levels.

Control arrangement. For all these systems, it appears that negative control arrangements are used and we assume so for clarity of exposition in the arrangement of the above 8 homeostatic mechanisms as shown in the figure below (to be provided by the reader!).

Figure 14.01
The major components of several homeostatic mechanisms involved in drinking behavior.

The physiological aspects of thirst and the activation of homeostatic mechanisms

The arrangement shown in Figure 14.01 consists of 8 homeostatic mechanisms regulating their respective variables in an ongoing manner and parallel to one another. It should therefore be evident that a control action taken by one system must affect some of the others. These affected systems would take restorative action in turn, each of which action would produce still further effects. Although we consider here only 8 HMs, and there may be many more of these, it is already clear that such a simple system can generate a dynamic of enormous complexity. This complexity can be fruitfully examined by manipulating some of the components of homeostatic mechanisms as will be discussed next.

Water deprivation is perhaps the easiest method to use for manipulating a regulated variable, but it should be emphasized that water itself is not a regulated variable. Therefore, it should be determined in which systems water deprivation generates regulation errors. The most likely are Osm_{plasma} and BV since Na^+_{plasma} is closely linked to water retention and water loss would also lead to natriuresis, hence no error in Na^+_{plasma} would arise. From Figure 14.01 we see that a BV error would lead to ATII release by the kidney, detection by the SFO and VP release. VP release is likely to be augmented by the detection of an Osm_{plasma} error by the SFO sensors as well. Since the normal regulatory processes cannot compensate for these errors, we postulate (and discuss in later chapters) that a hedonic state-generating mechanism exists and that the changes in overall error-status is transmitted to this mechanism. (The reader is encouraged to incorporate this putative hedonic state-generating mechanism in Figure 14.01.) The hedonic state-generating mechanism in turn activates compensatory behavior, i.e. drinking. Drinking hypotonic water, however, would cause a fall in Na^+_{plasma} levels and hence a Na^+_{plasma} regulation error leading to a reduction of pituitary OT release. The latter would curb natriuresis but cannot supply sodium to the system without behavioral activation. A salt-ingestive behavior is generated in a manner analogous to drinking as described above: the former termed "salt-appetite", the latter "thirst".

Na^+_{plasma} can be manipulated by the intravenous (i.v.) infusion of isotonic saline to generate a regulation error opposite to that described above. This would immediately affect at least the systems regulating Na^+_{plasma} and Osm_{plasma}, but subsequently possibly others such as BV and Na^+_{CSF}. Leaving the latter aside for the moment, we deduce from Figure 14.01 that Na^+_{plasma} system would cause the release of OT into the circulation leading to increased natriuresis. The Osm_{plasma} error would cause VP release as described previously, promoting water retention by the kidneys. If the infusion, in rate and/or Na^+ concentration, is such that the capacities of the respective regulating systems are exceeded in the short or long term, regulation errors triggering behaviors via hedonic states would arise as described previously. Drinking would then result in a reduction of plasma OT and VP levels as the Na^+_{plasma} and Osm_{plasma} errors decline.

Although these predictions are in general agreement with experimental findings, there is evidence that the cessation of OT and VP secretion occurs before any significant reduction in Na^+_{plasma} and Osm_{plasma} errors (Huang et al., 2000a, b). This presents a problem that can be addressed in at least 2 ways. The first possibility is that the Na^+_{gut} regulating system has multiple effectors and uses the pituitary, which is then shared with the Na^+_{plasma} and Osm_{plasma} systems, in addition to the visceral smooth muscles as shown in Figure 14.01. This would result in a reduction of plasma OT and VP levels as soon as ingested water affect gut Na^+ levels. Heeding Ockham's razor though, our preference, and the second possibility, is to consider that the Na^+_{plasma} and Osm_{plasma} systems do respond to the ingested water, but in a manner that reflects the *rate of change* in the Na^+_{plasma} and Osm_{plasma} errors. Therefore, even small Na^+_{plasma} and Osm_{plasma} changes may be sufficient to cause a significant reduction in OT and VP secretion as described for rate as opposed to proportional controllers in the explanatory article. We caution against concluding that a feedforward system or early inhibitory signal exists and suggest that the possibility of a rate (or adaptive) controller be eliminated first.

The psychological aspects of thirst and the selection of behaviors

If all behaviors are activated through the same final common pathway, how would an animal know whether to consume salt or water, for example? Consumption of water in the presence of a salt deficit would increase the Na^+_{plasma} error and increase the negative hedonic state following the behavior. The hedonic consequences of a behavior provide the first means of behavioral navigation. This process is further refined by associations that are formed between viscerosensory and somatosensory information on the one hand and the hedonic consequences that follow from a behavior executed under conditions providing the sensory information. Water and salt deficits would generate different ensembles of sensory activity whence their discrimination can be effected. This process is discussed in more detail later on.

References

Anderson, J. W.; Washburn; D. L. S.; Ferguson, A. V. 2000. Intrinsic osmosensitivity of subfornical organ neurons. Neuroscience 100: 539-547.

Cunningham, E. T.; Miselis, R. R.; Sawchenko, P. E. 1994. The relationship of efferent projections from the area postrema to vagal motor and brainstem catecholamine-containing cell groups: an axonal transport and immunohistochemical study in the rat. Neuroscience 58: 635–648.

Curtis, K. S.; Hunag, W.; Sved, A. F.; Verbalis, J. G.; Stricker, E. M. 1999. Impaired osmoregulatory responses in rats with area postrema lesions. American Journal of Physiology 277: R209-219.

Fitch, G. K.; Patel, K. P.; Weiss, M. L. 2000. Activation of renal afferent pathways following furosemide treatment I. Effects of survival time and renal denervation. Brain Research 861: 363-376.

Huang, W.; Sved, A. F.; Stricker, E. M. 2000a. Vasopressin and oxytocin release evoked by NaCl loads are selectively blunted by area postrema lesions. American Journal of Physiology 278: R732–R740.

Huang, W.; Sved, A. F.; Stricker, E. M. 2000b. Water ingestion provides an early signal inhibiting osmotically stimulated vasopressin secretion in rats. American Journal of Physiology 279: R756–R760.

Lawrence, A. J.; Jarrott, B. 1996. Neurochemical modulation of cardiovascular control in the nucleus tractus solitarius. Progress in Neurobiology 48: 21-53.

Marquez-Julio, A.; Whiteside, C. 1985. Diuretics. In H. Kalant; W. H. E. Roschlau; E. M. Sellers (eds.), Principles of medical pharmacology, pp. 463-477. Toronto: University of Toronto Press.

McKinley, M. J.; Pennington, G. L.; Oldfield, B. J. 1996. Anteroventral wall of the third ventricle and dorsal lamina terminalis: headquarters for control of body fluid homeostasis? Clinical and Experimental Pharmacology and Physiology 23: 271-281.

Peng, N.; Wei, C. C.; Oparil, S.; Wyss, J. M. 2000. The organum vasculosum of the lamina terminalis regulates noradrenaline release in the anterior hypothalamic nucleus. Neuroscience 99: 149-156.

Robertson, J. G.; Mosquedagarcia, D.; Ertl, R.; Robertson, A. C,. Biaggioni R. M. 1997. Hypovolemia in syncope and orthostatic intolerance: role of the renin-angiotensin system. American Journal of Medicine 103: 128-133.

Schimmer, B. P.; Sellers, E. A. 1985. Vasopressin and oxytocin. In H. Kalant; W. H. E. Roschlau; E. M. Sellers (eds.), Principles of medical pharmacology, pp. 503-514. Toronto: University of Toronto Press.

Schwartz, G. J. 2000. The role of gastrointestinal vagal afferents in the control of food intake: current prospects. Nutrition 16: 866-873.

Shapiro, R. E., Miselis, R. R. 1985. The central neural connections of the area postrema of the rat. Journal of Comparative Neurology 234: 344–364.

Stricker, E. M.; Sved, A. F. 2000. Thirst. Nutrition 16: 821-826.

Taylor, E. W.; Jordan, D.; Coote, J. H. 1999. Central control of the cardiovascular and respiratory systems and their interactions in vertebrates. Physiological Reviews 79: 855-916.

Weisinger, R. S.; Blair-West, J. R.; Burns, P.; Denton, D. A.; McKinley, M. J.; Tarjan, E. 1996. The role of angiotensin II in ingestive behaviour: a brief review of angiotensin II, thirst and Na appetite. Regulatory Peptides 66: 73-81.

PART II (continued)
THE MECHANISMS THAT GENERATE DRIVES
Advanced Mechanisms

CHAPTER 15
Stress and the norepinephrine system

Introduction

The notion of a hedonic system activating and guiding an organism through the generation of hedonic states that reflects the current aggregate physiological state of the organism is a pivotal aspect of understanding motivated behaviors. Its importance resides in the fact that it connects physiology and behavior via clearly specified general principles. These principles indicate when hedonic states arise, how they arise and subside, and how they instigate and terminate behavior. Specifically, hedonic states arise whenever a regulation system produces a chronic regulation error. This implies that the regulation system is unable to regulate an important physiological variable within the limits required to maintain the integrity of the organism. The hedonic states that arise in response to an increasing regulation error serve to co-opt the motor system and its cognitive resources. It is then up to the latter to select and execute the appropriate behaviors.

Any regulation error results in a physiological stress condition. This state of stress is assessed by the locus coeruleus (LC), situated in the dorsal pons, which acts as the somatic alarm system. The LC activates and hyperactivates a number of other systems necessary to deal with stress conditions. A general state of arousal with heightened processing capability is consequently generated.

The locus coeruleus and its noradrenergic projections

The LC is a nearly ideal candidate for relaying conditions of regulation failure to other brain centers. Since regulation failure is bound to generate physiological stress, the error relay center should be activated under such conditions. There are numerous reports delineating the activation of the LC by stressful events (e.g. Sandford et al., 2000; Tanaka et al., 2000). LC neurons are markedly activated under conditions of opiate withdrawal (Bremner et al., 1996; Heimer et al., 1997), neophobia (Cole and Robbins, 1987; Roozendaal and Cools, 1994; Steketee et al., 1989), hypovolemia and hypotension (Curtis et al., 1993; Curtis et al., 2001; Lawrence and Jarrott, 1996; Valentino et al., 1991), hunger (Wellman, 2000), footshock, pain, restraint stress, noxious stimuli (e.g. Passerin et al., 2000; see also Valentino and Aston-Jones, 2000 and their references), and other conditions of stress (Bremner et al., 1996; Heimer et al., 1997; Singewald et al., 1995). In short, any physiological stressor results in activation of the LC followed by physiological arousal (Curtis et al., 2001; Rouzade-Dominguez et al., 2001; see also Valentino and Aston-Jones, 2000 and their references), vigilance (e.g. Hasegawa et al., 2000; Servan-Schreiber et al., 1990; Usher et al., 1999), and possibly behavior (e.g. Neophytou et al., 2001; Delfs et al., 1998).

The LC projects widely, via the dorsal noradrenergic bundle, to many brain regions, especially those of systems whose heightened function would be beneficial or adaptive under conditions of stress as shown schematically in Figure 15.01. These include major projections to the raphe (set point and state), hippocampus (memory), amygdala (cognitive stress), cortex (heightened cognitive processing), thalamus (information relay), hypothalamus (humoral controllers), cerebellum (movement), and brainstem (visceral and somatic controllers)(Foote and Aston-Jones, 2000; Schroeter et al., 2000; Valentino and Aston-Jones, 2000; Van Bockstaele et al., 2001), but also less dense projections throughout the brain (e.g. Schroeter et al., 2000).

The purpose of this alarm system is primarily to activate a regulation-supportive behavior when homeostatic maintenance becomes inadequate. Therefore, afferents to the LC are expected to originate mostly from sites that function as the controller structures of HMs. In this context we have already mentioned the PVN and NTS in the chapter on thirst. Since these HMs may employ a diversity of neurotransmitters, it is to be expected that LC afferents would be chemically diverse as well. Both of these interpretations are in agreement with observations. In the context of controllers discussed above, both the NTS (Van Bockstaele et al., 1999a; Van Bockstaele et al., 2001) and the PVN (Schroeter et al., 2000; Van Bockstaele et al., 2001; see also Valentino and Aston-Jones, 2000 and their references) project to the LC and a variety of neurotransmitters are released in the LC including corticotropic releasing factor (CRF), NE, serotonin, enkephalins (ENK), glutamate (Glu), aspartate (Asp), g-amino butyric acid (GABA), neuropeptide Y (NPY), and possibly acetylcholine (Ach) (Arborelius et al.,

2000; Schroeter et al., 2000; Van Bockstaele et al., 2001; Wellman, 2000; see also Valentino and Aston-Jones, 2000).

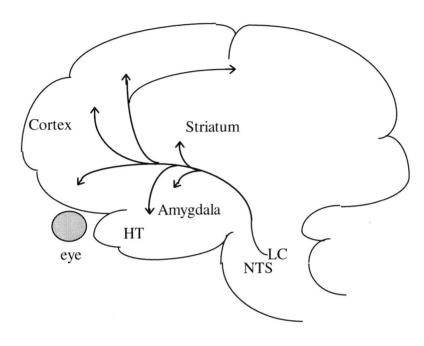

Figure 15.01
A simplified diagram showing projections of the LC via the dorsal noradrenergic bundle to different regions of the brain.

The behavior of noradrenergic neurons

CRF as well as NE are released in response to stress in the LC and they increase LC activity while ENK and opiates inhibit the LC and reduces NE levels (e.g. Van Bockstaele et al., 2001; Valentino and Aston-Jones, 2000). When a stressful event activates the LC, all neurons are activated similarly, i.e. the whole LC is activated (see Valentino and Aston-Jones, 2000 and their references). This effect probably reflects the electrotonic coupling of LC neurons (Van Bockstaele et al., 2001) and dendritic NE release (Schroeter et al., 2000) possibly also aids synchronization. Furthermore, synaptic contacts on LC neurons are both of a symmetric and asymmetric nature (Van Bockstaele et al., 1999b; see also Valentino and Aston-Jones, 2000 and their references) and suggests that all input signals to the LC are integrated irrespective of origin. The latter findings support our suggestion that the error-related stress indicator generated and propagated by the LC represents a 'global error' that indicates the average condition of stress experienced by the organism.

Conversely, when an error (i.e. stress) condition is terminated, LC neurons are quieted. This happens through the release of endogenous opiates in the LC upon the *termination* of stressful events (Curtis et al., 2001 - see Figure 15.02). We have pointed out before that an increase in regulation error generates a condition of (physiological) stress in an animal and that it sets up a negative hedonic state. The reduction of a regulation error reduces stress and sets up a positive hedonic state. Therefore, we interpret the release of CRF and NE as signals indicative of stress subsequent to regulation error increases (and also subsequent to psychological stressors) while the release of opioids is a signal of the reduction of regulation-error induced stress.

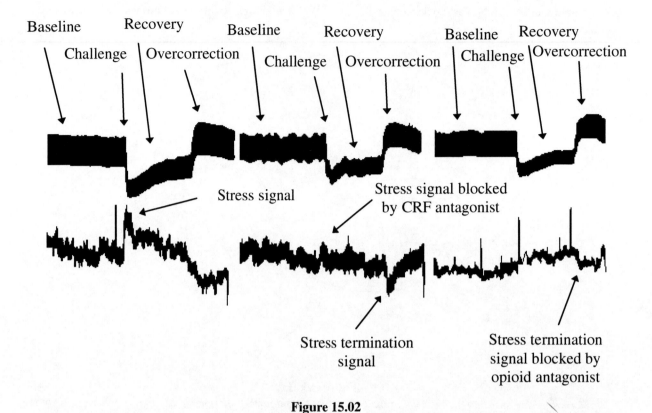

Figure 15.02

Challenging homeostatic regulation of blood pressure (top traces) with nitroprusside causes a sudden drop in blood pressure and an increase in locus coeruleus discharge rates (bottom traces) indicative of a stress condition. Locus coeruleus discharge rates are reduced upon termination of stress. CRF antagonists prevent the locus coeruleus from responding to stress while opioid antagonists prevent the locus coeruleus from responding to the termination of stress. (Composite figure after Curtis et al., 2001.)

In particular, an examination of the data obtained by inducing hypotensive stress through the application of nitroprusside to rats (Curtis et al., 2001) shows that LC discharge in these rats is a mirror of BP changes. Of considerable interest is the fact that over the period of infusion of nitroprusside, there is a gradual recovery of BP homeostasis as shown in Figure 15.02, top trace, a composite figure after Curtis et al. (2001). This is entirely consistent with the expected attempts by the BP homeostatic system to maintain the regulated variable near its set point (in our view the "opponent" process - Solomon, 1980; Solomon and Corbit, 1974). Note that LC discharge (bottom trace) varies proportionally to the BP regulation error. Upon the sudden termination of the infusion, there is an overcorrection of BP that is gradually eliminated. It seems from the traces that the overcorrection is of insufficient duration/intensity to induce overcorrection stress, nevertheless, we would fully expect high BP levels to produce physiological stress as well. These data provide strong support for our view that hedonic states are generated based on stress resulting from errors of regulation (see also the section on tolerance).

Increased activity of LC neurons results in increased NE release at projection targets (see Valentino and Aston-Jones, 2000 and their references). The cortex is a major target of LC projections and several lines of evidence indicate that cortical activation results in improved cognitive function. The ensemble activation of catecholamine neurons in the LC produces increased noise rejection (Servan-Schreiber et al., 1990, Usher et al., 1999) with concomitant gating of information and sharpening of sensory receptive fields such as those in the visual cortex (Hasegawa et al., 2000, Waterhouse et al., 1998).

A hypothesis concerning tolerance. It is generally accepted that neural pathways transmit information from a source to a destination. The theoretical limits of information transmission through a channel with noise were established by Shannon (1948). Some researchers subsequently extended these concepts to neural transmission. For example, viewing a neuron as a single channel lead to the interpretation of reaction times (Hick, 1952), firing patterns related to perception (Norwich 1991), and adaptational evolutionary processes (Schulze and

Mori, 1993) in information-theoretic terms. The reliability of communication channels can be improved by error detection and error-correction methods where the receiver acknowledges receipt of the transmitted information. Although error detection and error correction were introduced by Hamming shortly after Shannon's original work appeared (Hamming, 1950), to the best of our knowledge, error detection and error correction related to information transfer over neural circuits is virtually unexplored. We suggest that tolerance is a manifestation of error detection that arises in neural circuits with reciprocal connections.

The critical role of the LC in opiate tolerance phenomena is well-known (e.g. Christie et al., 1997; Haghparast, 1998; Ivanov and Aston-Jones, 2001; Khalili et al., 2001; Maldonado, 1997; Ruizortega and Ugedo, 1997; Tokuyama et al., 2001; Van Bockstaele et al., 2000). Evidence also suggests that the PGi is involved in the development of tolerance and associated withdrawal phenomena (e.g. Khalili et al., 2001; Liu et al., 1999; Ruizortega and Ugedo, 1997; Saiepour et al., 2001; Taguchi et al., 1999; Van Bockstaele et al., 1999b; Van Bockstaele et al., 2000). The PGi is reciprocally connected to the LC (Van Bockstaele et al., 1989) and a likely site of controllers for various HMs due to its extensive connections to nuclei with autonomic, visceral, and sensory-related functions (Van Bockstaele et al., 1989). We suggest therefore that information transmitted to the LC from the PGi is 'acknowledged' by the LC via its reciprocal connection to the PGi. NE and CRF are released in the LC in response to stress generated by homeostatic dysregulation and endogenous opioids are released in the LC in response to the termination of such stresses (see above).

Hence the administration of exogenous opioids to the LC reduces the level of NE in the LC and the activity of LC neurons (e.g. Ivanov and Aston-Jones, 2001; review by Maldonado, 1997), in essence providing a false 'termination of stress' signal. The receipt of information concerning a critical or chronic regulation error by one or more HMs regulating physiological variables therefore cannot be acknowledged by the LC. This would 'prompt' the PGi to gradually increase the information transmission level for a given size of error until reciprocal activity from the LC occurs. However, when afferent signals to the LC become strong enough to (re-)activate the LC, the attenuation of alarm states and concomitant subjective sense of relaxation cease. Consequently, a higher level of opiates is required to passivate the LC again for the same given size of error.

This view is consistent with many known withdrawal observations as well as those following. Chronic opiate administration leads to increased PGi neuron firing and hence the proposed increase in signal strength of PGi transmissions. These effects reflect the increased release of PGi-derived glutamate in the LC (Liu et al., 1999) probably mediated via cyclic adenosine monophosphate (cAMP) upregulation in the PGi as shown by the induction of withdrawal symptoms by intranuclear caffeine administration (Khalili et al., 2001).

During the withdrawal stage, there are reduced levels of opiates in the LC but an increased level of stimulation by the PGi to a given size of error. In fact, afferent controller-site nuclei such as the PGi increase glutamate release (Haghparast et al., 1998; Tokuyama et al., 2001). In general then, the LC will be hyperactivated under normal conditions during a state of withdrawal. This hyperactivation to normal error variations in the opiate-tolerant animal would be indifferentiable from the crisis-precipitated hyperactivation in the opiate-naive animal. Furthermore, the administration of opiate antagonists to the naive animal could not affect the 'acknowledgment' of LC neurons to activation by the PGi and no effect would be observed in such animals. In contrast, in the opiate-tolerant animal, opiate antagonists would unmask elevated levels of signal transmission from homeostatic controllers to the LC and lead to a state of hyperarousal. Again, these inferences are in agreement with the known effects of opiate withdrawal.

The behavioral effects of noradrenergic neuron activity

Activation of the LC often leads to a variety of behaviors as highlighted by opiate withdrawal (e.g. Khalili et al., 2001; Liu et al., 1999). In fact, we suggest that the induction of behavior through the activation of the LC by HM controllers that experience regulation difficulties is a central element of motivated behaviors. For example, extracellular levels of NE are increased in the rat PVN and peak shortly before dark and the onset of eating (Morien et al., 1995) when a condition of hunger could be expected and the maintenance of $glucose_{plasma}$ becomes more difficult. NE levels also increase with meal size in satiated rats, and meal size increases with NE levels in fasted rats (Morien et al., 1995). Both of these situations reflect increasing error conditions. Therefore, we do not view NE as being a signal facilitating or inhibiting eating (as various authors would suggest) since difficulties of explanation arise. In the former case, increased NE release in response to larger meals should further increase meal size and set up a dangerous positive feedback condition leading to internal organ damage. In the latter case, increased NE levels prior to eating would set up an equally dangerous but positive feedforward condition leading to starvation. The only tenable interpretation in our view is that NE release signals a condition of stress: in a satiated animal, larger meal size would lead to greater gut distention distress; and in a fasted animal, greater hunger would lead to greater levels of NE release prior to eating. It follows then that eating should lead to an eventual reduction in stress with commensurate decline in NE levels, but overeating with increased gut distention would re-induce stress with concomitant increases in NE levels - hence an adaptive behavior ensues.

References

Arborelius, L.; Skelton, K. H.; Thrivikraman, K. V.; Plotsky, P. M.; Schultz, D. W.; Owens, M. J. 2000. Chronic administration of the selective corticotropin-releasing factor 1 receptor antagonist CP-154,526: behavioral, endocrine and neurochemical effects in the rat. The Journal of Pharmacology and Experimental Therapeutics 294: 588–597.

Bremner, J. D.; Krystal, J. H.; Southwick, S. M.; Charney, D. S. 1996. Noradrenergic mechanisms in stress and anxiety: I. Preclinical studies. Synapse 23: 28–38.

Christie, M. J.; Williams, J. T.; Osborne, P. B.; Bellchambers, C. E. 1997. Where is the locus in opioid withdrawal. Trends in Pharmacological Sciences 18: 134-140.

Cole, B. J.; Robbins, T. W. 1987. Dissociable effects of lesions to the dorsal or ventral noradrenergic bundle on the acquisition, performance, and extinction of aversive conditioning. Behavioral Neuroscience 101: 476–488.

Curtis, A. L.; Bello, N. T.; Valentino, R. J. 2001. Evidence for functional release of endogenous opioids in the locus ceruleus during stress termination. The Journal of Neuroscience 21: RC152-RC157.

Curtis, A. L.; Drolet, G.; Valentino, R. J. 1993. Hemodynamic stress activates locus coeruleus neurons of unanesthetized rats. Brain Research Bulletin 31: 737–744.

Delfs, J. M.; Zhu, Y.; Druhan,J. P.; Aston-Jones, G. S. 1998. Origin of noradrenergic afferents to the shell subregion of the nucleus accumbens: anterograde and retrograde tract-tracing studies in the rat. Brain Research 806: 127–140.

Foote, S. L.; Aston-Jones, G. S. 2000. Pharmacology and physiology of central noradrenergic systems. Psychopharmacology - The Fourth Generation of Progress: The American College of Neuropsychopharmacology. [Found at http://www.acnp.org/g4/GN401000030/Default.htm]

Haghparast, A.; Semnanian, S.; Fathollahi, Y. 1998. Morphine tolerance and dependence in the nucleus paragigantocellularis: single unit recording study in vivo. Brain Research 814: 71-77.

Hamming, R. W. 1950. Error-detecting and error-correcting codes. The Bell System Technical Journal 26: 147-160.

Hasegawa, R. P.; Blitz, A. M.; Geller, N. L.; Goldberg, M. E. 2000. Neurons in monkey prefrontal cortex that track past or predict future performance. Science 290: 1786-1789.

Heimer, L.; Zahm, D. S.; Churchill, L.; Kalivas, P. W.; Wohltmann, C.; Maldonado, R. 1997. Participation of noradrenergic pathways in the expression of opiate withdrawal: biochemical and pharmacological evidence. Neuroscience and Biobehavioral Reviews 21: 91–104.

Hick, W. E. 1952. On the rate of gain of information. Quarterly Journal of Experimental Psychology 4: 11-26.

Ivanov, A.; Aston-Jones, G. 2001. Local opiate withdrawal in locus coeruleus neurons in vitro. Journal of Neurophysiology 85: 2388-2397.

Khalili, M.; Semnanian, S.; Fathollahi, Y. 2001. Caffeine increases paragigantocellularis neuronal firing rate and induces withdrawal signs in morphine-dependent rats. European Journal of Pharmacology 412: 239-245.

Lawrence, A. J.; Jarrott, B. 1996. Neurochemical modulation of cardiovascular control in the nucleus tractus solitarius. Progress in Neurobiology 48: 21-53.

Liu, N.; Ho, I. K.; Rockhold, R. W. 1999. Contribution of glutamatergic systems in locus coeruleus to nucleus paragigantocellularis stimulation-evoked behavior. Pharmacology Biochemistry Behavior 63: 555–567.

Maldonado, R. 1997. Participation of noradrenergic pathways in the expression of opiate withdrawal - biochemical and pharmacological evidence. Neuroscience and Biobehavioral Reviews 21: 91-104.

Morien, A.; Wellman, P. J.; Fojt, J. 1995. Diurnal rhythms of paraventricular hypothalamic norepinephrine and food intake in rats. Pharmacology Biochemistry and Behavior 52: 169-174.

Neophytou, S. I.; Aspley, S.; Butler, S.; Beckett, S.; Marsden, C. A. 2001. Effects of lesioning noradrenergic neurones in the locus coeruleus on conditioned and unconditioned aversive behaviour in the rat. Progress in Neuro-Psychopharmacology and Biological Psychiatry 25: 1307-1321.

Norwich, K. H. 1991. On the fundamental nature of perception. Acta Biotheoretica 39: 81-90.

Passerin, A. M.; Cano, G.; Rabin, B. S.; Delano, B. A.; Napier; J. L.; Sved A. F. 2000. Role of locus coeruleus in foot shock-evoked Fos expression in rat brain. Neuroscience 101: 1071–1082.

Roozendaal, B.; Cools, A. R. 1994. Influence of the noradrenergic state of the nucleus accumbens in basolateral amygdala mediated changes in neophobia of rats. Behavioral Neuroscience 108: 1107–1118.

Rouzade-Dominguez, M.-L.; Curtis, A. L.; Valentino, R. J. 2001. Role of Barrington's nucleus in the activation of rat locus coeruleus neurons by colonic distension. Brain Research 917: 206–218.

Ruizortega, J. A.; Ugedo, L. 1997. The stimulatory effect of clonidine on locus coeruleus neurons of rats with inactivated alpha(2)-adrenoceptors - involvement of imidazole receptors located in the nucleus paragigantocellularis. Naunyn-Schmiedebergs Archives of Pharmacology 355: 288-294.

Saiepour, M. H.; Semnanian, S.; Fathollahi, Y. 2001. Occurrence of morphine tolerance and dependence in the nucleus paragigantocellularis neurons. European Journal of Pharmacology 411: 85-92.

Sandford, J. J.; Argyropoulos, S. V.; Nutt, D. J. 2000. The psychobiology of anxiolytic drugs. Part 1: basic neurobiology. Pharmacology and Therapeutics 88: 197-212.

Schroeter, S.; Apparsundaram, S.; Wiley, R. G. Miner, L. H.; Sesack, S. R.; Blakely, R. D. 2000. Immunolocalization of the cocaine- and antidepressant-sensitive l-norepinephrine transporter. The Journal of Comparative Neurology 420: 211–232.

Schulze, G.; Mori, S. 1993. Increases in environmental entropy demand evolution. Acta Biotheoretica 41: 149-164.

Servan-Schreiber, D.; Printz, H.; Cohen, J. D.; 1990. A network model of catecholamine effects: gain, signal-to-noise ratio, and behavior. Science 249: 892-895.

Shannon, C. E. 1948. A mathematical theory of communication. The Bell System Technical Journal 27: 379-423.

Singewald, N.; Zhou, G. Y.; Schneider, C. 1995. Release of excitatory and inhibitory amino acids from the locus coeruleus of conscious rats by cardiovascular stimuli and various forms of acute stress. Brain Research. 704: 42-50.

Solomon, R. L. 1980. The opponent-process theory of acquired motivation. American Psychologist 35: 691-712.

Solomon, R. L.; Corbit, J. D. 1974. An opponent-process theory of motivation: I. Temporal dynamics of affect. Psychological Review 81: 119-145.

Steketee, J. D.; Silverman, P. B.; Swann, A. C. 1989. Forebrain norepinephrine involvement in selective attention and neophobia. Physiology and Behavior 46: 577–583.

Taguchi, K.; Kato, M.; Kikuta, J.; Abe, K.; Chikuma, T.; Utsunomiya, I.; Miyatake, T. 1999. The effects of morphine-induced increases in extracellular acetylcholine levels in the rostral ventrolateral medulla of rat. The Journal of Pharmacology and Experimental Therapeutics 289: 1539-1544.

Tanaka, M.; Yoshida, M.; Emoto, H.; Ishii, H. 2000. Noradrenaline systems in the hypothalamus, amygdala and locus coeruleus are involved in the provocation of anxiety: basic studies. European Journal of Pharmacology 405: 397–406.

Tokuyama, S.; Zhu, H.; Oh, S.; Ho, I. K.; Yamamoto, T. 2001. Further evidence for a role of NMDA receptors in the locus coeruleus in the expression of withdrawal syndrome from opioids. Neurochemistry International 39: 103-109.

Usher, M.; Cohen, J. D.; Servan-Schreiber, D.; Rajkowski, J.; Aston-Jones, G. 1999. The Role of locus coeruleus in the regulation of cognitive performance. Science 283: 549-554.

Valentino, R. J.; Aston-Jones, G. S. 2000. Physiological and anatomical determinants of locus coeruleus discharge: behavioral and clinical implications. Psychopharmacology - The Fourth Generation of Progress: The American College of Neuropsychopharmacology. [Found at http://www.acnp.org/g4/GN401000035/CH035.html]

Valentino R. J., Page ME, Curtis AL. 1991. Activation of noradrenergic locus coeruleus neurons by hemodynamic stress is due to local release of corticotropin-releasing factor. Brain Research 555: 25–34.

Van Bockstaele, E. J.; Bajie, D.; Proudfit, H.; Valentino, R. J. 2001. Topographic architecture of stress-related pathways targeting the noradrenergic locus coeruleus. Physiology and Behavior 73: 273-283.

Van Bockstaele, E. J.; Peoples, J.; Menko, A. S.; McHugh, K.; Drolet, G. 2000. Decreases in endogenous opioid peptides in the rat medullo-coerulear pathway after chronic morphine treatment. Journal of Neuroscience 20: 8659-8666.

Van Bockstaele, E. J.; Peoples, J.; Telegan, P.; Valentino, R. J. 1999a. Efferent projections of the nucleus of the solitary tract to peri-locus coeruleus dendrites in rat brain: evidence for a monosynaptic pathway. The Journal of Comparative Neurology 412: 410–428.

Van Bockstaele, E. J.; Saunders, A.; Telegan, P.; Page, M. 1999b. Localization of mu-Opioid Receptors to Locus Coeruleus-Projecting Neurons in the Rostral Medulla: Morphological Substrates and Synaptic Organization. Synapse 34: 154–167.

Van Bockstaele, E. J.; Pieribone, V. A.; Aston-Jones, G. 1989. Diverse afferents converge on the nucleus paragigantocellularis in the rat ventrolateral medulla: retrograde and anterograde tracing studies. Journal of Comparative Neurology 290: 561-84.

Waterhouse, B. D.; Moises, H. C.; Woodward, D. J. 1998. Phasic activation of the locus coeruleus enhances responses of primary sensory cortical neurons to peripheral receptive field stimulation. Brain Research 790: 33-44.

Wellman, P. J. 2000. Norepinephrine and the control of food intake. Nutrition 16: 837–842.

CHAPTER 16
Hedonic states and the dopamine system

Introduction

In our discussions of homeostatic mechanisms and their operation, which produce motivated behaviors, we have come to the conclusion that stimuli do not possess intrinsic hedonic values. This point of view is shared by others. "The reward value associated with a stimulus is not a static, inherent property of the stimulus. Animals can assign different appetitive values to a stimulus as a function of their internal states at the time the stimulus is encountered and as a function with their experience with the stimulus" (Schultz, et al., 1997). The assignment of hedonic values by neural circuitry were based on the error between actual and desired state of the HM involved in the regulation of a particular variable. In a previous chapter we saw how such a regulation error induced a state of somatic stress and reduction of the error a state of relief communicated by the LC to other brain areas.

One of these is the nucleus accumbens (NAC) where the state of stress is converted and calibrated to a drive state to induce the proper behaviors. Another site that responds to physiological stress communicated by the LC is the amygdala. Here external stimuli are associated with physiological conditions and are committed to memory via the hippocampus. This permits the organism to recognize external conditions that give rise to physiological states of stress/relief and to react to those appropriately. A third site is the ventral tegmental area (VTA) where external stimuli in conjunction with current physiological conditions are used to make predictions about future states of stress/relief. It appears that both the amygdala and the VTA generate hedonic states to indicate their respective imminent or expected future states of stress/relief. Note that an expected future state of stress is hypothesized to generate a current negative hedonic state, even if there is no current physiological state of stress, in order to activate a behavior to preempt the expected state of stress.

In this chapter we shall consider the possible mechanisms that could generate these hedonic states as they relate to the VTA. However, an integration between HMs and the dopamine system discussed in this chapter will only be attempted later. Nevertheless, the reader is advised to read the chapter where these systems are integrated at regular intervals and indeed after this chapter.

The dopamine systems of the brain

The brain contains dopaminergic neurons situated predominantly in three groups: the retrobulbar area (RA), the ventral tegmental area (VTA), and the substantia nigra (SN). Dopaminergic neurons of the SN send projections to brain structures such as the striatum, and they are mainly involved in the initiation and execution of movement. Dopaminergic neurons of the RA send projections to the hypothalamus, and they are mainly involved in the regulation of hormone secretion from the pituitary gland. Dopaminergic neurons of the VTA send projections mainly to the limbic system and associated areas and are involved in thought organization, mood, motivation, and goal-oriented behavior. Therefore, the ventral tegmental area (VTA) is a prime candidate for the neural circuitry responsible for the generation of hedonic states. Figure 16.01 shows the SN and VTA and projections emanating from them.

The distribution of dopamine and dopamine receptors in the living brain can be determined with the use of radioactive isotope tracers. These tracers emit positrons which are detected and used to form an image of regions of the brain where the tracers accumulate. This procedure is called positron emission tomography (PET) (e.g. Volkow et al., 1996). For instance, the dopamine neurons of the brain use the amino-acid tyrosine to synthesize dopamine. If a volunteer is given radiolabeled (radioactive) tyrosine to ingest, it will be taken up by the body and transported across the blood-brain barrier into the brain. There it will be taken up by dopamine neurons where it will be converted into dopamine. Because the radiotracers accumulate in dopamine neurons, they can be detected by the instrumentation. Consequently a map showing the distribution of dopamine neurons in the brain can be made.

Evidence for dopamine as the "reward" neurotransmitter comes from several lines of research on humans and other animals. Drugs like amphetamine and cocaine exert their addictive actions in part by prolonging the influence of dopamine on target neurons. Furthermore, neurons associated with dopamine pathways are among the best targets for electrical self-stimulation (where a rat can voluntarily apply a tiny shock to a part of its brain, where an electrode is implanted, by pressing on a lever). Finally, animals treated with dopamine receptor blockers learn more slowly to press a lever to obtain food.

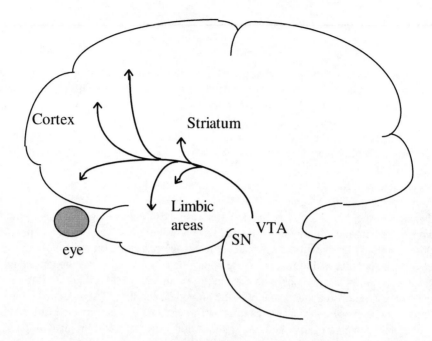

Figure 16.01
A simplified diagram showing projections of the VTA and SN to different regions of the brain.

In order to survive in its environment, an organism must be able to engage in adaptive behaviors. We have considered what such adaptive behaviors may be and how an animal could tell that a behavior was adaptive under the given circumstances. The ability to predict events and thereby take preparatory adaptive behavior, may further enhance the fitness of an organism. One important, but simple, prediction that an organism can make is the probable time and magnitude of future rewarding events. Some theories of reward-dependent learning suggest that learning occurs from the unpredictability of events: no further learning takes place when the reward is entirely predicted by a sensory cue(s). Engineered systems that are designed to optimize their actions in a complex environment face the same challenge as animals, except that in the former case reward is determined in terms of design goals. The temporal difference algorithm (TDA) is a method used by such artificial systems to learn prediction (e.g. Schultz et al., 1997; Suri et al., 2001).

The behavior of dopamine neurons

In electronic recordings made from single dopamine neurons in alert monkeys while they engaged in different behaviors, it was found that such neurons produced short increases in activity above baseline levels when the monkeys were presented with some rewarding stimulus such as a piece of fruit. (These responses are also produced by novel orienting stimuli.) After repeated pairings of such rewards with preceding visual or auditory cues, dopamine neurons change the time of their short bursts of activity from just after receipt of the reward (unconditioned stimulus) to just after the presentation of the cue (conditioned stimulus) as shown in Figure 16.02.

That is, neurons shift the activation forward in time relative to the reward. There is also a concomitant change in behavior of these monkeys: as soon as the cue is given, they put out their hands to receive the reward, instead of when the reward itself is given. When the neurons have learnt to predict a reward from a cue, and the reward is not given, the neurons show depressed activity relative to the baseline very shortly after the reward would have occurred.

These findings suggest that dopaminergic neurons encode expectations about external stimuli or rewards. From a computational perspective, it seems that dopamine neurons produce an output that encodes an error or deviation between the actual reward received and predictions of the time and magnitude of the reward. Neurons are activated only if the time of the reward is uncertain (no preceding cues) and they are depressed if the reward does not occur when expected. They indicate therefore how well learned predictions anticipate environmental conditions.

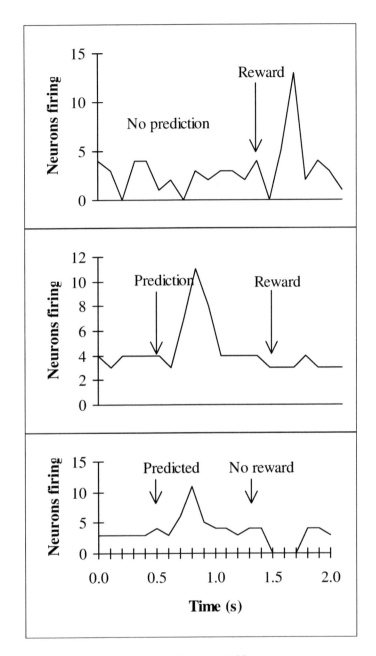

Figure 16.02

Recordings from dopamine neurons showing baseline activity and increased activity following an unexpected reward (top), increased activity following the predictive cue (middle), and depressed activity following omission of the reward (bottom). Figures drawn after Schultz (1998).

A computational model of dopamine systems

   The model. The TDA has been used to interpret the functional role played by the dopamine signal in terms of the information it transmits (Schultz et al., 1997). There are 3 main assumptions in the TDA. The first is that the goal of learning is to use sensory cues to predict a discounted sum of all future rewards V(t) within a learning trial. The second is that future sensory cues and rewards depend only on the present but not the past sensory cues. The third that V(t) shows consistency over time. We can now formalize these concepts:

$$V(t) = [\gamma^0 r(t) + \gamma^1 r(t+1) + \gamma^2 r(t+2) + ...] \qquad (16.1)$$

$$\underline{V}(t) = \sum_i w_i x_i(t) \qquad (16.2)$$

$$V(t) = [r(t) + \gamma V(t+1)] \qquad (16.3)$$

where V(t) is the discounted sum of all future rewards based on the cue at time t, $\underline{V}(t)$ is the *estimated* discounted sum of all future rewards based on the cue x_i at time t, and $0 \leq \gamma \leq 1$ is the discount factor which makes rewards that arrive sooner more important than those that arrive later. The TDA error, an error between the discounted sum of future rewards and the estimate of this sum, can now be defined as:

$$\delta(t) = V(t) - \underline{V}(t)$$
$$= r(t) + \gamma V(t+1) - \underline{V}(t).$$

However, since V(t+1) is unknown and also has to be predicted, the error of prediction is approximated by

$$\delta(t) = r(t) + \gamma \underline{V}(t+1) - \underline{V}(t) \qquad (16.4).$$

To understand the discount factor, consider the following: if you are given the opportunity to choose between getting $100 today or getting $100 next year, which would you choose? Most people would wish to receive their reward immediately because the future is uncertain and they may not be around next year to collect their reward. Now, if you were given the choice between $100 today and $150 next year, which would you choose? You may still opt for $100 today. However, if you had to choose between $100 today or $200 next year, you may think it more worthwhile to wait until next year. This means that $200 given to you next year is as valuable to you now as $100 given to you today. The $200 is then discounted by a factor of 0.5.

Anatomical interpretation of the model. The anatomical arrangement of inputs and outputs of the VTA is given in Figure 16.03 and can be interpreted in the following way: M_1 is a part (containing a large population of neurons) of the brain's cortex that calculates or produces the discounted estimate $\gamma \underline{V}(t+1)$. For instance, M_1 can be a neural network (neural networks will be discussed in Part III of this book) that takes an input from the sensory systems (e.g. a cue such as smell) and produces the output $\gamma \underline{V}(t+1)$ based on Equation 16.2. M_2 is another part of the cortex that calculates or produces the estimate $\underline{V}(t)$ also based on Equation 16.1. It too can be thought of as a neural network that produces an output, in this case $\underline{V}(t)$, from the input of sensory cues.

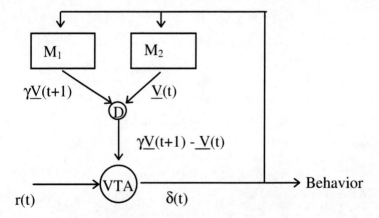

Figure 16.03
The anatomical arrangement of inputs and outputs of the VTA showing the connection between anatomy and the temporal difference algorithm (adapted from Schultz et al., 1997).

The node marked "D" in Figure 16.03 takes $\gamma\underline{V}(t+1)$ obtained from M_1 and subtracts $\underline{V}(t)$ obtained from M_2. In other words, node D determines the difference between the entities calculated by M $_1$ and M_2. This node can be a neuron whose dendrites make contact with axons from M_1 and axons from M_2. The output of the neuron is $\gamma\underline{V}(t+1) - \underline{V}(t)$ and is called a temporal difference or temporal derivative. The neuron sends its output to the VTA. The VTA adds this input to the information it receives from still a third part of the brain about the size of the current reward r(t). The output that the VTA produces is then $r(t) + \gamma\underline{V}(t+1) - \underline{V}(t)$ which is the error $\delta(t)$. The value calculated for $\delta(t)$ is then used to guide behavior but also relayed back to M_1 and M_2 to make further calculations based on adjusted weights. It is assumed that the output from the VTA is actually $\delta(t) + b(t)$ where b(t) is the baseline firing rate.

An inspection of Figure 16.03 may reveal it as being somewhat awkward, and we suggest, without loss of generality, a modified interpretation as shown in Figure 16.04. In the modification, at every time period t, $\underline{V}(t)$ is calculated once only, based on the presence of cues and their importance as given in Equation 16.2. Let us assume that M_1 calculates the entity $\underline{V}(t)$ and sends it to M_2 and a discounted copy, $\gamma\underline{V}(t)$, to D. During the next time period, $t+1$, a new value of $\underline{V}$ (now $\underline{V}(t+1)$) is calculated. A copy of $\underline{V}(t+1)$ is sent to M_2 and a discounted copy $\gamma\underline{V}(t+1)$ is sent to D. When $\underline{V}(t+1)$ arrives at M_2, M_2 sends its current content, namely $\underline{V}(t)$, to D and $\underline{V}(t+1)$ becomes the current content of M_2. As before, D performs a subtraction to produce the temporal derivative $\gamma\underline{V}(t+1) - \underline{V}(t)$ at the VTA.

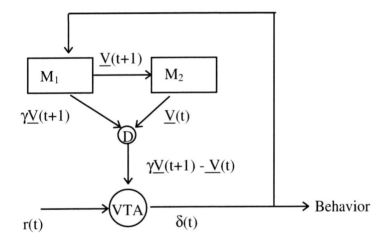

Figure 16.04
The anatomical arrangement of inputs and outputs of the VTA showing the connection between anatomy and the temporal difference algorithm (adapted from Schultz et al., 1997).

Example
A mother entertains her toddler by placing a candy under one of 3 colored boxes. The toddler is then allowed to turn the boxes over until s/he finds the candy. Once the candy is found and consumed, this game is repeated once more. Since the mother knows under which box the candy is going to be on both trials, she knows what V(t) is. However, the toddler does not know and has to make an estimate $\underline{V}(t)$, based on the sensory cues it receives. It forms an expectation of the candies it may get for the entire game and may initially weight every box equally. This expectation we get from Equation 16.2:

$$\underline{V}(t) = \sum_i w_i x_i(t)$$
$$= w_1 x_1(t) + w_2 x_2(t) + w_3 x_3(t)$$
$$= 0.33(box_{red}) + 0.33(box_{green}) + 0.33(box_{blue}).$$

Should the toddler know that there will be 2 trials, it may also form a separate expectation of $\underline{V}$(t+1), the rewards to be obtained on the second (and further, if any) trial(s). (If there are not to be any more trials, the expectation of rewards, $\underline{V}$(t+1), will simply be zero.) However, the second trial and the candies that could be recovered during that trial will seem more remote to the toddler. Consequently, its expectation of the rewards to be obtained during the second trial will be weaker (or future discounted). To reflect this, the second or future attempt is discounted by the factor γ. M_1 and M_2 of the toddler's brain now determine $\gamma\underline{V}$(t+1) and $\underline{V}$(t) respectively and the difference is sent to the VTA. The box is turned over and the reward information r(t) also arrives at the VTA.

The toddler can now determine the error of prediction. When the error is known, the weights of the cues can be adjusted. If the error is large, the weights need much adjustment. If there is no error, the weights need no adjustment. Thus, the weights are adjusted based on the size of the error. If the mother is in the habit of concealing the candy under the red box, the toddler will come to weight the red box more, for example, to give

$$V(t) = 0.75(box_{red}) + 0.1(box_{green}) + 0.15(box_{blue}).$$

Once the toddler has learned that the red box is most likely to conceal a candy, it will experience a sense of excitement (increased dopamine release from the VTA) at the *sight* of the red box. If s/he then proceeds to *find* the candy under that box, it will be as expected and little excitement (normal baseline-level dopamine release) would be engendered. However, if the candy is *not* where expected, s/he will experience disappointment (decreased dopamine release).

The example above is conformant with Figure 16.03. However, the explanation of the TD algorithm provided here is somewhat simplified, particularly regarding Equation 16.2, and the interpretation of sensory cues and their internal representations. The interested reader is referred to the original (Schultz, et al., 1997).

References
Schultz, W. 1998. Predictive reward signal of dopamine neurons. Journal of Neurophysiology 80: 1–27.
Schultz, W.; Dayan, P.; Montague, P. R. 1997. A neural substrate of prediction and reward. Science 275: 1593-1599.
Suri, R. E.; Bargas, J.; Arbib, M. A. 2001. Modeling functions of striatal dopamine modulation in learning and planning. Neuroscience 103: 65-85.
Volkow, N. D.; Fowler, J. S.; Gatley, S. J.; Logan, J.; Wang, G.-J.; Ding, Y.-S.; Dewey, S. 1996. PET evaluation of the dopamine system of the human brain. The Journal of Nuclear Medicine 37: 1242-1256.

CHAPTER 17
System states and the serotonin system

Introduction

The discussion of the previous chapter lead us to suspect that the dopamine reward systems of the brain, particularly that of the VTA, may be responsible for generating the positive hedonic states in an organism when the CP of a variable moves toward the SP. However, when the CP moves away from the SP, a negative hedonic state is generated. When we consider the generation of hedonic states more closely, it becomes apparent that several questions need to be addressed.

First, if a positive hedonic state is absent, is the resultant hedonic state neutral or negative? That is, does one neurotransmitter cause a positive hedonic state by its presence and a negative hedonic state by its absence? This seemed to be the case with the dopamine system. Second, it is also possible that 2 neurotransmitters independently generate hedonic states, for example, a neurotransmitter, say NTX, could produce a negative hedonic state with its presence and a positive hedonic state with its absence which is the opposite of dopamine. Third, we may furthermore wish to know whether the changing of the SP of a system also affects the hedonic states generated in an organism or not. We shall consider these issues in this chapter, but, alas, not find an answer to all of them.

The serotonin systems of the brain

Serotonin cells. The brain contains serotonergic neurons situated predominantly in the raphe nuclei of the midbrain. The caudal raphe nuclei project to the spinal cord and there is evidence that these descending systems inhibit pain transmission. Most of the rostral raphe nuclei project to the cortex, the limbic system, and the hypothalamus. These latter nuclei are responsible for many of the other effects of serotonin, such as those on temperature regulation, mood, sleep cycles, sexual behavior, and food intake. The locations of the raphe nuclei in the brain and their major known projections are shown in Figure 17.01.

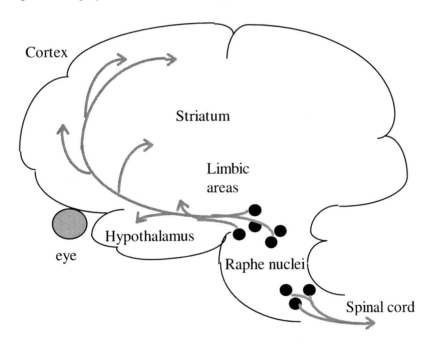

Figure 17.01
A simplified diagram showing projections from the rostral raphe nuclei to different regions of the brain and from the caudal raphe nuclei to the spinal cord.

Serotonin receptor types. Serotonin neurons contain a variety of receptors (analogous to the receptors discussed in the context of bacterial chemotaxis) which mediate their operation. Serotonin binds to all of these receptors, but some drugs will bind only to one type or a subset of types. These drugs can therefore be used to investigate which functions are regulated by which serotonin receptor subtypes. If one can then determine where in the brain these receptor subtypes are located, one can identify some of the neural structures involved in the functions mediated by these receptors. There have been, to date, 14 types of serotonin receptors identified. They are given in Table 17.01 below along with some of the behaviors mediated by them.

The behavior of serotonin neurons

The activity of serotonin neurons depends on the vigilance state of the animal: they are less active during sleep than during the waking state. During the waking state, serotonin acts as a gain suppressor, inhibiting almost all activities and emotions (see Panksepp, 1986). In contrast to dopamine neurons which respond exquisitely well to external stimuli and can even learn to predict them (see the chapter on dopamine), serotonin neurons generally seem not to react to such stimuli. Instead, electrical recordings show that these neurons produce slow, regular, self-generated, and state-dependent rhythms.

Table 17.01
Serotonin receptor subtypes and functions that are mediated by them.

Receptor type		Function(s) mediated
5-HT$_1$		
	5-HT$_{1A}$	eating, aggression, mood, sex
	5-HT$_{1B}$	eating, sex, aggression, mood
	5-HT$_{1Da}$	
	5-HT$_{1Db}$	eating
	5-ht$_{1E}$	unknown
	5-ht$_{1F}$	unknown
5-HT$_2$	generally:	mood, anxiety, perception
	5-HT$_{2A}$	eating, hormone release, sex
	5-HT$_{2B}$	
	5-HT$_{2C}$	eating, sex, hormone release
5-HT$_3$		sex
5-HT$_4$		
5-HT$_5$		
	5-HT$_{5a}$	
	5-ht$_{5b}$	unknown
5-HT$_6$		
5-HT$_7$		

Behavioral effects of serotonin

Increasing serotonin levels in the brain cause a pronounced decrease in many behaviors and emotions. Serotonin-mediated activity in the brain can be increased by a number of methods such as increasing the amount of precursor (from which serotonin is synthesized), increasing the amount of serotonin, activating serotonin receptors with drugs, or blocking the breakdown of serotonin. We shall consider some of the effects of serotonin on behavior now.

Eating. Activating serotonin pathways with the anti-depressant drugs fluoxetine and sertraline, or other serotonin agonists, produces hypophagia (see Blundell and Hartford, 1998). This reduced eating is the result of increased satiation (the inhibition of eating that causes meal termination) and increased satiety (the post-meal suppression of appetite). Of interest are indications that with some drugs, but not others, the reduction in food intake may be dependent on dietary composition: fat intake, rather than protein or carbohydrate intake, appears to be selectively reduced. Furthermore, the serotonergic drug dexfenfluramine has been reported to reduce the frequency and intensity of urges to eat in obese women, mostly in the afternoon and evening. It appears that in humans, 5-HT$_{1B}$ and 5-HT$_{2C}$ receptors are primarily involved in the suppression of appetite.

Sex. Increasing serotonin levels in the brain generally produces a decline in sexual behavior in both females and males. In males, the administration of fluoxetine (a selective serotonin re-uptake inhibitor and anti-depressant) attenuates premature ejaculation (Yilmaz et al., 1999), and reduces sexual motivation (Matuszcyk ct al., 1998). Furthermore, serotonin inhibits both spinal reflexes which produce penile erection (see Mckenna, 1998) and, through the median and dorsal raphe projections to hypothalamic and other regions, ejaculation (Kondo and Yamanouchu, 1997).

The activation of serotonin receptor subtypes influences sexual behavior differently in males and females. Activation of 5-HT$_{1A}$ receptors decrease sexual behavior (lordosis) in female rats (Wolf et al., 1998). Activation of 5-HT$_{2A/2C}$ receptors in the ventromedial hypothalamus increases lordosis in females (Maswood et al., 1998) and, given systemically, reduces sexual behavior in male rats (Gorzalka and Hanson, 1998). Finally, activation of 5-HT$_3$ receptors in female rats facilitate lordosis and blocking of these receptors inhibits lordosis (Maswood et al., 1998).

Sleep. An increase in brain serotonin generally facilitates short wave sleep and reduces paradoxical sleep. Thus, depletion of serotonin with parachlorophenylalanine induces insomnia (e.g. Imeri et al., 1997) while a reduction in dietary tryptophan, the precursor of serotonin, reduces short wave sleep, increases paradoxical sleep, and wakefulness (Voderholzer et al., 1998). Experience with anti-depressants suggests that activation of post-synaptic 5-HT$_{1A}$ receptors increase slow wave sleep as does blocking 5-HT$_{2C}$ receptors (Staner et al., 1999). An increase in slow wave sleep causes increased growth hormone release (see Vancauter et al., 1998). Of interest too, is that aspects of sleep are considered to be under homeostatic control (e.g. Aeschenbach et al., 1996).

Temperature regulation. Serotonin increases in the brain tend to produce hyperthermia. An increase in serotonin in the medial preoptic area increases brain temperature (Imeri et al., 1999). Reducing serotonin release in the hypothalamus is accompanied by a decrease in body temperature due to decreased heat generation and increased heat loss (Hsieh et al., 1998). In particular, it appears that activating 5-HT$_2$ receptors in the hypothalamus produces hyperthermic effects while activating presynaptic 5-HT$_{1A}$ receptors (which causes a reduction in serotonin release) produces hypothermic effects (Lin et al., 1998). Subcutaneous administration of the 5-HT$_{2A/C}$ agonist DOI produces hyperthermia in rats and the selective HT$_{2A}$ antagonist amperozide blocks this effect (Salmi and Ahlenius, 1998). Finally, in humans, the street drug ecstasy, a potent serotonin agonist, causes hyperthermia and psychiatric syndromes. These syndromes probably result from lasting nerve damage caused by the induction of profound energy losses in serotonin neurons that prevent them from maintaining homeostasis, ion gradients, and repair functions, as has been demonstrated in rats (Huether et al., 1997).

Interactions with other systems

There is considerable evidence indicating that the serotonin systems interact with other neural systems. For example, a number of neurotransmitter systems, all of which serve to reflect the nutritional state of the body, seem to be connected with serotonergic systems (see Blundell and Hartford, 1998). Cholecystokinin (CCK) is released by the gut in response to the presence of fat in the diet and sends a satiety signal to the brain, while neuropeptide Y (NPY) is a strong phagogenic agent, causing increased food intake. Furthermore, we have seen before (in the chapter on hunger) how the peptide leptin functions as a signal indicative of body fat content. Decreased food consumption caused by increased levels of CCK and/or leptin can be countered by serotonin antagonists, while increased food consumption due to increased levels of NPY can be blocked by serotonin agonists.

There also appear to be interactions with the dopamine reward systems. When animals are given food in a specific place, they come to develop a preference for that location, even when food is not present. This place preference can be blocked with a dopamine antagonist in (food-) deprived rats, but not in sated rats (see Nader et al., 1997 and references therein). We have also seen that serotonin agonists tend to reduce feeding in (deprived) animals, hence presumably also reducing acquired place preferences. Thus, it appears that both serotonin agonists and dopamine antagonists block place preferences in deprived animals.

Serotonin and hedonic states

Serotonin's role as a general inhibitor of behavior and suppressor of pain suggests that it plays a role in the formation of hedonic states. In particular, numerous studies on eating behavior clearly show that increases in serotonergic activity inhibits eating. For example, when obese patients were put on a very low calorie diet for 8 weeks, they lost weight sharply. When dexfenfluramine or placebo was given starting at week 8, the body weights of those receiving the drug continued to fall, but those receiving placebo regained weight. A qualitative interpretation of the results observed by Finer et al. (1992) is shown in Figure 17.02.

The question now is what role serotonin plays in the formation of hedonic states. There seems to be 2 possibilities: (i) serotonin generates hedonic states directly and so changes the hedonic curve of a system; for instance, serotonin may generate negative hedonic states that work in synergy with the positive hedonic states generated by the dopamine system; or (ii) serotonin affects hedonic states indirectly by adjusting the SP of a system. Of these 2, the latter seems the more plausible.

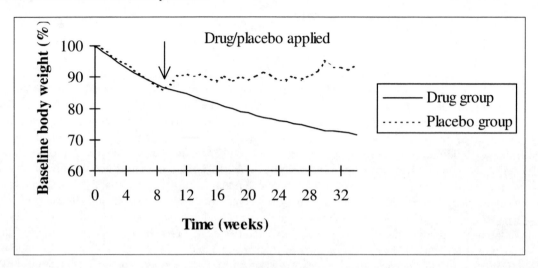

Figure 17.02

The qualitative effects (after Finer et al., 1992) of dexfenfluramine on body weight when given to obese humans after 8 weeks on a very low calorie diet. Those receiving placebo tended to resume normal eating and gained weight; those on the drug continued to lose weight.

We hypothesize, specifically, that an increase in serotonin activity would adjust the SP in the direction that normal non-goal interactions with the environment would drive the CP. This implies, in general terms, that increasing serotonin activity decreases various SPs. For example, normal interactions between an animal and its environment cause a depletion of glucose reserves, hence a decrease in the glucose CP. Increasing serotonin activity in the system regulating glucose levels reduces the SP of that system. This would reduce the tendency of the organism to eat. We furthermore conjecture that the different serotonin receptor subtypes mediate the SPs of different control systems, individually or in combination. For example, the 5-HT$_{2C}$ receptors may be involved in producing the glucose level SP, while the 5-HT$_{2A}$ receptors may be involved in producing the body temperature level SP. A SP signal could also be produced by a combination of activities in 2 or more subsystems, much like color is produced by the firing, in different proportions, of the primary-color-sensitive rods in the eye.

Figure 17.03 illustrates how the SP is adjusted through increased serotonergic activity. In the example, only the SP, not the shape of the hedonic curve, is changed. If an animal normally consumes 5 "glucose units" of glucose before the old SP is reached, it will now feel overstated with the same amount of food. Instead, it would tend to consume less food, thus accounting for the reduction in food consumption produced by serotonin administration. If the animal maintains the same activity level, its body weight would decrease until some equilibrium with the new SP is reached.

More specifically, say for example that behavior is activated when the negative hedonic state increases above 50 "hedonic units". Then, with the old SP, eating would be activated when the CP has fallen below 3 glucose units. If the CP falls further to below 1 glucose unit, liver metabolism is modified to generate glucose from fat (see the chapter on hunger). In this case, behavior is activated before fat stores are utilized. If, however, the SP is changed from 5 to 3 glucose units, eating behavior would only be activated when the CP has fallen below 1 glucose unit. In this case, where the new SP is effective, fat stores would tend to be drawn on *before* eating occurs. Thus, over time, they would become depleted and hence account for the reduction of body weight.

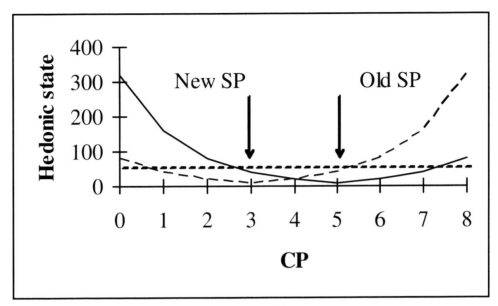

Figure 17.03

The figure shows how the SP of a control system is decreased from the normal value (solid line) to a new value (dashed line) through increased serotonergic activity. The dotted line indicates the level of negative affect above which there is a large likelihood that behavior would be activated.

Since it is also possible that serotonin could change the shape of the hedonic curve of a HM such as flattening it, we should consider the implications of such an effect. Figure 17.04 shows a situation where the administration of serotonin flattens the hedonic curve. If the reader finds Figure 17.04 rather wanting, s/he should furnish it.

Figure 17.04

The figure shows the hypothetical flattening of a hedonic curve from the normal value (solid line) to a new value (dashed line) through increased serotonergic activity. The SP remains unaltered. The dotted line, as in Figure 17.03, indicates the level of negative affect above which there is a large likelihood that behavior would be activated.

        If we assume, as we did above, that behavior is activated when the negative hedonic state increases above 50 hedonic units, the administration of serotonin would cause eating behavior to be activated only when the CP has fallen below 1 glucose unit. The animal would then consume 4 glucose units in order to restore its glucose CP to the glucose SP. In contrast, with the normal hedonic curve, eating would be activated when the CP falls below 3 units and the animal would then consume 2 units of glucose. If the rate of energy expenditure remains the same under the normal and flattened hedonic curves, the administration of serotonin would lead to an animal consuming fewer, but larger meals. Consequently, no change in body weight would occur, but a change in feeding pattern would result. This analysis argues against the view of serotonin as producing hedonic states and lends support to the view of serotonin as adjusting the SPs of HMs.

Serotonin as SP indicator

        Let us now briefly review the evidence that exist and can be garnered in support of the hypothesis that serotonin is a determinant of SP level. First, serotonin neurons tend to be autoactive, not responsive to external stimuli, but instead to physiological states. This is certainly consistent with SP signals which appear to be in some sense autonomous . It is also consistent with the fact that a SP is not permanently fixed, but can be adjusted based on the state of the system (e.g. thermostat SP set lower at night, higher in the morning). Second, applied serotonin inhibits many behaviors. This is consistent with the lowering of a SP, which would, for as long as the system is in excess (CP higher than SP), inhibit behavior. Over time, some aspects of behavior may return to normal, but the system will now have different parameters than before (e.g. reduced body weight). Third, there is evidence that selective serotonin agonists influence dietary composition by suppressing the intake of macronutrients unevenly. This is consistent with the possibility that the different SPs of the HMs controlling these macronutrients are dependent on neurotransmission at different serotonin receptor subtypes. Fourth, although increased brain serotonin levels are considered to produce hyperthermia, some authors, who have found that subcutaneous tryptophan increased rat tail skin temperature and reduced their colonic temperature, believe that administering this serotonin precursor reduces the set point for body temperature (Fregly et al., 1996). Fifth, serotonin neurons appear to be completely inhibited during paradoxical sleep (see Lucki, 1998). If serotonin systems function as SP signals for HMs, the inhibition of serotonin neurons during paradoxical sleep would imply a disruption of homeostatic control systems during this period of sleep. There is indeed abundant evidence that homeostasis is suspended during paradoxical sleep (e.g. Amici et al., 1998). Some view this release of individual cells from their functions in homeostatic systems as the major purpose of paradoxical sleep - it permits cells to perform essential maintenance and repair functions (see Reiner, 1984) and in this manner safeguards the homeostatic systems themselves. Our own views are in agreement with those expressed above. Furthermore, we believe that dreaming reflects the testing of suspended homeostatic systems during and after maintenance and repair and before they are brought into service again. These are rather similar to the testing performed by an auto mechanic after a repair, and before the vehicle is returned to the owner, to see if the problems are fixed satisfactorily.

        Some facts, on the other hand, may be problematic for the view that serotonin systems act as SP signal generators. Two examples are given here. First, serotonin-induced hypophagia can be blocked by the CCK_A (cholecystokinin) antagonist devazepide and counteract the influences of other serotonin systems (see Blundell and Hartford, 1998). Second, and perhaps most problematic, dietary-induced obesity occurs in response to significantly increased food consumption when rats are given access to a variety of foods other than their normal diet (Rogers and Blundell, 1984). The reader is encouraged to attempt to explain the phenomenon of dietary-induced obesity in terms of homeostatically driven behavior. Nevertheless, the views espoused here regarding serotonin as SP indicator are in some agreement with that of Azmitia (1999) who argues that serotonin plays a pivotal role in the homeostasis of neural tissue.

References

Aeschenbach, D.; Cajochen, C.; Landolt, H.; Borbely, A. A. 1996. Homeostatic sleep regulation in habitual short sleepers and long sleepers. American Journal of Physiology - Regulatory Integrative and Comparative Physiology 39: R41-R53.

Amici, R.; Zamboni, G.; Perez, E.; Jones, C. A.; Parmeggiani, P. L. 1998. The influence of a heavy thermal load on REM sleep in the rat. Brain Research 781: 252-258.

Azmitia, E. C. 1999. Serotonin neurons, plasticity, and homeostasis of neural tissue. Neuropsychopharmacology 21: 33S-45S.

Blundell, J. E.; Hartford, J. C. G. 1998. Serotonin and appetite regulation: implications for the pharmacological treatment of obesity. Pharmacology and Pathophysiology 9: 473-495.

Finer, N.; Finer, S.; Nauova, R. P. 1992. Drug therapy after very-low-caloric diets. American Journal of Clinical Nutrition 56: 1955-1985.

Fregly, M. J.; Rowland, N. E.; Cade, J. R. 1996. Relationship between drinking and increase in tail skin temperature of rats treated with L-5-hydroxytryptophan. Pharmacology 52: 69-77.

Gorzalka, B. B.; Hanson, L. A. 1998. Sexual behavior and wet dog shakes in the male rat: regulation by corticosterone. Behavioral Brain Research 97: 143-151.

Hsieh, M. T.; Chueh, F. Y.; Lin, M. T. 1998. Magnolol decreases body temperature by reducing 5-hydroxytryptamine release in the rat hypothalamus. Clinical and Experimental Pharmacology and Physiology 25: 813-817.

Huether, G.; Zhou, D.; Ruther, E. 1997. Causes and consequences of the loss of serotonergic presynapses elicited by the consumption of 3,4-methylenedioxymethamphetamine (MDMA, Ecstasy) and its congeners. Journal of Neurotransmission 104: 771-794.

Imeri, L.; Bianchi, S.; Mancia, M. 1997. Muramyl dipeptide and IL-1 effects on sleep and brain temperature after inhibition of serotonin synthesis. American Journal of Physiology - Regulatory Integrative and Comparative Physiology 42: R1663-1668.

Imeri, L.; Gemma, C.; De Simoni, M. G.; Opp, M. R.; Mancia, M. 1999. Hypothalamic serotonergic activity correlates better with brain temperature than with sleep-wake cycle and muscle tone in rats. Neuroscience 89: 1241-1246.

Kondo, Y.; Yamanouchi, K. 1997. Potentiation of ejaculatory activity by median raphe nucleus lesions in male rats - effect of p-chlorophenylalanine. Endocrine Journal 44: 873-879.

Lin, M. T.; Tsay, H. J.; Su, W. H.; Chueh, F. Y. 1998. Changes in extracellular serotonin in rat hypothalamus affect thermoregulatory function. American Journal of Physiology - Regulatory Integrative and Comparative Physiology 43: R1260-1267.

Maswood, N.; Caldarolapastuszka, M.; Uphouse, L. 1998. Functional integration among 5-hydroxytryptamine receptor families in the control of female rat sexual behavior. Brain Research 802: 98-103.

Matuszcyk, J. V.; Larsson, K.; Eriksson, E. 1998. The selective serotonin reuptake inhibitor fluoxetine reduces sexual motivation in male rats. Pharmacology, Biochemistry and Behavior 60: 527-532.

Mckenna, K. E. 1998. Central control of penile erection. International Journal of Impotence Research 10: S25-S34.

Nader, K.; Bechara, A.; van der Kooy, D. 1997. Neurobiological constraints on behavioral models of motivation. Annual Review of Psychology 48: 85-114.

Panksepp, J. 1986. The neurochemistry of behavior. Annual Review of Psychology 37: 77-107.

Reiner, P. B. 1984. Behavioral neurobiology of the feline locus ceruleus complex. Ph. D. thesis, University of Pennsylvania, Appendix pp. 160-168.

Rogers, P. J.; Blundell, J. F. 1984. Meal patterns and food selection during the development of obesity in rats fed a cafeteria diet. Neuroscience and Biobehavioral Reviews 8: 491-508.

Salmi, P.; Ahlenius, S. 1998. Evidence for functional interactions between 5-HT$_{1A}$ and 5-HT$_{2A}$ receptors in rat thermoregulatory mechanisms. Pharmacology and Toxicology 82: 122-127.

Staner, L.; Luthringer, R.; Macher, J. P. 1999. Effects of antidepressant drugs on sleep EEG in patients with major depression - mechanisms and therapeutic implications. CNS Drugs 11: 49-60.

Vancauter, E.; Plat, L.; Copinschi, G. 1998. Interrelations between sleep and the somatotropic axis. Sleep 21: 553-566.

Voderholzer, U.; Hornyak, M.; Thiel, B.; Huwigpoppe, C.; Kiemen, A.; Konig, A.; Backhaus, J.; Riemann, D.; Berger, M.; Hohagen, F. 1998. Impact of experimentally induced serotonin deficiency by tryptophan depletion on sleep EEG in healthy subjects. Neurospychopharmacology 18: 112-124.

Wolf, A.; Jackson, A.; Price T.; Trevino, A.; Caldarolapastuszka, M.; Uphouse, L. 1998. Attenuation of the lordosis-inhibiting effects of 8-OH-DPAT by TFMPP and quipazine. Brain Research 804: 206-211.

Yilmaz, U.; Tatlisen, A.; Turan, H.; Arman, F.; Ekmekcioglu, O. 1999. The effects of fluoxetine on several neurophysiological variables in patients with premature ejaculation. Journal of Urology 161: 107-111.

PART III

THE MECHANISMS THAT GENERATE GOALS

CHAPTER 18
Artificial neural networks (basics)

Introduction

In Part I of this book, we have discussed the interactions between an organism and its environment. We have pointed out that the environment poses certain problems of information processing that have to be successfully solved by an organism in order to survive. We have adopted as a central theme that innate psychological mechanisms have evolved to perform these information processing problems. In Part II we have assumed that some of these innate psychological mechanisms are homeostatic mechanisms and we proceeded to explain the need for homeostasis. We have also linked homeostasis and behavior with the concept of hedonic states. HMs, we saw, were mechanisms generating motivational drives.

Taken together, it means that the environment provides stimuli that disturb homeostasis (e.g. heat), but as inferred from the dopamine system, also cues to stimuli and these stimuli themselves, that could restore homeostasis. The task now is one of finding and interacting with those stimuli by attending to cues that can be used to classify and predict them. This brings us to Part III and the mechanisms that generate goals. We shall see that these mechanisms are essentially general computational mechanisms capable of recognition and prediction. The ways, aside from the formation of internal representations, in which these mechanisms operate to generate goals will be discussed in a later chapter.

Neurons

The computational units of biological neural networks are nerve cells or neurons. A neuron, shown in Figure 18.01, consists of three parts: the cell body or soma, an input region of dendritic protrusions from the soma, and a single output conduit, the axon. The axon terminates on the somata and dendrites of other cells but for a minute gap (about 50 nm), the synaptic cleft. The points of contact between cells are called synapses.

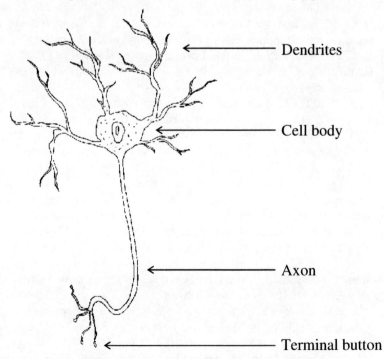

Figure 18.01
A neuron showing the cell body, the dendrites, and the axon. The terminal button is the point of contact with another cell.

Networks of neurons

Neurons are often highly organized into structures in many brain areas. The cerebral cortex, for instance, clearly consists of six layers (Kelly, 1985a). The cerebellum, which plays an important role in motor control, shows exquisite organization in the arrangement of Purkinje cells and lateral fibers (e.g. Pellionisz and Llinas, 1979). In the tectum, input neurons terminate in a highly organized manner to form topographical maps of various sensory modalities (see Camhi, 1984). Similarly, inputs from the retina to the six layers of the lateral geniculate body of the thalamus form six maps of the contralateral visual hemifield in vertical register (Kelly, 1985b).

An example of an organized network of cells is the primate retina, shown in Figure 18.02. It shows a 3-layered structure with an input layer consisting of the rod and cone receptor cells, a hidden layer consisting of the bipolar cells, and an output layer consisting of the ganglion cells. The axons of the ganglion cells form the optic nerve which transmits visual information via the thalamus to the visual cortex. The receptors register the "input data", the hidden layer processes these data, and the output layer sends the processed data somewhere else (e.g. the visual cortex).

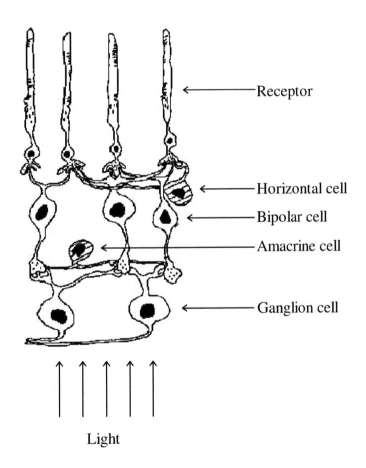

Light

Figure 18.02

A simplified rendition of the primate retina showing a 3-layered structure. The input layer consists of the rod receptor cells, the hidden layer consists of the bipolar cells, and the output layer of the ganglion cells. The axons of the ganglion cells form the optic nerve. The receptors detect light, and it is curious that the system is oriented such that light has to pass through the output and hidden layers to reach the receptors.

Artificial neural networks

Artificial neural networks are very basic simulations of real neural networks. An artificial neural network (ANN) consists of a number of interconnected computational elements called nodes. Such a network is not an amorphous collection of randomly interconnected nodes, but has a well-defined structure. Most neural networks consist of three layers of nodes: the input; hidden; and output layers. In general, every node in the input layer is connected to every node in the hidden layer. Hidden and output layers are likewise fully connected. Furthermore, every connection has a certain weight or strength. Figure 18.03 shows an example of a neural network producing an output from experimentally obtained data.

Data are introduced to the network at the input layer. These data are propagated, via the connections between the input and hidden nodes, to the nodes of the hidden layer. Here the data are combined and transformed before being relayed to the output nodes. At the output nodes, the data from the hidden nodes are further combined and transformed to produce the network output. From input to output then, the data go through a sequence of combinations and transformations, details of which will be provided in subsequent sections.

Every connection in the network is weighted to indicate the strength of the connection. Data propagated along a connection is multiplied by the connection weight. Because the connection strengths (or connection weights) between nodes are initially set to small random values, the output from an untrained network is nonsensical. Networks, therefore, have to be trained to perform useful tasks. In essence, training consists of providing the network with a number of training "examples". Every example consists of a series of input measurements or data and the corresponding "response" or output required of the network. "Learning" occurs by using the differences between the network output and the desired output (this difference is called the output error) to adjust the connection weights between the nodes such that the output error is reduced. In backpropagation networks, this adjustment occurs from the output layer backwards.

In addition to classification problems, networks can also perform function estimations which make predictions possible. The similarity with the dopamine system of prediction and reward should not be lost on the reader and s/he is encouraged to perform a mapping of the anatomical interpretation of the dopamine prediction system onto an ANN.

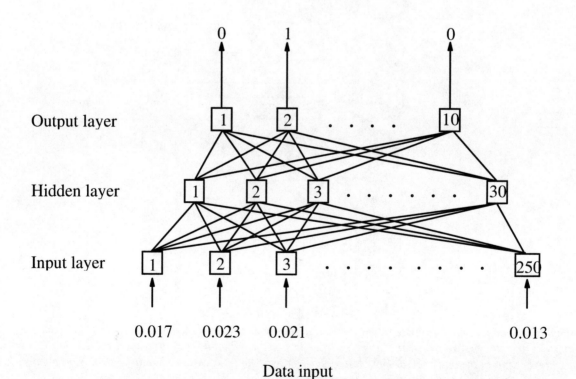

Figure 18.03

This figure shows an artificial neural network with 250 input nodes, 30 hidden nodes, and 10 output nodes. This network performs a classification task: each output node corresponds to one of 10 different classes (e.g. type of tree). Also shown are measurements (average length of leaves, width of leaves, weight of seeds, etc.) obtained from a tree and being given as input to the network.

The examples in the training set are repeatedly presented to the network in a random order. Training is periodically stopped and the network is tested with a validation set of examples to cross-validate its performance. The examples in the validation set are often fewer in number and generally similar, *but not identical*, to those in the training set. A network is considered optimally trained, not when the output error generated by the training set reaches a minimum, but when the validation set output error reaches a minimum as shown in Figure 18.04. This procedure prevents overlearning (the network learns the training set so well that nothing else is recognized) and improves generalizing (Schoner, 1992). Training is ideally terminated when the network generalizes well to new data and the cross-validation method is a way to estimate when this occurs. In practice, one often takes all the available measurements, randomly assigns 80% to the training set, and 10% each to the validation and testing sets.

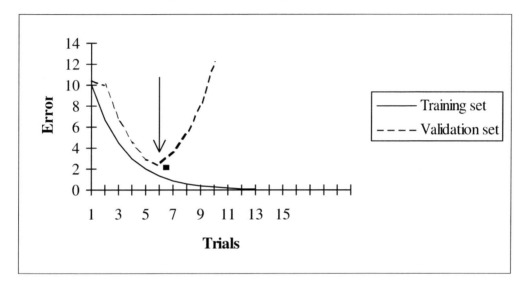

Figure 18.04

The average error for all the samples in a set changes with the number of learning trials. A network is not trained with, but periodically tested with, the samples of the validation set. However, since the samples in the validation set are similar to those in the training set, the error of the validation set will initially decline in a manner similar to that of the training set. Once training proceeds beyond a certain point, the error of the validation set will start to increase, while that of the training set continues to decrease. When training is terminated where the validation set error reaches a minimum (indicated by the arrow), the network could be expected to generalize best to the testing set. At this point, the error produced on the testing set (indicated by the square) can be expected to be similar to that of the validation set.

The structure of a network, that is, the number of layers it has and the way in which the nodes are interconnected, is known as the architecture of the network. Networks can have more than one hidden layer. Furthermore, not every node in one layer has to be connected to every node in the next layer, therefore, not every network is fully connected. In networks with local connections, only a small number of nodes in one layer are connected to a node in the next layer. In recurrent networks, there are connections from the output layer back to the input layer. The architecture of a network is an important determinant of its abilities.

Network computations

Local perspective. Every node in a network is a computational unit (Rumelhart et al., 1988) and some data processing occurs at every node. A hidden layer node (e.g. hidden layer node 1), as shown in Figure 18.05, performs the following computations: the data transferred from every input node are combined (usually by addition) into a single value. The output from input node 1 (the value 3), multiplied by the connection strength between input node 1 and hidden node 1 (the value 0), is added to the outputs from input nodes 2, 3, and 4 multiplied by their respective connection weights to give ([3 x 0] + [1 x 1] + [0 x 1] + [1 x 0] = [1]). This value (1) is passed through the transfer function $F(X) = 2X$ to determine the hidden node's output $F(1) = 2 \times 1 = 2$. The product of the hidden node output and the connection strength between the hidden node and a node in the next layer is then passed on to that next node. At this next node, all the inputs are again combined and the process repeated. In essence then, a node simply performs a computation on the combined inputs from the previous layer, and sends the result to every node of the next layer (Rumelhart et al., 1988). It is implicitly assumed that the network in this example has 4 nodes in the input layer, at least 1 node in the hidden layer, and 3 nodes in the output layer. Although the neural network structure described here allows all the nodes in a particular layer to perform their computations in parallel, hence parallel distributed processing (Rumelhart et al., 1988), such computations are serially implemented on computers, except those with specialized hardware.

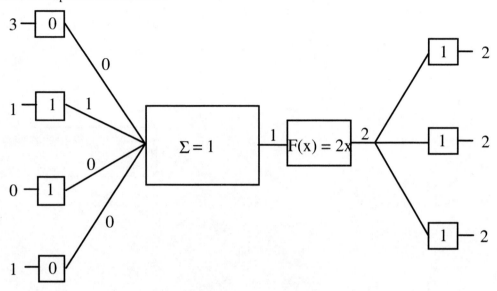

Figure 18.05

This figure shows (from left to right) the computations performed at hidden layer node 1. The data transferred from each of the 4 input nodes, multiplied by the respective connection weights (in small squares), are added to give a single value at this hidden node. This value is passed through the transfer function F(x) to determine the hidden node's output. As before, this output is multiplied with the connection weights (in small squares) and transferred to the 3 output nodes.

Global perspective. On a global level, the computations performed by all the nodes of a neural network as described above, are equivalent to a number of matrix operations. The reader familiar with matrix operations can easily verify this. The matrix of input layer values, which consists of the training examples, is multiplied by the matrix of weights (between input and hidden layers) to give a matrix of hidden layer values. The matrix of hidden layer values are transformed with a transfer function before being multiplied with another matrix of weights (between hidden and output layers) to give the matrix of output layer values. The latter matrix values are transformed again with a transfer function to give the final output of the network. The ability of networks to perform non-linear computations are due to the use of non-linear transfer functions, mostly for the hidden and output layers. The most appropriate transfer function(s) for a particular application has to be determined by trial and error, however, the sigmoidal transfer function is frequently used and a good initial choice. The entire computational process can be schematically represented as shown below (read [X] as matrix of X):

[Input layer values] x [***weights 1***] = [hidden layer values]

↓

transfer function 1

↓

[transformed values] x [***weights 2***] = [output layer values]

↓

transfer function 2

↓

[final network output]

Above, *weights 1* refers to the connection weights between the input and hidden layers and *weights 2* to those between the hidden and output layers. These weights are initially randomly assigned and adjusted during training until good values are found. Also above, transfer 1 refers to the transfer function between hidden and output layers, and transfer 2 to that of the output layer. The transfer function between input and hidden layers is almost always a linear function, hence is omitted from this diagram.

The global view of ANN computations implies that real neural networks most likely perform sequences of matrix operations. Thus Pellionisz and Llinas (1979) developed the tensor network model of motor control by the cerebellum, while Churchland (1986) suggested that the brain encodes by means of phase-space positions implemented by laminar structures and computes by means of phase-space coordinate transformations implemented by neural matrices.

References

Camhi, J. M. 1984. Neuroethology. Sunderland, MA: Sinauer.

Churchland, P. M. 1986. Cognitive neurobiology: a computational hypothesis for laminar cortex. Biology and Philosophy 1: 25-52.

Kelly, J. P. 1985a. Anatomical basis of sensory perception and motor coordination. In E. R. Kandel; J. H. Schwartz (eds.), Principles of neural science, pp. 222-243. Amsterdam: Elsevier.

Kelly, J. P. 1985b. Anatomy of the central visual pathways. In E. R. Kandel; J. H. Schwartz (eds.), Principles of neural science, pp. 356-365. Amsterdam: Elsevier.

Pellionisz, A. and Llinas, R. 1979. Brain modeling by tensor network theory and computer simulation. The cerebellum: distributed processor for predictive coordination. Neuroscience 4: 323-348.

Rumelhart, D. E., Hinton, G. E.; McClelland, J. E. 1988. A general framework for parallel distributed processing. In D. E. Rumelhart; J. E. McClelland (eds.), Parallel distributed processing, pp. 44-76. Cambridge, MA: MIT.

Schoner, W. 1992. Reaching the generalization maximum of backpropagation networks. In I. Aleksandr; J. Taylor (eds.), Artificial neural networks, 2, pp. 91-94. Amsterdam: Elsevier.

CHAPTER 19
Artificial neural networks (continued)

Introduction

In the previous chapter, we have seen that artificial neural networks consist of an interconnected collection of simple processing units, called nodes, which are arranged in layers. Data is fed into the network at the *input layer*. The response of the network to the input pattern is made available as an output pattern at the *output layer*. If there are layers between the input and output layers, they are called *hidden layers* (because they are not in direct contact with the outside world).

We shall review previous concepts and discuss further important ones pertaining to ANNs in this chapter, show some examples, and discuss various applications.

Network types

When a network is trained by giving it examples of the output patterns, required in response to given input patterns, it is called a supervised network. When a network "figures out" a consistent output by itself, it is called an unsupervised network. When information is fed from the input layer forward to the next layer and so on until it reaches the output layer, it is called a *feedforward* network (e.g. Figure 18.03). When the output of a network is connected back to the input, it is called a *recurrent* network because it has feedback loops. In a supervised neural network, the difference between the output of the network and the example output is called the *error*. This should immediately remind the reader of HMs as well as the dopamine system. Of the 7 components of a HM, there are at least 2 that s/he should be able to identify easily in a neural network "in training". We recommend that the reader attempts to perform a mapping of a feedforward supervised neural network onto a HM at this point.

Training and testing

A network is typically trained with a set of input data. The set of input data is divided into a training set (about 80% of the data) and validation and testing sets (the remaining 20%). This is important, because the network must be tested on completely new data, i.e. data that has never before been presented to it, to test whether it can generalize. A large network with many connection weights take longer to train than a smaller network with few connection weights.

Learning, learning rules, and learning rates

Learning takes place according to a learning rule. The learning rule specifies how the connection weights between the nodes must be updated. In a backpropagation neural network, the error is used to calculate the amount with which each weight should be updated, by backpropagating the error from the output to the hidden and then to the input layer. The amount by which to update the weights can be multiplied by a scaling factor called the learning rate. If the scaling factor is larger than one, learning of the network is sped up. If the scaling factor is less than one, learning is slowed down. Scaling factors that are too large cause networks to "overshoot" their targets and training to become unstable. A good approach is to use a larger scaling factor initially, and a smaller one when the network starts to converge.

Convergence

Convergence is an important concept. During learning, the weights are adjusted to make the error smaller. This means that the weights gradually take on values which produce the desired output. Therefore, the weights converge to those values required to produce a small error. The network is said to converge on a solution and the error converges to some small value as shown for the training, and, less so, for the validation set in Figure 18.04. Keep in mind the complication of terminating training before the error of the validation set starts to diverge again.

Optimization

When a network has converged to a solution (for both training and validation sets) it is said to be optimized. Optimization can be a difficult problem. Optimization depends on a number of different things, such as: (i) the learning rule and learning rate used; (ii) the architecture of the network; and (iii) the appropriateness of the examples given as training input (e.g. Baum and Haussler, 1989; Hush and Horne, 1993; Lippmann, 1987).

Finding the optimum weights for the connections of a neural network constitutes an optimization problem in multidimensions, the number of dimensions being the number of connection weights to be optimized. Hence, aside from the various backpropagation methods, a whole array of multidimensional optimization methods can be brought to bear on the problem of optimal network training (e.g. Baldi, 1995). These optimization methods represent different approaches whereby the individual weights are adjusted to reduce the network's output error.

Pruning is a method of architecture optimization where one starts with a large network, trains it, and then deletes one of the hidden layer nodes or one of the connections. The smaller network is then trained again. Pruning is repeated until the network does not show convergence any longer. This means that the previous network had the optimal architecture.

Generalization and overlearning

An optimally pruned and trained network can perform correctly on the testing data. Such a network is said to be capable of generalization because it generalizes from the training to the testing set. A network with too many weights and trained too long can learn all the input examples very well, but when given the test examples, it is unable to recognize them. It is said to be overtrained (e.g. Kamruzzaman et al., 1992; Ogawa and Yamasaki, 1992). The validation set enables the user to estimate at which point overlearning will start to occur. A network with too few nodes or connections will not converge and thus cannot be trained and it will perform poorly on both training and testing data.

Mapping

A neural network has the ability to map any arbitrary set of vectors (set of input patterns or input examples) onto any other arbitrary set of vectors (set of output patterns or desired outputs). What is interesting, however, is that in the process of mapping a subset of the domain (the training data set) onto a subset of the range (the desired network outputs), a well-trained network manages to map the *entire* domain onto the entire range. In this case, new data will generate the correct output when presented to the network and the network is said to be capable of generalizing from the training data set.

A network with three layers performs two sequential mappings of the input data. The first mapping is that of the input data onto 'hidden data". The second mapping is from the 'hidden data" to the output data. The 'hidden data" or the mapping at the hidden layer forms an *internal representation* of the input pattern (Rumelhart et al., 1988). Multiple hidden layers enable a network to perform more complex mappings between input and output, as do some nonlinear transfer functions (Lee, 1992). This ability of relatively simple simulations of real neural networks to perform complex sequential mappings makes them such powerful information processing systems.

Algorithms

An algorithm is a computational recipe. It is simply the sequence of steps that have to be performed in order to arrive at the desired result. For example, the steps to use to do long division constitutes an algorithm.

The algorithm for a supervised backpropagation network is given below:
1. Initialize the weights to small random numbers.
2. Present a training pattern at the input nodes and evaluate the network output.
3. Determine the difference between the output and the desired output (error).
4. Adjust all the weights based on the size of the error.
5. Periodically stop training and test the network with the validation set. If the network's error on the validation set starts to increase, stop training.
6. Go to step 2.

Keep in mind that every step of the algorithm above can be divided into smaller steps, and so on until every step is completely specified, understood, and can be executed.

Applications

Neural networks are generally used in 2 types of problems: (i) classification/identification and (ii) function estimation. Examples of classification/recognition applications are the following: the classification of cells as cancerous or non-cancerous; the recognition of fingerprints, speech, handwriting, and others; the classification of species of flowers; the discrimination between tanks and trees (used in smart bombs); the compression of data; the reconstruction of images; the recognition of chemicals based on their spectra; and a host of other applications (e.g.

Bhandare et al., 1993; Bilgen and Hung, 1994; Lerner and Lu, 1993; Liu et al., 1993; Schulze et al., 1994; Tanabe et al., 1992). Examples of function estimation are: the prediction/forecasting of exchange rates; the interpolation or extrapolation of process variables used in process control; the prediction of merchandise inventory levels; the assessment of delinquency risk, and many more (e.g. Berthiau et al., 1994).

Demonstration example

    Assignment. There are 3 species of the iris flower found on Canada's Gaspe Peninsula: Virginica, Versicolor, and Setosa. The species differ in that their petals and sepals are of characteristic width and length and these have been measured (Anderson, 1935). You are required to construct an ANN to classify any iris as belonging to one of the 3 species based on measurements of its petals and sepals. You are given the data shown in Table 19.01 collected by researchers in the field.

Table 19.01

Sample measurements: 100 from each of the 3 different species of the iris flower.

Measurement	Petal length (cm)	Petal width (cm)	Sepal length (cm)	Sepal width (cm)	Species
1	8.3	2.1	5.5	2.5	Versicolor
2	8.1	2.0	5.7	2.1	:
:	:	:	:	:	:
100	8.2	2.2	5.4	2.2	:
1	9.3	2.5	5.7	2.4	Virginica
2	8.9	2.6	5.8	2.4	:
:	:	:	:	:	:
100	9.1	2.5	5.6	2.3	:
1	7.9	2.6	5.3	2.8	Setosa
2	8.1	2.5	5.5	2.9	:
:	:	:	:	:	:
100	8.9	2.6	5.1	2.7	:

    Approach. Construct a backpropagation network (as shown in Figure 19.01) with 4 input nodes (one each for petal length, petal width, sepal length, and sepal width) and 3 output nodes (one each for Versicolor, Virginica, and Setosa). It is difficult to know how many nodes to have in the hidden layer, a good rule is to take half of the sum of input and output nodes (rounded up to give 4 hidden nodes). The logistic or sigmoidal function is most frequently used for the transfer functions between the layers and we shall here do the same.

    Select, in a random manner, 80 measurements from every species and put them into a training file. Randomly choose 10 of the remaining measurements from every species and put them into a testing file. Construct a validation file from the remainder. The desired output for a measurement is 1 0 0 for Versicolor, 0 1 0 for Virginica, and 0 0 1 for Setosa. An example of an entry in one of these files is given in Table 19.02.

Table 19.02

Sample entry from a network training, validation, or testing file.

Input data				Desired output		
8.3	2.1	5.5	2.5	1	0	0
7.9	2.6	5.3	2.8	0	0	1
:	:	:	:			
8.9	2.6	5.8	2.4	0	1	0

Start training the network according to the algorithm given earlier. The initial and final output from the network may look like that given in Table 19.03. Because the weights are given small random initial values, the initial output of the network is meaningless - the network appears to be confused . As learning progresses, the output values from the network start to approach the desired output values. When training is terminated according to the criteria stipulated in the backpropagation algorithm, the network output will be close, but not identical, to the desired network output as shown in Figure 19.01.

Table 19.03
Sample of the initial and final output from a network.

Input data				Desired output			Initial output			Final output		
8.3	2.1	5.5	2.5	1	0	0	0.5	-0.9	0.1	0.9	0.0	0.1
7.9	2.6	5.3	2.8	0	0	1	-0.3	-0.6	0.7	0.1	0.2	0.8
:	:	:	:	:	:	:	:	:	:	:	:	:
8.9	2.6	5.8	2.4	0	1	0	0.4	0.6	0.5	0.0	0.9	0.1

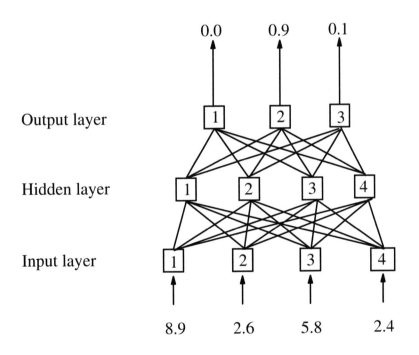

Network output

Data input

Figure 19.01
A fully connected backpropagation network for the classification of irises. The network shows an output indicating that the input measurements of petal length, petal width, sepal length, and sepal width, from left to right respectively, are from a flower belonging to the species Virginica.

References

Anderson, E. 1935. The irises of the Gaspe Peninsula. Bulletin of the American Iris Society 59: 2-5.

Baldi, P. 1995. Gradient descent learning algorithm overview - a general dynamical systems perspective. IEEE Transactions on Neural Networks 6: 182-195.

Baum, E. B.; Haussler, D. 1989. What size net gives valid generalization? In D. S. Touretzky (ed.), Advances in neural information processing systems 1, pp. 81-90. San Mateo, CA: Morgan Kaufmann.

Berthiau, G., Durbin, F., Haussy, J.; Siarry, P. 1994. Learning of neural networks approximating continuous functions through circuit simulator SPICE-PAC driven by simulated annealing. International Journal of Electronics 76: 437-441.

Bilgen, M.; Hung, H. S. 1994. Neural network for restoration of signals blurred by a random shift-variant impulse response function. Optical Engineering 33: 2723-2727.

Bhandare, P., Mendelson, Y., Peura, R. A., Janatsch, G., Kruse-Jarres, J. D., Marbach, R.; Heise, H. M. 1993. Multivariate determination of glucose in whole blood using partial least-squares and artificial neural networks based on mid-infrared spectroscopy. Applied Spectroscopy 47: 1214-1221.

Hush, D. R.; Horne, B. G. 1993. Progress in supervised neural networks. IEEE Signal processing. 10: 8-39.

Kamruzzaman, J., Kumagai, Y.; Hikita, H. 1992. Study on minimal net size, convergence behavior and generalization ability of heterogeneous backpropagation network. In I. Aleksandr; J. Taylor (eds.) Artificial neural networks, 2, Elsevier, Amsterdam, pp. 203-206.

Lee, S. 1992. Supervised learning with Gaussian potentials. In B. Kosko (ed.), Neural networks for signal processing. Prentice Hall, Englewood Cliffs, NJ., pp. 189-223.

Lerner, J. M.; Lu, T. 1993. Practical neural networks aid spectroscopic analysis. Photonics Spectra 27: 93-98.

Lippmann, R. P. 1987. An introduction to computing with neural nets. IEEE ASSP, 4: 4-22.

Liu, Y., Upadhyaya, B. R.; Naghedolfeizi, M. 1993. Chemometric data analysis using artificial neural networks. Applied Spectroscopy 47: 12-23.

Ogawa, H.; Yamasaki, K. 1992. A theory of over-learning. In I. Aleksandr; J. Taylor (eds.) Artificial neural networks, 2, Elsevier, Amsterdam, pp. 215-218.

Rumelhart, D. E., Hinton, G. E.; Williams, R. J. 1988b. Learning internal representations by error propagation. In D. E. Rumelhart; J. E. McClelland (eds.), Parallel distributed processing, MIT, Cambridge, MA, pp. 318-362.

Schulze, H. G., Blades, M. W., Bree, A. V., Gorzalka, B. B., Greek, L. S.; Turner, R. F. B. 1994. The characteristics of backpropagation neural networks employed in the identification of neurotransmitter Raman spectra. Applied Spectroscopy 48:50-57.

Tanabe, K., Tamura, T.; Uesaka, H. 1992. Neural network system for the identification of infrared spectra. Applied Spectroscopy 46: 807-810.

CHAPTER 20
Goals

Introduction

Goals and goal-oriented behaviors lay at the heart of motivational psychology. A motivated behavior is a behavior for which a goal exists and for which a drive to achieve such a goal can be activated. In Part II we have considered the mechanisms that generate drives and in Part III we consider the mechanisms that generate goals. A major mechanism of goal formation is exemplified by the artificial neural network. In this chapter, we shall consider the various aspects and attributes of goals (see Austin and Vancouver, 1996), the processes of goal formation, and interpret them in terms of HMs and ANNs.

Goals are defined as internal representations of desired states. States can be outcomes, events, or processes. Internally represented desired states can be biological set points for internal processes (e.g. body temperature) or complex representations of desired outcomes (e.g. to earn a degree). The reader is familiar with both of these: the former from discussions about homeostatic mechanisms and the latter from discussions about artificial neural networks and the representations formed at their hidden layer nodes.

The structure of goals

The Operational Structure of Goals. Control theory, under which homeostatic mechanisms fall, has been important in the development of the psychology of motivated behaviors. There are 2 basic types discussed in the literature: the one is a discrete system (Miller et al., 1960) and the other is a continuous system (Powers et al., 1960). The discrete system is known as the Test-Operate-Test-Exit (TOTE) system. In this system, a stimulus is evaluated by comparison with a goal, operated on to reduce the error between stimulus and goal, and retested. This procedure is repeated until the error is considered "small enough" after which the process is terminated. In the continuous model, the error between current and reference signals is continuously tested and the process is never terminated, even if the error is negligibly small. These 2 systems are shown in Figure 20.01.

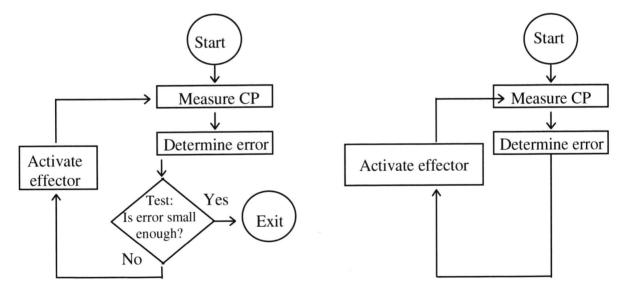

Figure 20.01
Flow diagrams of the discrete Test-Operate-Test-Exit cybernetic system (left) and the continuous cybernetic system (right).

In these views, the difference between the desired state and the current state drives the organism towards reducing that difference. These views, however, do not explain how this difference drives the organism. They differ therefore from our view which postulates the generation of hedonic states by the error dynamics to produce the drives. In both the discrete and continuous views, the desired states and current states must be internally represented in order to permit a comparison. The reader should compare the concepts of desired and current states with set points and desired network outputs, and current points and current network outputs, respectively - see for example McFarland (1989). Therefore, the internal representations are often considered as results of the operation of the systems. This is consistent with the implications drawn from ANNs where internal representations form at the hidden layers during training: from the initial nonsensical representations to the later meaningful ones.

This has important implications: normally we view a goal as pre-existing and serving to guide our behaviors. The view from control systems implies that, if goals are identified with set points, they exist initially. In contrast, the view from artificial neural networks suggests that, if goals are identified with hidden layer representations, they form as a consequence of action or training. It seems that it may be necessary to refine our terminology to differentiate between these 2 types of goals or to associate the term "goal" with concepts either from ANNs or the homeostatic view, but not both. The other implication, of the view of goals as internal representations forming in response to actions, is that initial actions must be either random or preprogrammed. This is also consistent with the behavior of ANNs where the initial output or behavior is random due to the random weights assigned initially.

If goals form in response to behaviors, one certainly must ask what good they are then in the production of behavior. Here too, ANNs may supply an answer. A *trained* ANN can produce a proper response to a stimulus almost instantaneously. The formation of goals, if we are to identify them with internal representations at the hidden layer of an ANN, facilitate and reflect fast and accurate responses. The formation of "wrong" goals implies fast but inaccurate action, perhaps eventually accurate by happenstance. A well-trained network, then, will have "correct" goals, but it may be meaningless to ask whether the goals help to produce proper behavior, or whether proper behavior produces correct goals. In some sense, the one *is* the other, rather than *causes* the other. (Upon reflection, the reader may realize that the connection between internal representation and accurate operation in ANNs is rather analogous to that between internal representation and toxin-evading operation in bacteria - see the chapter on bacterial chemotaxis.) Furthermore, a single trained net can produce outputs to input patterns or members from several (tens/hundreds/thousands or more) different categories, thereby meeting several constraints on behavior simultaneously and reducing the likelihood of conflict. Accessing one output pattern necessarily accesses all output patterns because they are all encoded in the same set of connection weights.

The Organization of Goals. Given that multiple goals can exist simultaneously in the same person (or organism), it may be necessary to organize them to prevent conflicts. We have discussed the possible hierarchies in which homeostatic mechanisms can be activated. It is generally considered by motivational psychologists that goals are structured into hierarchies with the most important goals at the top (pass the course), followed by subgoals (pass the exam), followed by still lower-order goals (understand the lecture). The lowest order goals tend to be goals of muscle movement (hold the pen, take down class notes). This hierarchy of goals is sometimes referred to as the action hierarchy and sometimes as the perceptual hierarchy. Some researchers believe that a separate hierarchy of emotional and other goals exist that influence the allocation of attention and resources to the pursuit of action-hierarchy goals. Goals in any level can be connected and interact with goals in any other level. This may remind the reader of the connections between the nodes of artificial neural networks where each node could be a goal and every layer could represent the status of the goals.

However, it may make more sense to think of an ANN with several hidden layers: here the lower order goals are the representations forming in the hidden layers adjacent and closer to the input and output layers, while the higher order goals are those that form in the middle or central hidden layers. The ability of a trained ANN to simultaneously satisfy many constraints on behavior has been mentioned already. The reader is reminded then, that conflict resolution may occur, not only in a hierarchical or serial manner such as in HMs, but also simultaneously and in parallel as in ANNs.

In general, psychophysics and cognitive psychology focus on the lowest order goals, motivational psychology on the intermediate level goals, and personality psychology on the higher-order goals.

The components of goals

Goals may not be single monolithic entities, but may have different components or dimensions. This does not refer to sub-goals and lower-level goals, but to the goal itself. Statistical analyses have produced from 4 - 6 factors of importance in goals. For instance, Austin and Vancouver (1996) have identified 6 dimensions of goals. I have relabeled 5 of these goal components somewhat in the list below:
1. Importance
2. Difficulty

3. Clarity
4. Time-span
5. Awareness

   This ought not to be problematic. If we identify goals with the internal representations that form at the hidden layers of networks, then a hidden layer with more than one node will technically have goals with multiple dimensions (i.e. as many dimensions as there are hidden nodes). However, it is generally difficult to understand the internal states of networks in terms of external conditions (Sumpter and Noid, 1996). The dimensions of goals discussed here are therefore not likely to correspond to the number of hidden nodes in a network in an easily accessible manner.

   Importance. The importance of a goal allows prioritizing of a goal. The importance of a goal may also determine the commitment made to a goal. The importance of a goal could be rated by an external observer (e.g. rating how much effort one expends in studying). The importance of a goal could be determined internally in terms of the amount of pain or gain associated with the error (in HM terms, the intensity of the hedonic state). The degree to which goals attain permanence is seen by some as constituting personality, while others view personality as a characteristic style of social behavior (see the chapter on temperament).

   Difficulty. The difficulty of a goal determines the probability of attainment. There is usually a trade-off: a more difficult goal generally demands more resources but has a greater potential benefit. The personal agency beliefs of an individual come into play here. The more a person views him/herself as capable in achieving a specific goal (e.g. produce a paper on "The Neurobiology of Fear"), the more likely he/she is to accept that goal. The more a person views the situation (e.g. class/instructor/course load/personal circumstances) conducive to the attainment of a goal, the more likely s/he is to initiate pursuit of that goal. Finally, the level of success achieved in the pursuit of that goal is then directly related to the level of difficulty of that goal. We wish to leave it to the reader to explain "difficulty" in terms of ANNs.

   Clarity. Some goals are much better spelled out than others and as such they possess greater clarity. Quantitative goals are more specific than qualitative goals. Qualitative goals such as "do your best" are more easily attained than quantitative goals such as "get more than X% ". However, more specific goals lead to improved performance on tasks. In my opinion, this may be the result of closer monitoring of progress (e.g. better feedback) that may be possible with better specified or clearer goals. One could also reason that the better a network is trained, the more well-formed and less random, hence clearer, its internal representations would be.

   Time-span. Goals change with time. In addition, some goals are long-term and some are short-term. Higher order goals tend to be longer-term than lower-order goals. Think about the absurdity of having a lifelong goal of crossing a "t" in your class notes and having a very brief goal of achieving the top level of performance in your job. Lower-order goals must operate faster than higher-order goals to prevent the system from becoming unstable. Goals that change over time can easily be understood in terms of ANNs: a network in training continually adjusts its weights, hence its internal representations. If we see humans as networks that are being trained in a changing environment over the course of an entire lifespan, we could expect goals that change over time.

   Awareness. Although most people would find it hard to deny that conscious goals are motivating, goals are often not limited to those that are conscious only. Some processes are merely beyond the attention level of the individual. Goals may also move in and out of awareness as required. Often, goals which are initially conscious, become automated with practice. Conversely, goals can be unconscious and become conscious over time. We have seen that hedonic states may serve to bring goals to consciousness.

The contents of goals

   The contents of goals are what we normally think of as "goals". The contents of a goal may be complex, just as the structure is. In order to understand the nature of goal contents, goals are often classified. Here the problem is how to determine the number of classes to use for such categorization. Some psychologists classify goals as promoting self-realization or harmony seeking: self-realization wants to optimize the benefit to the self, while harmony seeking wants to minimize conflict. Other researchers categorize goals based on life domains such as family, work, recreation, etc. A third group of psychologists aim to classify goals based on self-constructing systems as viewed by developmental psychology. The reader is encouraged to explain goal content in terms of ANNs.

Emotion and affect

Emotion and affect (feeling) have always been considered important in motivated behavior. We have incorporated emotion and affect indirectly through hedonic states. Others (Ford and Nichols, 1987) believe that "entertainment" goals are activated when an individual's level of arousal drops below some set point while "tranquillity" goals are activated when arousal has increased above the set point. This implies that emotion can be seen as a goal in itself, i.e. a goal that contains an emotional state as objective.

Consider the latter point more carefully. If one looks at a HM designed to heat a water tank by activating a heating coil when the water temperature drops below a certain set point, then, under normally fluctuating environmental conditions, it may appear as if the system is trying to regulate "activity" (as opposed to water temperature). An external observer could argue that the system is actually trying to maintain an optimal level of activity or arousal: when it has been inactive for a certain period of time, it tries to increase its activity level by switching the heating coil on; and if it has been active for a while, it tries to reduce its activity level by switching the coil off! In this case, however, it is known that the system is regulating water temperature and not activity level. The same could possibly be true for emotion and affect, i.e. that they are consequences of homeostatic action rather than variables that need to be regulated themselves. In the case of the water tank HM, the activity level is determined by how fast the external temperature fluctuates.

Assessing goals

In order to classify goals, it is necessary to identify goals. The following test (in the form of an algorithm) has been given in the literature (see Austin and Vancouver, 1996) as a relatively precise method to identify goals. This test is very reminiscent of HMs and it is given here, slightly modified, to fit HM terminology:
1. hypothesize a regulated variable;
2. manipulate (disturb) the regulated variable;
3. identify actions intended to restore the regulated variable to its set point;
4. identify whether the individual can sense the current state (of the regulated variable);
5. block the sensing mechanism (sensor);
6. repeat 2; and
7. verify that no corrective action takes place.
Since goals are also associated with ANNs , the reader is encouraged to apply the test given here also to ANNs. Such an undertaking may reveal the extent of overlap between goals as conceptualized in terms of SPs and goals as conceptualized in terms of hidden layer representations.

The processes of goals

Goal establishment. In order to have a goal, a goal has to be established. How is a goal selected and accepted? The discussion hereto has implied that goals are generated as a consequence of activity in a specific environment. This fits the artificial neural network model of cognitive function and internal representation: through training goals become formed and established. However, the set point of a HM can also be seen as a goal, but this seems to be externally given or determined by evolutionary processes rather than internally developed through training. This highlights the difference between the homeostatic mechanism view and the artificial neural network view of motivated behaviors. The first is a view of the functioning of a mature or developed system. The second is a view of the development of a system from immature to mature. The challenge is to combine them. Note that the environment plays a crucial role in both cases: in the first by evolutionary means; in the second by providing "desired network outputs".

External goals often become internal goals through compliance with the goal, identification with the goal, and finally internalization of the goal. Here the goal goes through stages of redefinition. You should consider the question of where the external goal comes from: - another external source? This generates an infinite regress unless one accepts that some external event or personage (e.g. God) provides or initially provided external goals. A finer distinction may need to be drawn here: internal goals develop via interactions with the external world or environment, and hence can be seen as ultimately externally derived. Therefore, internally developed goals are in a sense external goals also, the difference being that the latter are given "fully formed" (e.g. the desired network outputs; set point value) while the former are given "incipiently formed" (e.g. representations forming at the hidden nodes; controller output). This analysis also highlights the role of the environment in shaping behavior.

The level of commitment given to a goal may reflect the degree to which the (external) goal has been accepted. In our opinion, a goal cannot be accepted if its pursuit does not involve hedonic states - these may be either positive or negative since a goal could be avoided as much as sought. Some researchers claim that goals have valences, which could be positive, neutral, or negative, and probabilities associated with them. These valences seem to be rather similar to the concept of hedonic states, while the probabilities can be seen as weights given to these hedonic states based on the likelihood of success of a particular action. For instance, if hunger could be satisfied by the ingestion of either rice or potatoes, then, if rice is present, consuming rice would have a greater probability of success in relieving hunger. Some people would consider eating rice then as the goal - in terms of HMs, eating rice is not the goal, but satisfying hunger is. The commitment to a goal may therefore reflect the valence of a goal as well as the difficulty - hence probability of success - of that goal. There seems to be some interaction between valence and task difficulty. It is generally considered better to succeed at a more difficult task than an easier one, hence the more difficult task will have a greater valence associated with it. Conversely, it is considered better to fail at a more difficult task than at an easier one. At the same time, if you could take a short-cut to accomplish a task, why would you follow a more lengthy route? Both of these seem to be true, yet they appear to be conflicting! Can they be resolved?

Planning and monitoring. Planning, as often used in the literature, is defined as specific alternative behavioral actions that could be employed in pursuit of a goal. In this respect, planning ties higher order goals (pass the course) to lower-order goals (take notes) without actively pursuing any of these. You may wish to consider the role that the construction and evaluation of alternative behavioral paths play in planning. Construction is important, especially in the sense that it puts together a sequence of operations that can be executed within the available period of time without generating conflicts. Evaluation is important, because it provides a way of testing alternative actions without actually incurring the cost of acting.

In many models of goal-based behavior, evaluation as used in planning is considered to be the same as monitoring, with the exception that the outcome of an action is determined by recourse to memory while with monitoring the outcome of an action is evaluated physically. Many simple behaviors can be connected to form more complex behaviors which are often called scripts. Repertoires of stored scripts (and their consequences) provide a person with more alternatives and greater flexibility in planning their goals.

Monitoring of actions often enhance goal achievement. Goals can be monitored at all different levels - from the highest-order to the lowest muscle-contraction level. Feedback provided implicitly or explicitly by the environment can improve the quality of monitoring. It is our opinion that the more unfamiliar the task or the more insecure the person, the greater the degree of feedback required.

Persistence. Goals can be pursued as conceived, revised to suit changing circumstances, or abandoned altogether. Often, a persistent error or persistent failure to attain a goal leads to disengagement from the goal. The incentive disengagement cycle (Klinger, 1987) suggests that disengagement from a goal proceeds along a standard sequence, (stated here with annotation):
1. heightened effort (to meet the goal);
2. anger and aggression (when failing to meet the goal after increased effort);
3. depression and reduced activity (to conserve the remaining resources);
4. feelings of help- and hopelessness (when the goal is abandoned); followed by
5. a gradual recovery (when a new goal develops).

This cycle is linked to a pattern of change in goal importance - from being important enough to pursue to being abandoned. If an error is persistent, the goal may be abandoned; if the error is well-managed, then the pursuit of the goal is persistent. How would you interpret this in terms of homeostatic theory and neural networks? The implication for a HM is that an old set point is abandoned and a new set point established in response to a persistent error. Neural networks establish internal representations, which could be seen as goals, in response to training with examples. If the error between the output of the network and the desired or example output cannot be reduced, it implies that more training is required (e.g. increased effort) or that the backpropagation of the error is not effective. In the latter case the learning rule has to be changed or the architecture of the network needs to be changed (e.g. a new hidden node needs to be added). This means that the weights of the network need to be re-initialized (reduced activity followed by meaningless output) and that a new internal representation would form during training (hence a new goal would form and a gradual recovery in network performance). Conflict between goals may also lead to the modification or abandonment of goals.

References

Austin, J. T.; Vancouver, J. B. 1996. Goal constructs in psychology: structure, process, and content. Psychological Bulletin 120: 338-375.

Ford, M. E.; Nichols, C. W. 1987. A taxonomy of human goals and some possible applications. In M. E. Ford and D. H. Ford (eds.), Humans as self-constructing systems: putting the framework to work, pp. 289-311. Hillsdale, NJ: Erlbaum.

Klinger, E. 1987. Current concerns and disengagement from incentives. In F. Halisch and J. Kuhl (eds.), Motivation, intention, and volition, pp. 337-347. Heidelberg: Springer.

McFarland, D. 1989. Problems of animal behavior. New York: Longman Scientific and Technical Publishers.

Miller, G. A., Galanter, E.; Pribram, K. H. 1960. Plans and the structure of behavior. New York: Holt.

Powers, W. T.; Clark, R.; McFarland, R. 1960. A general feedback theory of human behavior II. Perceptual and motor skills monograph 11 (3).

Sumpter, B. G.; Noid, D. W. 1996. On the design, analysis, and characterization of materials using computational neural networks. Annual Review of Material Science 26: 223-277.

CHAPTER 21
Process control

Introduction

Almost all scientific and technical fields have made use of ANNs in some form, often with considerable success (Sumpter and Noid, 1996). One such area where ANNs have found application is in chemical process control (Hussain, 1999; Zoriassatine and Tannock, 1998). At first sight, chemical process control may seem to have nothing to do with psychology. On second thought though, one realizes that a chemical plant involves the transportation of fluids through conduits - likewise fluids circulate through the body; the synthesis of new chemicals - like neurotransmitters, proteins, and other substances in the body; the decomposition of chemicals - like many toxins by the liver; the exchange of gases - as do the lungs; the exchange of mass - as do the kidneys; the exchange of heat - as does the skin; the detection of temperature, pressure, chemical composition, and many others - as do the senses; and so on. Clearly, chemical plants can be very complex, the processes that occur in them are often non-linear, and the control of these processes to generate the desired products can be daunting. When processes also include biotechnology and living organisms (e.g. bacteria, yeasts), they can become exceedingly complex (Karim et al., 1997).

The approaches taken by engineers to apply ANNs to complex chemical process control problems may therefore be of interest to us. Besides, it seems only fair that having benefited from the concepts of neural networks, borrowed from psychologists, engineers have a debt to repay!

Learning in process control

The same ANNs that have been discussed in previous chapters are used in process control (PC). As before, supervised and unsupervised networks can be used, as well as feedforward and feedback systems. Of these, the backpropagation network, a supervised multilayer feedforward network learning by error backpropagation, is definitely the most common (Hussain, 1999). As alluded to above, chemical processes are often multivariate (involving several regulated variables simultaneously), non-linear systems and ANNs are especially useful for such applications.

Due to the complexity of many chemical plants and the processes occurring in them, engineers often need to construct accurate mathematical models of these chemical processes. Such models allow them to determine what to do when certain things go wrong with the processes. This could save a lot of time, energy (e.g. electricity), and chemicals, and allow the plants to be operated more safely and efficiently. Obviously, such models could bring about enormous cost savings. However, it is often very difficult and costly to generate these models. ANNs, in contrast, can extract complex information about chemical processes from normally available data in a more efficient manner.

In PC, ANNs are then often used to provide "models" of the chemical processes, in the sense that they can be trained to produce the same outputs as chemical plants when given the same inputs as the plants. They are not true mathematical models because it is not presently understood what the meaning of the weights in ANNs is, although we do understand that ANNs encode information in their connection weights, and can produce the correct responses from certain inputs, and we do understand how these connection weights are adjusted. Sometimes, ANNs are used to provide inverse models of chemical plants. In this case, the network is given the (desired) output from the plant and trained to indicate what the inputs should be to produce this output. Finally, ANNs are also used to act as controllers or augment them, as we have suggested in an earlier chapter on homeostatic mechanisms. These 3 major categories of PC, that is model-predictive control, inverse-model control, and adaptive control, are shown schematically in Figure 21.01 and will be discussed next.

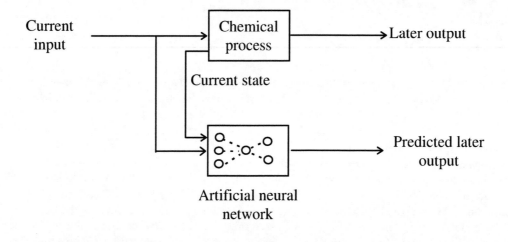

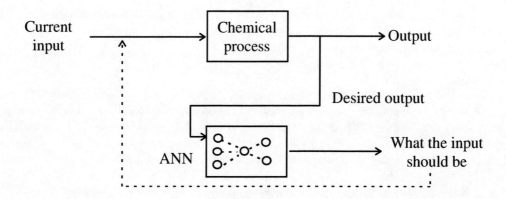

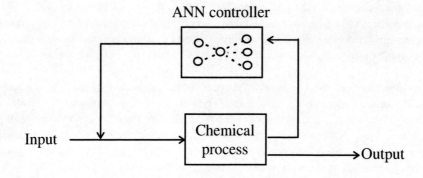

Figure 21.01

A schematic illustration of the 3 major techniques of process control and how they can incorporate ANNs: model-predictive control (top); inverse-model control (middle); and adaptive control (bottom).

Categories of process control

        <u>Model-predictive control techniques.</u> These are the most common control techniques and an example is shown in Figure 21.02. In this approach, one tries to predict what actions the controller should take now to minimize the future deviations of the CP of a regulated variable from its SP. For example, if the temperature of a water stream coming from a heated tank is being regulated, and that temperature is too low, the controller has to activate the heating mechanism. It may take a long time, let's say 30 minutes, before the water temperature has risen to the required level (the lag of the system). One may wish, therefore, to know what to do now to minimize the error 30 minutes hence. What should be done now depends on the current conditions of the process (e.g. temperature in the tank, water level in the tank, amount of water coming in, temperature of the water coming in, and power of the

heating mechanism). The current conditions will determine the outlet water temperature in 30 minutes' time, and knowing what that will be, the controller can take corrective action now.

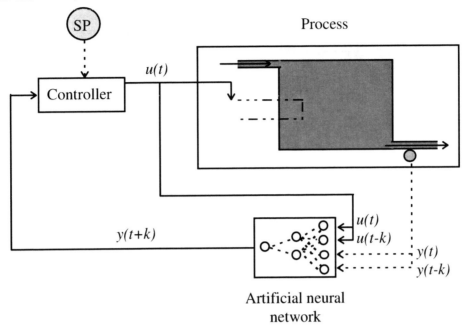

Figure 21.02

A schematic illustration of the use of an ANN in model-predictive control.

ANNs are now trained to predict the outlet temperature given the current conditions in the plant (water temperature, water level, heating power) and the current input to the plant (inlet water temperature, amount of water coming in). To do this, one needs the input and desired output data to train the net. The input data consist of the input to the plant and the conditions in the plant, and the desired output is the outlet water temperature that would occur 30 minutes later. This implies that some tests have to be done to gather the required data. A properly trained ANN would then predict what the outlet water temperature would be 30 minutes later, given the current conditions. Based on this predicted CP, control action could be taken now to minimize the error later. This should be no surprise: humans too, use their neural nets to predict what would happen later (e.g. how thirsty one would be) given current conditions (how thirsty one is now) and current inputs (how hot it is) in order to take action to minimize discomfort.

Figure 21.02 gives a schematic diagram of an ANN used to model a chemical process in order to predict its output at a later stage based on current conditions. In the figure, the action taken by the controller at some point in time t (usually the current time) is indicated as $u(t)$, at some earlier point in time as $u(t-k)$, and at some future point in time as $u(t+k)$ (e.g. $t + 30$ *minutes*). Likewise, $y(t)$ indicates information about the process at time t, and so on. In the figure, the conditions $y(t)$ are obtained from the outlet water temperature sensor only, but normally includes information from many other sources also (water level, inlet water temperature, etc.). Compare this figure also to Figure 21.01.

Inverse-model control techniques. In this case, the ANN learns to supply at its output the appropriate control action $u(t)$, given the desired future process conditions $y(t+k)$, and the current $y(t)$ and past $y(t-k)$ process conditions. In other words, the network is given information about what one wants the process conditions $y(t+k)$ to be like, and it is then trained to indicate what control actions $u(t)$ to take in order to obtain these conditions. For example, if one wants the outlet water of a tank to be 50 °C in 30 minutes' time, and the current water temperature, water level, inlet water temperature, amount of incoming water, and heating rate are known, the trained network should indicate how much electricity or steam to send to the heating coil to reach the target temperature at the required time. Figure 21.03 illustrates such a set-up. The reader will realize that the trained ANN can replace the controller.

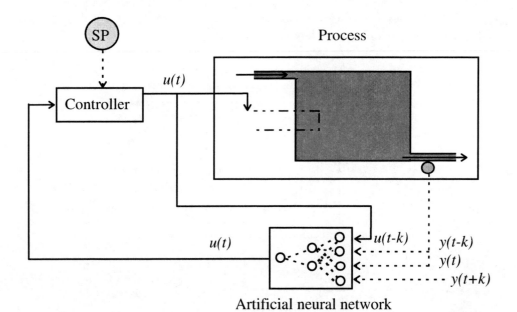

Figure 21.03
A schematic illustration of the use of an ANN in inverse-model control.

Adaptive control techniques. This technique is similar to the inverse-model in the sense that the ANN is used as the controller. The major difference is that in the adaptive technique training of the ANN is ongoing, even while it is operating (as opposed to being trained once and then used). The weights are adjusted on-line using the plant conditions and the desired plant conditions. The benefit of this method is that it adjusts to changes that occur in the plant as they occur. For example, if the heating coil in the water tank is gradually rusting, causing the heating process to change (e.g. deteriorate), the control actions of an ANN that is trained first and then used as a controller will eventually become unsuitable. On the other hand, in adaptive process control the ANN is continuously trained and it remains updated and capable of providing efficient PC. The adaptive control method, using an ANN, is shown in Figure 21.04.

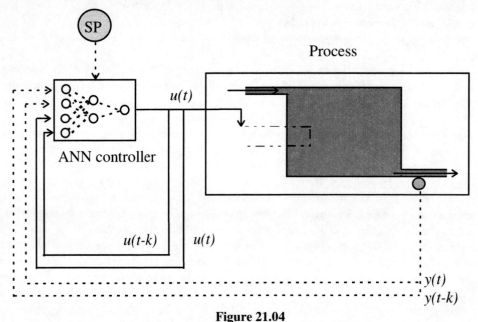

Figure 21.04
A schematic illustration of the use of an ANN in adaptive process control.

ANNs and control chart pattern recognition

Control charts. Control charts are widely used to record critical process variables and to determine whether the process is out of control and requires intervention. The chart consists of a plot of the critical variable(s) over a period of time along with upper and lower limits for this variable much like a medical chart of a patient may display their temperature over a period of time. Every process has "common causes" which are natural to the process and cause some natural fluctuations of the regulated variables. These fluctuations vary within certain ranges which can be statistically characterized to give the upper and lower limits plotted on the control chart. "Special causes" on the other hand, are unusual events that cause the regulated variables to transgress these limits. When the variables exceed one of these limits, the process should be stopped and the cause of the unusual behavior found. For example, if the water tank used in previous examples should spring a large leak causing the tank to empty, regulating the temperature of the outlet water would become impossible (even with an adaptive control technique). This would cause the water temperature or amount of outgoing water to exceed its normal limits, indicating a problem. The system must then be stopped to find and rectify the problem. Figure 21.05 shows an example of a control chart.

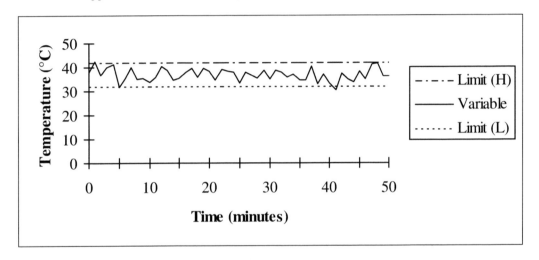

Figure 21.05
A control chart for a regulated variable (the outlet water temperature from a water tank regulated at 37 °C) showing the normal behavior of the regulated variable over a period of time. The upper and lower limits, which the variable should not exceed, are also shown and are set at 2 times the standard deviation of the variable's fluctuations.

Average run lengths. In some cases, however, certain non-random patterns exist in control charts that do not breach the control limits, but are nevertheless indicative of unsound process conditions. For example, these patterns could be gradual trends, sudden jumps, of a cyclical nature, and so forth. They indicate special causes at work in the process and may even predict a catastrophic failure. Obviously, one does not want a catastrophic failure to occur before the plant is taken off-line and the problem fixed. Therefore, being able to recognize these abnormal patterns, especially ones caused by special causes of consequence, would be of great advantage.

The normal fluctuations of a regulated variable may, by chance, show a non-random pattern. These occasional chance patterns need to be told apart from real abnormal ones. It is known that the occurrences of accidental non-random patterns, but not those of a 'defective' pattern, are dramatically reduced when more points are taken into account. The number of points taken into account in determining the nature of a pattern, normal or aberrant, is known as the average run length (ARL). The ARL should be as long as possible because this reduces the chances that a random pattern will be classified as abnormal (thus producing a 'false alarm' or Type I error). On the other hand, the ARL should be as short as possible to detect abnormal conditions as soon as possible (and so to avoid 'misses' or Type II errors). How the appropriate ARL is determined shall not concern us here. Instead we shall assume that the ARL for a process is known and that patterns are interpreted based on this ARL.

ANNs, excellent for pattern recognition, are obvious candidates for identifying pathological process conditions based on the appearance of abnormal patterns. They are even more useful when several abnormal patterns can occur simultaneously. Consequently, they have been trained to automate control chart interpretation in PC applications (Zorriassatine and Tannock, 1998). Examples of abnormal patterns are shown in Figure 21.06. The reader should realize here that ANNs can be used in 2 capacities for PC: as function estimators to aid in or provide control commands and/or as pattern classifiers to detect abnormal conditions.

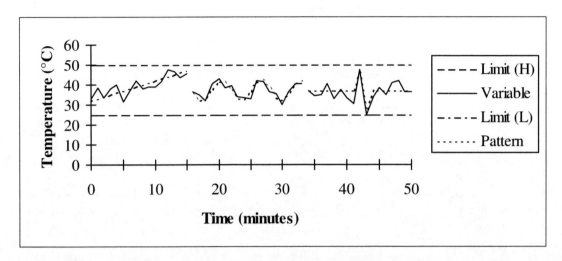

Figure 21.06

A control chart showing some abnormal behavior patterns of the regulated variable over a period of time. These are (i) a trend; (ii) a cycle; and (iii) a discontinuity (jump) and they are superposed on the graph. The average run length is taken to be 15 minutes. The upper and lower limits, which the variable should not exceed, are also shown.

Internal models

As a final point of interest, albeit speculative, let us consider a complication of some of the applications of ANNs to PC. Sometimes the model-predictive and inverse-model techniques are combined to produce the internal-model control technique. In this case, the system has 2 ANNs, one to model the plant, and the other to act as controller as shown in Figure 21.07. The predictive model provides estimates of future plant conditions to the ANN controller which combines this information with current plant conditions and past control signals to determine the current set of control signals. This produces an ANCM with predictive abilities, efficient control signal generation, and memory: in short, an intelligent control mechanism.

It is further interesting to consider the possibility that the predictive model could function as the self' by providing a model of the plant (i.e. the body). Recent evidence indicates that the sensation of self depends on the convergence of inputs from different sensory modalities (Botvinick and Cohen, 1998), possibly on the same neural structure(s). It also suggests that phantom limb pain could originate from the internal model' of the body (e.g. Flor et al., 1995). For example, if a piece of equipment in the plant fails and is removed, the model may not be aware' of this, and it would continue to produce outputs as if that piece of equipment was still present. This problem can only be overcome if the model is trained anew on the behavior of the plant as it now is with the broken equipment. It suggests to us that phantom sensations can only be modified with retraining, perhaps by providing vigorous stimulation to the stump of the amputated limb, to generate a new internal model of the body.

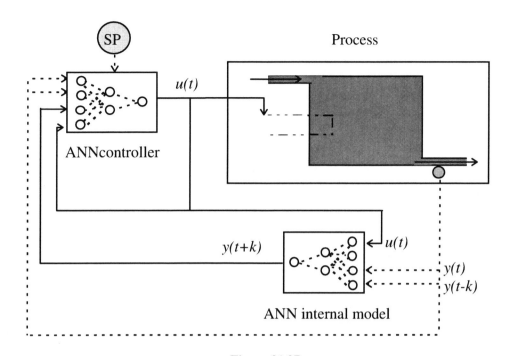

Figure 21.07
A schematic illustration of an ANCM using the internal-model control technique.

References
Botvinick, M. M.; Cohen, J. D. 1998. Rubber hands feel touch that eyes see. Nature 391: 756.
Flor, H.; Elbert, T.; Knecht, S.; Wienbruch, C.; Pantev, C.; Birbaumer, N.; Larbig, W.; Taub, E. 1995. Phantom-limb pain as a perceptual correlate of cortical reorganization following arm amputation. Nature 375: 482-484.
Hussain, M. A. 1999. Review of the applications of neural networks in chemical process control - simulation and online implementation. Artificial Intelligence in Engineering 13: 55-68.
Karim, M. N.; Yoshida, T.; Rivera, S. L.; Saucedo, V. M. ; Eikens, B.; Oh, G.-S. 1997. Global and local neural network models in biotechnology: application to different cultivation processes. Journal of Fermentation and Bioengineering 83: 1-11.
Sumpter, B. G.; Noid, D. W. 1996. On the design, analysis, and characterization of materials using computational neural networks. Annual Review of Material Science 26: 223-277.
Zorriassatine, F.; Tannock, D. T. 1998. A review of neural networks for statistical process control. Journal of Intelligent Manufacturing 9: 209-224.

PART IV
THE INTEGRATION OF TOPICS

CHAPTER 22
A theory of behavior

Introduction

  Motivational psychology is the study of goals, drives, and the actions associated with these. Motivated behaviors occur within a specific environmental context, and the formative nature of this context is reflected in the phenomenon of adaptation. In Part I we discussed the relationship between an organism and its environment. In particular, we suggested that some of the innate psychological mechanisms that developed in the course of an organism's adaptational history, could be HMs. The principles of HMs were covered in Part II where it was observed that even simple HMs could produce sophisticated control. Of import here was the conjecture that HMs activate behaviors through the generation of hedonic states. We then investigated the nature of these hedonic states and found that the brain's dopamine system was the logical candidate for generating hedonic states. The serotonin system, on the other hand, appeared to be the prime candidate for the generation of SP signals. We saw in Part III that goals, when defined as internal representations of desired states, could be interpreted in terms of the activities of the hidden layer nodes of ANNs. This lead to the insight that goals develop as a consequence of experience and that they may facilitate the attainment of future similar tasks. We also examined the extraordinary ability of ANNs to interpret a multitude of signals as exemplified in chemical PC. These signals, reflecting the state of the environment and that of the system, are then transformed into the appropriate control actions necessary for the (future) preservation of the system. The task now remains to combine these hypotheses, concepts, and facts into a coherent whole. We shall attempt to do so in this chapter, and by doing so, construct a theory of motivated behavior implemented in the form of a model.

Assumptions

  In order to deal with the complexity of the issues and to strive for coherence, we shall formally make the assumptions following below. The basis on which an assumption is made is also given. These assumptions are neither exhaustive nor necessarily complete: they merely provide a starting platform for the process of model construction and may warrant, at any point, further scrutiny.

  <u>Assumption 1.</u> In the chapters on homeostatic mechanisms, we have defined 'behavior' as the operation of a HM. We have also established that a single HM could have 2 or more effectors, thus produce 2 or more different behaviors. We shall here assume that the controller(s) of every HM affect physiological processes only and that behaviors are generated by other control systems.

  <u>Assumption 2.</u> Based on the chapters regarding artificial neural networks, we shall furthermore assume that the behavioral controller is an ANN, and that the physiological controllers may be so.

  <u>Assumption 3.</u> We assume that a negative hedonic state is generated when the CP of a regulated variable moves away from the SP and hence a regulation error arises. A positive hedonic state arises in the opposite case. This was discussed in the chapter on homeostatic mechanisms and behavior.

  <u>Assumption 4.</u> We shall assume that regulation errors are communicated by the LC as discussed in the chapter on norepinephrine and stress.

  <u>Assumption 5.</u> We shall also assume that the dopaminergic neurons of the VTA are responsible for the generation of hedonic states. This is in agreement with many views of this system as being the 'reward' system and based on the discussions in the chapter on dopamine and hedonic states.

  <u>Assumption 6.</u> The chapter on serotonin and system states provided support for the view of serotonin being the neurotransmitter mediating SP signals. We shall therefore assume that the serotonergic systems of the brain provide the SPs for various HMs and that they could be differentiated on the basis of the serotonin receptor subtypes involved in signal transmission. We shall also provisionally assume that an increase in serotonergic activity generally results in a lowering of the SP of a HM.

  <u>Assumption 7.</u> We shall assume that receptors could be associated with ANNs that perform "preprocessing" of information before it is relayed to the controller. This was alluded to in the chapter on dopamine where the concept of 'sensory modalities' was used.

Assumption 8. Finally, in accordance with the concepts discussed in the chapters on hormonal cascades and temperament, especially the former, we assume that various components of the system, to be constructed are sensitive to the actions of hormones that could modulate their operation.

The basic model

As discussed in the chapter on HMs and behavior, a HM, generating hedonic states, can be used to explain behavior: when the CP of a regulated variable moves away from its SP, a negative hedonic state is generated and when the CP moves toward the SP, a positive hedonic state ensues. Chapter 16 on dopamine systems indicated that the VTA may be the generator of these hedonic states. The behavior of the organism brings it into contact with the "reward". As a result of its commerce with the reward, the error between SP and CP is affected.

The basic model is therefore obtained by concatenating the concepts of HM with that of hedonic state: these are most clearly embodied in Figure 10.01 and Figure 16.03, respectively, and this basic model is shown in Figure 22.01. To integrate these two systems, it appears necessary to postulate neural mechanisms that can account for a *change in the size of the error*. This is accomplished by the systems E_1 and E_2 in the figure. This information is relayed by the locus coeruleus to other brain sites, including the VTA, as discussed in the chapter on norepinephrine and stress. The difference between E_1 and E_2 reflects the nature of the current 'reward' (i.e. stress or relief). This difference is the entity r(t) encountered in the dopamine system of prediction and reward as discussed ina previous chapter. The VTA combines r(t) with information on sensory cues obtained via the cortical sensory modalities M_1 and M_2 to produce the reward signal $\delta(t)$, the prediction error signal. The reward signal $\delta(t)$ activates the behavioral effector producing a behavior that has an impact on the error between SP and CP. The effector immediately associated with the controller can be considered a physiological effector (such as producing more concentrated urine to prevent water loss). The physiological effector is activated first, and when it fails to keep the CP near the SP, the resulting increasing error is transmitted to E_1 and E_2 to produce the reward signal $\delta(t)$ which serves to activate a behavior (such as drinking water).

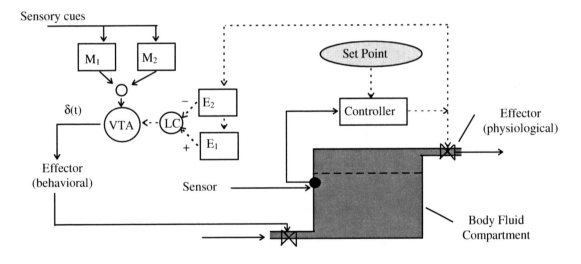

Figure 22.01
A concatenation of Figures 10.01 and 16.03 forms the basic model of motivated behavior.

Through combining the concepts of the chapters on HMs, norepinephrine and stress, and dopamine and reward, this concatenation produces a HM capable of generating hedonic states when normal physiological regulation is no longer sufficient to maintain an important variable within a safe range of values. It therefore fuses the control sophistication of HMs with their various controller types (i.e. proportional, integral, derivative) and control configurations (i.e. feedforward, feedback) with the predictive capabilities of the dopamine reward system conferred by hedonic states and learning. It also combines a sensitivity to internal states (i.e. physiological sensors and effectors) with an ability to act and react to external stimuli (i.e. sensory systems and behavioral effectors) in an integrated manner.

Augmentation 1

We shall now augment our model with the major concept of the chapters on artificial neural networks. In particular, we shall consider the controller as being an ANN. We shall also consider the sensory modalities M_1 and M_2 (independently or in combination) as being ANNs. Aspects of Figure 21.04 are therefore incorporated into Figure 22.01 to yield Figure 22.02.

This modification makes more explicit the abilities of the sensory modalities and associated processing systems for learning to permit pattern classification and function estimation (prediction). It brings the advantages of ANNs to the model and confers on the system the ability to form internal representations of the external world and hence the ability to generate goals. In a rudimentary sense the model is now complete: it can account for the generation of drives mediated by HMs as well as the generation of goals mediated by ANNs. In this manner it accounts for the essentials of a motivated system. In addition to motivation, the model is also capable of cognition and so establishes a relationship between processes of cognition and motivation. It should be noted here, however, that the important issue of emotions and their generation (in so far as they be dissociated from cognition and hedonic states) remain to be addressed in a satisfactory manner.

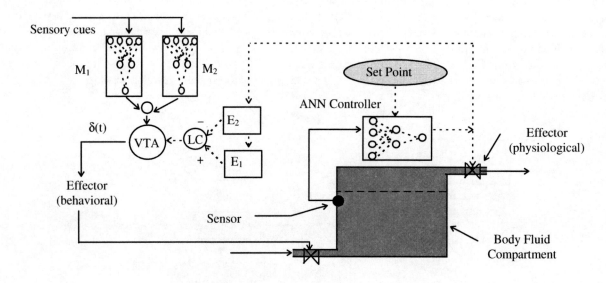

Figure 22.02
*Augmentation of the basic model of motivated behavior shown in
Figure 22.01 with the ANN elements from Figure 21 4.*

Augmentation 2

The next major modification to be made to the model is incorporating information about serotonin systems, covered in the chapter on serotonin and system states, into the SP of the system. As mentioned before, we assume that the SP signal is produced by serotonin-releasing neurons acting via serotonin receptor subtypes to generate individual SPs for specific homeostatic systems.

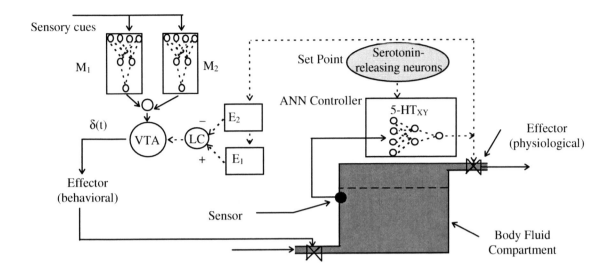

Figure 22.03

Augmentation of the homeostatic model of motivated behavior shown in Figure 22.02 with a serotonin-based SP generating system.

Figure 22.03 is meant to indicate that information from the physiological sensor(s) of the system is fed into some of an ANN s input nodes. At this stage no declaration is made regarding the neurotransmitters or receptor types mediating sensor input. However, we do conjecture that the SP signal is also fed into one or more of the input nodes of the controller ANN, and that at least one of these SP-related input nodes contains serotonin receptors of a specific subtype(s).

While we are addressing the issue of neurotransmitters, let us have a look at some of the others that may be involved. It has been pointed out in the chapter on hunger that the homeostatic explanation, unlike the hunger and satiety centers hypothesis, can account for neurotransmitters. At least 3 neurotransmitters have now explicitly been accounted for: norepinephrine which conveys the cumulative regulation error of physiological processes, dopamine which produces a prediction error output that activates behavior, and serotonin, which provides SP information to the ANN controller. An inspection of Figure 22.03 also suggests that 2 more are involved: acetylcholine, which is released at the neuromuscular junction, must be involved in the output from the behavioral effector and glutamate in the output from the cortical sensory modalities M_1 and M_2.

Augmentation 3

The penultimate augmentation to be made at this point, is to acknowledge the likelihood that the behavioral effector may be of considerable complexity to permit the formulation and execution of behavior. We shall therefore also assume that the behavioral effector is an ANN which receives multiple sensory inputs and produces elaborated and complex motor outputs. At least some of the input nodes of the effector ANN must receive dopaminergic input from the VTA, the signal that activates behavior. This suggests immediately that dopamine receptor subtypes could be accommodated in the model, the particulars of which will have to be determined. The other inputs to the effector ANN may be visual, kinematic, tactile, and so forth. Figure 22.04 represents our final, but still incipient, model of motivated behavior.

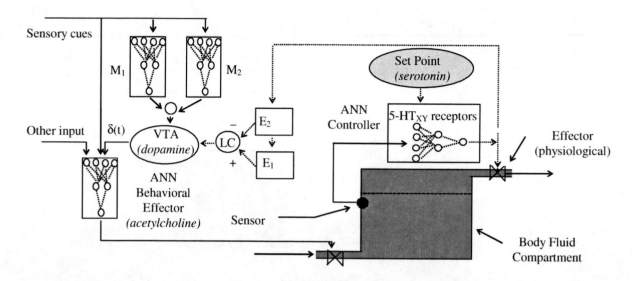

Figure 22.04

Augmentation 3 of the homeostatic model of motivated behavior shown in Figure 21.03 with an ANN serving as behavioral effector.

Augmentation 4

   The final augmentation we make now is to incorporate an internal model into the system. It is quite likely that the internal model is implemented by cortical structures since it is known that somatosensory and motor cortex contain representations of the body (e.g. Kandel, 1985). Since M_1 and M_2 are associated with cortical sensory modalities, we subsume them into the internal model. The internal model receives a wide variety of external input from the senses and internal input from the sensors of HMs and produces an output that influences the behavioral effector. We show this augmentation in Figure 22.06.

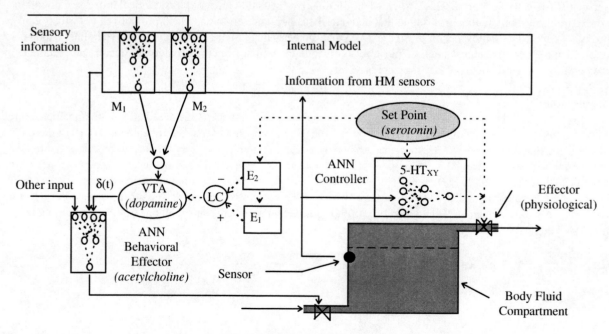

Figure 22.05

Final augmentation of the homeostatic model of motivated behavior shown in Figure 21.04 with an ANN serving as internal model incorporating concepts from Figure 21.07.

We find that the model as shown in Figure 22.04, despite being nascent, is already complicated and that it is necessary to simplify it to see what it boils down to. An inspection of Figure 22.04 reveals that the model could be broken down into 2 HMs regulating the same variable. The first and obvious one being the physiological HM; the second being the behavioral HM. This simplification is shown in Figure 22.06.

Behavioral Homeostatic Mechanism   Physiological Homeostatic Mechanism

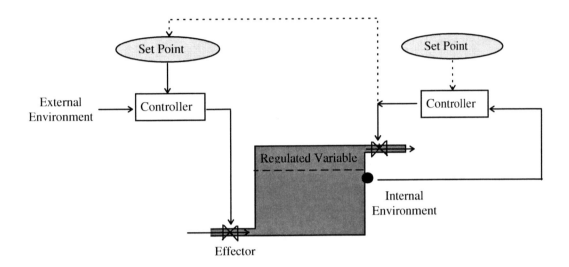

Figure 22.06

A conceptual simplification of the model shown in Figure 22.04. This figure shows that the model essentially consists of 2 HMs regulating the same variable: one regulates this variable through the manipulation of internal (physiological) conditions, the other regulates the same variable through the manipulation of external conditions (which has an eventual impact on internal conditions).

Figure 22.06 suggests that we can, somewhat loosely, view cognitive psychology and motivational psychology as the study of different aspects of the behavioral HM. In particular, Cognitive Psychology is the study of the External Environment-Controller-Effector system while motivational psychology is the study of the Set Point-Controller-Effector system. Keep in mind that the behavioral SP incorporates drives which originate from the physiological HM. We are also of the opinion that the model as shown above indicates that emotion/drive/"heart" directs an organism, and that the mind/intellect is an instrument that permits the organism to respond to its drives in the most efficient manner, given its specific lifespan, physiology, and environment. We suppose where one's heart indicates one course of action and the mind another, some conflict between heart and mind has arisen in the sense that short-term benefit appears of equal strength as long term gain, but that the former requires a course of action which may preclude the course of action required for the latter.

We should also note that the physiological HM tends to be domain specific, while the associated behavioral HM is more domain general. However, since the behavioral HM tends to become activated as a result of the operation of the physiological HM, it may become more limited in scope and not be truly domain general. The physiological HM, therefore, generates a focusing or attentional effect. The modification of the behaviors of both HMs may be further influenced by the release and actions of hormones as described in Chapter 7. In Chapter 7 we saw that external stimuli influence the physiological state of the organism, this in turn hinders or promotes the release of hormones. The hormones, in their turn, modify sensory and/or motor pathways that has the effect of bringing the organism into contact with different stimuli, thus perpetuating the cycle. The reader is encouraged to examine the system shown in Figure 22.04 for internal consistency and for consistency with the material in previous chapters, and to explain its operation in detail.

Finally, we wish to remind you, the reader, that describing a system as a HM makes the basic claim that the system can be formalized or represented in terms of a HM. This means that the system may in fact be something quite different. We are merely saying that the operation of the system, e.g. organism, can be approximated to the desired degree (or a better degree than existing alternatives) by the chosen formalism. If the formalism is a largely accurate description of the system, it would be possible to increase the correspondence between reality and model through successive refinements of the model. If the formalism is a poor description of the real system, then the approximation between formalism and reality will remain poor, despite the use of many refinements. In such a case, a new formalism ultimately needs to be devised, or, if already in existence in another field, imported. It is up to the reader to make this judgment, and, where and if necessary, make refinements or apply a new formalism to the understanding of motivated behavior.

References

Kandel, E. R. 1985. Central representation of touch. In E. R. Kandel; J. H. Schwartz (eds.) Principles of neural science, pp.316-330. Amsterdam: Elsevier.

CHAPTER 23
Living systems theory

Introduction

We have started this text out with a discussion of motivation in bacteria. We then proceeded to cover in length motivational mechanisms in multicellular organisms such as humans, and we shall now extend these views to also include groups of multicellular organisms such as organizations, companies, and governments.

Living systems such as cells, humans, organizations, and societies, all have in common the fact that they can maintain some internal constancy despite fluctuations in their environments. The difference between a desired state and the current state of the system is converted into an action to reduce that difference. Therefore, living systems theory is concerned with self-regulating systems.

The basic, self-regulatory structure is a natural phenomenon. The fact that it describes both humans and societies is an isomorphism. That is, isomorphisms are 2 or more things with the same structure. Keep in mind that structure can mean "physical" structure such as a body or a "functional" structure such as a process. For instance, humans and water tanks have different physical structures, but, as far as water level regulation is concerned, very similar functional structures. Because of such isomorphisms, living systems can be expected to have in common: (1) purposeful behavior; (2) control mechanisms; (3) hierarchies of control mechanisms; (4) learning. Figure 23.01 shows a schematic diagram of a general control system that may apply to all living systems.

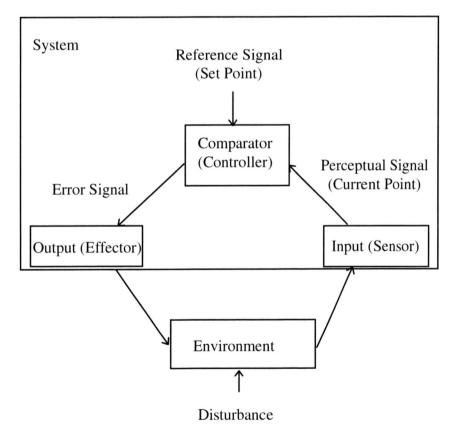

Figure 23.01
A diagram of a general control system.

Purposeful behavior

Bacteria, as we have seen, are capable of producing purpose-like behavior. Humans, we assume, are capable of purposeful behavior. Organizations, like humans, are often described as purposeful. Think of a small business such as a bakery that is trying to operate. The business consists of a manager, a buyer, a baker, and a clerk. The clerk is responsible for ensuring that there is, at all times, enough flour for the bakery. If the bakery runs short, the clerk should advise the manager who will then instruct the buyer how much flour to order. The baker is responsible for baking bread and in the process uses flour. In terms of homeostatic mechanisms, the clerk acts as the sensor of the business, the buyer as the effector, and the manager as the controller. The flour is the regulated variable and some thought may suggest that the daily demand for bread is possibly determining the set point for flour. But what about hedonic states? It is our suspicion that *a profit represents a positive hedonic state* for the system and *a loss represents a negative hedonic state* for the system.

Does this make sense? If the CP moves away from the SP, for example, if flour gets used up faster than it can be replenished, the bakery will run out of bread. If it has no product to sell but must pay rent and wages, it will incur a loss. Therefore, the system should modify its behavior. If the CP moves away from the SP because too much flour is being ordered, more flour has to be paid for than is sold as bread and a loss would also occur. It seems therefore at least partly plausible to regard profit and loss as organizational hedonic states. If self-regulation by the business is successful, it will survive.

Hierarchies of control systems

In our discussions about homeostatic mechanisms, we have considered the possibility of different HMs sharing components such as sensors and/or effectors. We have also considered the possibility of different HMs acting simultaneously but in incompatible ways. Arranging HMs in a hierarchy and activating them accordingly has been considered as one possible way to resolve conflicts between such control mechanisms. Furthermore, in our discussion of goals, we have considered the multiple levels at which goals exist: from higher-order goals to lower-order goals. Often the term "goal" is used interchangeably with "reference signal" or "set point" (e.g. Vancouver, 1996). If we accept this usage, it implies that for every goal in every level there must be a corresponding set point (compare this usage of the term 'goal' to that in the chapter on goals.

One way of connecting all the goals in a hierarchy is to let the output of higher-order goals combine to form the set points for lower order goals. The outputs of the lower-order goals combine to form the set points for still lower-order goals until the goals at the level of muscle contractions are reached (these are the lowest-order goals). When many control systems are all connected up like nodes in layers, it is reminiscent of neural networks. In this case, every node of the neural network consists of a HM. (We have seen before - e.g. the dopamine system - that HMs in turn may consist of networks of nodes) The reader's knowledge of neural networks should also inform her/him of the possibility that each connection between different HM nodes can be weighted. Figure 23.02 is a schematic diagram of the interconnected HM nodes of a Human System.

The reader should note that the system shown in Figure 23.02 does not conform to an ANN in some important respects. The system above does not produce an output at the top layer, despite the label "behavior". It could be modified by having outputs to the outside world coming from the last "output" nodes (in addition to feeding the output from the same nodes back to the previous comparator as a set point) or from the lowest level output (effector) nodes. The input is not modified, but fed "directly" to every input node in every layer. In a neural network, the output from one layer is typically the input to another layer - thus the input is not fed directly or unmodified to higher layers. The system could be modified by connecting the effector output from a node in the previous layer to the sensor input of a node in the next layer. In the latter case, the bias should connect to each comparator and serve as an internal set point. At the very end, an external source acts as external set point (the training examples). This suggests that the system above needs to be modified to accommodate such an external set point. Finally, as with a neural network, the connections could be weighted. A modified system is shown below in Figure 23.03. You, the reader, should now consider Figure 23.03 and the various modifications indicated to select, with justification, that modification most congruent with the material discussed in the current and previous chapters.

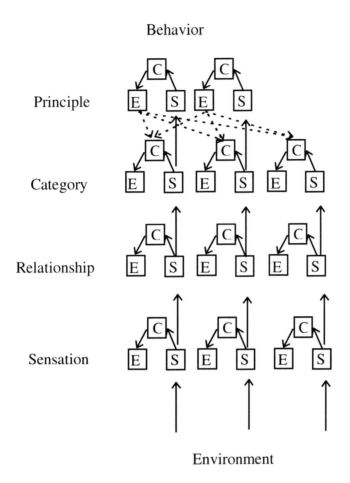

Behavior

Principle

Category

Relationship

Sensation

Environment

Figure 23.02

A highly simplified schematic diagram of the interconnected HM nodes of a Human System. Weighted connections are shown only between the top two layers for the sake of clarity, however, all layers have weighted connections (adapted from Vancouver, 1996).

As with humans, organizations consist of hierarchies of control units. At the top, the goal is represented as a mission statement. For every department there are goals to enable meeting the mission statement. For every unit within a department, there are goals to enable meeting the departmental goals. This continues to the level of each individual having her/his goals that contribute ultimately to meeting the organization's mission statement.

You may appreciate that motivating the people in an organization can play an important role in allowing that organization to meet its mission statement. You should also consider a human being as an "organization" of cells (e.g. "bacteria"). If the human then is motivated, this implies that eventually every cell of the human body must be "motivated". Having seen from bacterial chemotaxis that even cells can act in a motivated-like manner, the notion of every cell in a person being motivated should not come as a complete surprise.

According to organizational role theory, each member of an organization is associated with a role set composed of various other members of the organization. Think of every voter in the country having some idea of the role a prime minister should fulfill. Together, all the voters form a role set that sends the role to a particular individual and measures that individual against the sent role. The sent role acts as a set point and the prime minister individual constantly tries to act in a manner which brings his current role in line with the sent role. The individuals that make up a member of the organization's role set are defined by the information flow and authority structure of the organization.

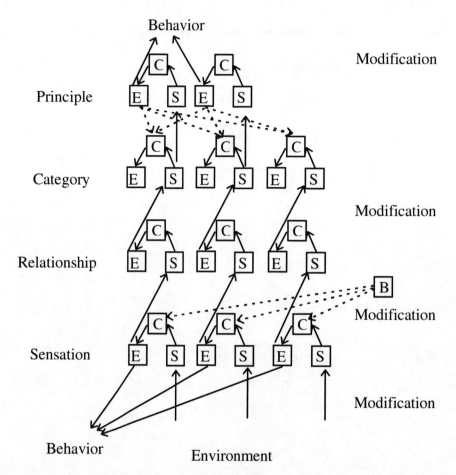

Figure 23.03

A highly simplified schematic diagram of the interconnected HM nodes of a Human System modified according to neural network concepts. Although all the modifications could be enacted simultaneously, consider Figure 23.02 with only, in turn, one of the modifications shown above.

In an organization, supervisors often act as senders of roles for the organization. The role communicated to a subordinate serves as a set point or reference signal and the behavior or performance of the subordinate serves as current point or current signal for *both* the supervisor and subordinate. This is important: if the performance of the subordinate conforms to the role sent by the supervisor, the supervisor gets feedback telling him/her that he/she has successfully sent the role; for the subordinate it means that he/she has successfully performed the required role. The role sending episode is shown in Figure 23.04.

In the diagram above, the "environment" of Figure 23.01 includes now another Human System. The role sending episode above also suggests that role-sending eventually occurs at the level of each individual cell. This could be explained in terms of lower-order goals: the lowest order goals of humans (i.e. muscle contractions) may be the highest-order goals of cells. This also suggests that not only muscle contractions, but all cellular functions such as action potential generation, hormone secretion, etc. are the lowest-order goals of the human system (and the highest-order goals of the cell systems).

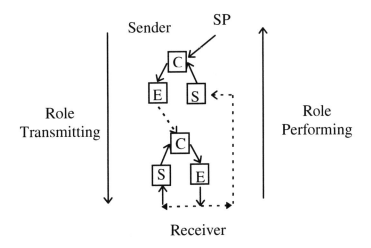

Figure 23.04

A schematic diagram of the role episode: sending and receiving a role.

What about hedonic states? In my opinion, praise/reprimand, promotion/demotion, and salary increases/decreases function as hedonic states. These probably operate either individually or in combination to produce hedonic states at the level of the subunits of an organization. At the level of the individual human being, these translate into the positive and negative hedonic states of feeling good or feeling bad, respectively. However, some are of the opinion that it is not necessary to postulate affect at the level of an organization (Vancouver, 1996) while others (e.g. Ostroff, 1992) believe that a homogeneity of affect emerges from the interactions of human subsystems. This homogeneity of affect could be, in sum, positive or negative and act as the hedonic state of the organization.

Regarding the position of an individual in an organization, keep in mind that set points need not be fixed, but could vary over time. For instance, if one has influenza and is feverish, one may wish to increase the set point of ones apartment's thermostat. When one has recovered, one may reduce the set point again. It seems likely to us that if an individual can handle more complex set point variations, then s/he would be found higher up in the hierarchy of the organization.

The complexity of system performance.

The reader may recall from our earlier discussions of HMs that controllers can be one or a combination of 4 types: on-off, proportional, derivative, and reset. Also, they can be feedforward or feedback depending on where the sensors and effectors are located relatively to one another. Furthermore, feedforward systems are capable of anticipating future events while feedback systems react to past events. The period of time it takes a system to react to an event is called the *lag* of the system. The period of time with which the system can anticipate an event is called the *lead* of the system (Deutsch, 1966). At the system level, lag determines how responsive the system is to a disturbance. Lead reflects the system's ability to anticipate and counter disturbances. In both cases, a system protects itself by maintaining stability, i.e. it prevents external disturbances from causing internal disturbances in important variables (Ashby, 1952).

Clearly, "an ounce of prevention is better than a pound of cure" because in the case of cure, damage has been done, while in the case of prevention, damage has not yet occurred. For these reasons, the anticipatory system (system with lead) is considered more sophisticated than the reactive system (system with lag). Note also that we are talking about a reactive system: the same terminology (unintentionally so) as that used in the chapter on temperament. This immediately raises the question of whether reactive/non-reactive temperaments can be stated in terms of living systems theory (and hence in homeostatic terms). It furthermore suggests that we can ask whether someone with a reactive temperament is likely to be "reactive" (i.e. quick) to anticipate things. The person with the reactive temperament may not only "overreact" to events but may also tend to worry more about future events. Note how the investigation of one topic (living systems/control theory) has provided an unanticipated and thus surprising possible insight into another (temperament).

For both lead and lag, memory is important. In memory is stored perceptual signals, system responses, and outcomes of these responses. For instance, one signal may be sunshine producing thirst, the response may be eating candy, and the result may be even greater thirst. Another signal may be sunshine producing thirst, the response may be drinking water, and the result may be reduced thirst. In the future, sunshine may then inhibit the eating of candy and promote the drinking of water, even before thirst has occurred (lead), or the inhibition of eating candy and the promotion of drinking water after thirst has occurred (lag). In either case, the living system benefits from memory. As we have seen in the chapter on process control, learning permits more sophisticated control, especially where the controller itself is a neural network capable of learning.

We want to conclude with a question on leadership. Leadership is often seen as requiring the ability to motivate people. Given the material covered in the current and preceding chapters, how could this be accomplished? The reader is implored to consider the qualities necessary in a leader of any group of people, and how such a leader could most efficiently go about exercising these attributes.

References
Ashby, W. R. 1952. Design for a brain. New York: Wiley.
Deutsch, K. W. 1966. The nerves of government: models of political communication and control. New York: Free Press.
Ostroff, C. 1992. The relationship between satisfaction, attitudes, and performance: an organizational level analysis. Journal of Applied Psychology 77: 963-974.
Vancouver, J. B. 1996. Living systems theory as a paradigm for organizational behavior: understanding humans, organizations, and social processes. Behavioral Science 41: 165-204.

CHAPTER 24
The failure of motivation

Introduction

The field of abnormal psychology encompasses a wide range of disorders. These disorders have been classified according to characteristic patterns that emerge in cognition, behavior, and affect. Since one can conceive of some of these disorders as resulting from the failure of systems that produce motivated behaviors, it may be of interest to attempt explanations of them in those terms. The reader is therefore encouraged to apply his/her knowledge of homeostatic systems and hedonic states, drawn together in the model presented in Chapter 22, towards the understanding of psychological disorders and the specific dynamic interplay between their environmental, physiological, and behavioral processes. The reader may immediately realize the breadth of possibilities for testing and research since the broad categories of cognition, behavior, and affect can be directly derived from, or related to, various systems within the model. The success or failure of such an effort at explanation in terms of the model would at the same time provide an interesting and useful test of the integrated model of motivational mechanisms presented hitherto.

One of the ways in which the mechanisms that generate motivated behaviors could fail is simply by not producing signals when supposed to, or by producing signals either too strong or too weak than required for normal functioning. In order to examine how motivational mechanisms can "fail" to produce appropriate behavior, we will perform a behavioral analysis of *bulimia nervosa*, an eating disorder that we believe could be interpreted in terms of signals of disproportionate intensity and fluctuation relative to one another. Since we have already considered, in Chapters 13 and 14, how the homeostatic view can be applied to the concepts of "normal" hunger and thirst, we may draw on our understanding of these normal processes when attempting to explain the observed characteristics of this psychological disorder.

Homeostatic theory and "weight" regulation

The concept of weight regulation is associated with eating disorders and eating in general. Many researchers believe that there is a stability of body weight within adults, hence the reader may frequently encounter such views in the literature. The intake of food, expenditure of energy, and metabolic processes influence one another and contribute to this stability of weight. From this observation, it would seem logical that homeostatic processes are involved in regulating weight. Set point theory has been used to describe such processes, proposing that changes in physiological and metabolic systems result from the compensatory mechanisms to regulate weight around an established set point (Keesey and Powley, 1986; Mrosovsky and Powley, 1977).

Some researchers believe that the set points for weight are not so established as early applications of set point theory have proposed. Keesey and Powley contend that fluctuations can occur and that exercise, diet, and changes over time have an effect on weight set points (Keesey and Powley, 1986). The involvement of homeostatic mechanisms with regard to the regulation of weight appears as a logical assumption. If weight appears to be stable, then wouldn't there be homeostatic mechanisms involved that are regulating this stability? As a result, a number of studies show that weight appears to be regulated, since the intake and loss of weight is accompanied by both metabolic/energy changes and compensatory behaviors.

However, viewing weight as a regulated variable with an established set point can be shown as problematic when applying our augmented model involving physiological and behavioral homeostatic mechanisms. The assumption of homeostatic mechanisms involved in the regulation of weight has to be analyzed. Homeostatic mechanisms, as described in Chapter 10, involve the regulation of specific variables in which deviations from set points lead to control actions to maintain the set point. However, caution should be exercised when determining what specific variables are being regulated. The stability of a variable, such as weight, may suggest that there is a set point for a particular variable and that it is being regulated. This may be deceiving, since the presence of "phantom" variables can lead to an erroneous application of homeostatic analysis.

Weight, in our view, is not being regulated. Instead, homeostatic mechanisms regulating other variables contribute to the appearance of weight stability and regulation. The homeostatic systems regulating specific carbohydrates, essential amino acids, Na$^+$ and fatty acids, blood volume, osmolality, and others have a composite effect on weight. In order to 'test' if a variable is being regulated, the essential components of a homeostatic mechanism must be identified. An initial and important way of establishing if an apparent regulated variable is a true regulated variable, is by determining if sensors detecting an aspect of that particular variable exist. It is unlikely that "weight" sensors exist, however, there do exist body receptors that act as "sensors" for specific carbohydrates, amino acids, etc. Hence we conclude that weight in itself is not being regulated, but that other variables that contribute to body weight, are.

Physiological and behavioral analysis

We believe that behaviors are driven by at least two important sources (see also below): one being physiological, the other psychological, especially cognitive. The physiological sources are ultimately related to homeostatic mechanisms regulating a myriad of physiological variables within physiologically safe ranges. The other source is cognitive and it develops on the basis of learning associations between actions and their consequences.

Homeostatic mechanisms affecting weight include those that regulate essential nutrients, water balance, and blood volume. These systems may have complex interactions and influence the operation of one another. For instance, they may be sharing components such as effectors and sensors. When these systems fail at regulation, the behavioral system is activated. Signals of physiological stress conditions are transmitted to the locus coeruleus, which activate other brain centers and eventually, behaviors are likely to ensue (i.e. exercise, dieting).

Cognitive mechanisms affecting weight include those that generate hedonic states. These hedonic states are generated because environmental stimuli (i.e. food, advertisements, social contexts) strongly evoke similar past stimuli that have frequently been followed with particular hedonic states. That is, in the past, these stimuli have been tagged with particular hedonic valences and committed into memory via the hippocampus. An individual may have been exposed to negative situations such as shame elicited from family and friends when he/she would eat. Therefore, some stimuli may trigger expectations of displeasure as a result of associated unrewarding consequences. Other stimuli may trigger expectations of positive hedonic states as a result of associated rewarding experiences. For instance, when an individual did not "overeat", he/she might have been given praise and social rewards for such behavior. Therefore, an individual would seek to engage in behaviors that would lead to positive hedonic states or that would avoid or reduce negative hedonic states based on the array of present stimuli.

Bulimia nervosa

Bulimia nervosa is an eating disorder, along with *anorexia nervosa* and the atypical eating disorders, characterized by oscillating episodes of fasting and gorging. All eating disorders have much in common and the atypical eating disorders are often very similar to *anorexia* or *bulimia nervosa* but may not meet the criteria for the former disorders in all respects (e.g. Fairburn and Harrison, 2003). Below are DSM-III-R (American Psychiatric Association, 1987) criteria for diagnosing individuals with *bulimia nervosa* followed by a table summarizing the cognitive, behavioral, and affective characteristics of the disorder:

1. Recurrent episodes of binge eating (rapid consumption of a large amount of food in a discrete period of time);
2. Feeling of lack of control over eating behavior during the eating binges;
3. Regular self-induced vomiting, use of laxatives or diuretics, strict dieting or fasting, or vigorous exercise in order to prevent weight gain;
4. Minimum average of two binge eating episodes a week for at least three months;
5. Persistent overconcern with body shape and weight.

In the diagnostic criteria listed by Fairburn and Harrison (2003), *anorexia nervosa* also has to be ruled out as possible diagnosis before a diagnosis of *bulimia nervosa* is made.

Table 24.01

Summary of cognitive, behavioral, and affective characteristics of bulimia nervosa

Cognition	Behaviors	Affect
Unrealistic thoughts about one's weight and body	Binges Vomiting Use of Laxatives Excessive Exercise	Feelings of anxiety Feelings of insecurity Feelings of depression

Typical stages of bulimia nervosa and application of the homeostatic model

The cyclical episodes of gorging and fasting evident in *bulimia nervosa* have been divided into different stages with characteristic attributes. These stages and their attributes are shown below in Table 24.02. We will attempt to explain these stages of bulimia nervosa with the aid of the model expounded in Chapter 22. In particular, we will pay particular attention to the origin of different signals that drive behavior as mentioned above. From Figure 22.05 it is clear that signals activating the behavioral controller may originate from one of three different sources: they arrive from homeostatic systems involved in the regulation of physiological variables via the LC and VTA; from the internal model via cortical projections; and possibly from other sources. We suggest that an essential aspect of *bulimia nervosa* may be the way in which the relative intensities of these incoming signals change.

For example, a strongly inhibitive signal coming from the cortex may override physiological signals of nutrient deficiencies. Such an inhibitory signal may be the result of prior negative experiences such as punishment and social disapproval that have become associated with the act of eating. Hence, eating is continually inhibited by a signal from the internal model that is strong enough to override other signals unless these other signals can overcome the inhibition. We believe this tonic inhibitory signal sets the background tone for the disorder since it ought not to be present in normal individuals.

Table 24.02

The stages of bulimia nervosa and their characteristic attributes

Stage	Attributes
Early pre-binge	Fear of becoming fat Fasting
Later pre-binge	Increasing hunger Increasing motivation to eat
Binge	Nutrient deficit Intense hunger Intensive food consumption
Purge	Feelings of shame and regret Motivation to undo "shameful" behaviors Physiological over-satiation

Early pre-binge stage

During the early pre-binge stage, the influx of environmental stimuli with adverse eating-related associations produce high continuous activity in the prefrontal cortex. This high degree of stimulus-driven cognitive functioning produces the fear of becoming fat due to negative associations with eating, a belief that eating will lead to weight gain, and a perception that "fatness" is socially undesirable. For example, Tuschen-Caffier et al. (2003) found that bulimics, when exposed to their body image using a video recording, experienced a significantly increased sense of insecurity compared to controls. Moreover, the heightened sense of insecurity also seemed to take longer to return to baseline levels compared to control subjects (Tuschen-Caffier et al., 2003).

These expectations that negative hedonic states will follow eating thus inhibit eating. Hence fasting provides a means to avoid negative hedonic states and to gain the positive feelings of social approval. This interpretation allows us to account for both the presence of a fear of becoming fat and the accompanying process of fasting.

Later pre-binge stage

When nutrient-related physiological variables are in balance, it is easy to see how cognitive processes can inhibit eating. This is so since the homeostatic systems experience no regulation errors and would produce no drive signals to initiate eating. Even small drive signals to start eating could thus be easily blocked by cognitive inhibition. If the inhibitory cognitive signal is strong, drive signals to induce eating will also have to be commensurately stronger.

The growth of regulation errors in nutrient-related physiological variables (i.e. deficits in glucose levels, lipid levels, amino acid levels, mineral levels, and so on) will generate compound regulation errors that would lead to the gradual emergence of a condition of physiological stress and the concomitant growth of a related negative hedonic state. The function of this negative hedonic state, of course, is to activate the mechanisms leading to eating behavior. Hence, during the late pre-binge stage, as this negative hedonic state is becoming increasingly stronger, but is not yet strong enough to overcome the inhibitory cognitive signal, one could expect feelings of increasing hunger and an increasing motivation to eat to develop. Hence we can also account for the attributes of the late pre-binge stage.

Although the individual now experiences an increasing negative hedonic state associated with physiological nutrient deficits, one should remember that under normal conditions, eating, when hungry, is generally followed by positive hedonic consequences. Hence, at this stage, cognitive processes may also start to generate expectations of positive hedonic states that will follow eating based on prior experiences of hunger and its relief due to eating. For instance, when hungry, the sight of food has an enticing attribute as a stimulus: the individual thinks about food, and how desirable it will be to eat. This is done at the same time that cognitive processes are also taking place in which an individual is thinking about how unrewarding eating is due to environmental (i.e. social/family) influences. Therefore, the late pre-binge stage may also be characterized by an increasing degree of cognitive conflict (keep fasting *versus* start eating).

Binge stage

Binging starts when the growing negative hedonic state due to increasing nutrient deficits starts to exceed the inhibitory cognitive signal. In other words, the negative feelings experienced due to hunger are now worse than the negative feelings due to the fear of becoming fat. In addition, the expectation of positive feelings consequent upon satiating the hunger may also become larger than the current positive feeling associated with maintaining the fast.

Sustained periods of dieting and exercise have now intensely increased the physiological nutrient deficit. As a result of the learned rewarding consequences of dieting, it has required an increasingly higher negative hedonic state to be sufficient to override dieting behavior and for the individual to engage in eating behavior. Since the physiological deficits are unusually large, the individual will now be motivated to engage in the consumption of large amounts of food (binge).

Our application of the model allows us to account for the nutrient deficits, intense feelings of hunger, and large amounts of food consumed during the binging stage. It also permits us at this point to suggest that following food consumption the feelings of hunger will be pacified and the inhibitory cognitive signals that lead to fasting will reemerge - hence to predict that the early pre-binge stage would follow. What we are not able to predict though, is the intensity with which the early pre-binge stage would reemerge.

Purge stage

The reemergence phase of the early pre-binge stage has been labeled the purge stage because of the characteristic efforts to undo the binging behavior. In fact, the inhibitory cognitive signals reemerge with such force that the individual often tries to undo the "shameful" act of eating by purging. Purging can be effected either by way of inducing vomiting or by taking laxatives. Although it is unclear why purging emerges, the consequences of over-eating may contribute to the development of this stage. Due to the excessive intake of food, especially if the foods consumed do not amount to a balanced diet, it is likely that a number of regulated physiological variables will return to normal and then overshoot their mark as digestion continues while other nutrient deficits would persist. In both cases, i.e. due to both excess and deficit, regulation errors and physiological stress will ensue. Since nausea is more likely to be associated with an excess than a deficit of some nutrient or another, it is possible that the excesses generated by bingng would generate some degree of nausea. One could then suggest that the induction of vomiting is an extension of this natural process that follows the sudden increase in nutrient concentrations to excessive and possibly toxic levels.

During the purge stage, the individual experiences feelings of shame and regret. The individual is once again strongly motivated to diet, and the cognitive processes continue, in which there is contemplation about how the hedonic state associated with the rewarding effects of dieting was insufficient to thwart eating behavior. There is also anticipation of negative social consequences of the binge behavior which increases the negative hedonic state related to eating behavior. As a result, the individual is now motivated to again try hard to diet and exercise since the rewarding consequences of these behaviors have a more intense hedonic state than those associated with eating. Our application of the model then allows us to explain the occurrence of over-satiation and it hints at how the purging behavior itself may develop, but does not explain the feelings of shame and regret that follows binging. It is possible that these feelings of shame and regret that follow (binge) eating are, just like the feelings of fear of becoming fat, learned. This seems like a parsimonous interpretation and we shall assume it to be the case unless compelled by better evidence otherwise.

Implications of using a model

Having a model with which to explain the operation of a normal system permits one also to investigate how abnormal conditions may develop. Hence we have seen that an application of our model does indeed allow us to make sense both of eating and the eating disorder *bulimia nervosa*. It is also important to note that it allows us not only to explain the different stages of the disorder, but also under which conditions transitions to other stages will occur. For example, the transition from the late pre-binge stage to the binge stage occus when the drive to eat exceeds the drive to fast due to the associated changes in hedonic states and expected hedonic states as explained above. More importantly, a model or theory could be seen, in contrast to a single hypothesis, as a set of interlocking hypotheses. All of these hypotheses could therefore be experimentally tested and to the extent that they be confirmed, will support the theory. Hence a theory also has the benefits of allowing one to make predictions about how the course of events could be altered by intercession at some or another specific point. In the case of a disorder, such predictions may suggest new avenues for treatment or avenues that should be avoided as discussed below. In other words, the model allows one to understand where and how to intervene in the process to alleviate the symptoms of the disorder and how to potentially correct it.

During the early pre-binging stage, the eating-inhibition cognitive signal is considered to be reinforced by external stimuli. One could therefore postulate that avoiding stimuli that have negative associations with eating and positive associations with fasting may help in retarding or preventing the disorder from developing if applied early enough. However, once the disorder is full-blown, such stimulus-shielding may have little benefit. The early pre-binge stage is also characterized by a fear of becoming fat and a fear of social rejection and allaying or reversing these fears may be the single most important treatment for individuals with the disorder since it would remove the background tone that sets up the dynamics of the disorder. This view is congruent with the findings that cognitive therapies appear to be the most successful in dealing with eating disorders (Fairburn and Harrison, 2003), although the theoretical bases for these therapies differ from ours (Fairburn et al., 2003), that stimuli associated with negative body imagery induce insecurity in bulimics (Tuschen-Caffier et al., 2003) and that neuroticism and low self-esteem are major risk factors in the development of eating disorders (Cervera et al., 2003).

Increasing feelings of hunger and a conflict between drives to eat and to fast are prevalent in the later pre-binge stage. Since binging involves the excessive consumption of food, and since it is postulated that extreme hunger contributes to this excessive intake, one could suggest that measures to avoid the development of excessive hunger may prove helpful. In other words, one could try to tip the balance in favor of eating and against continued fasting earlier on, perhaps by supplying a small but very enticing treat.

Once eating starts though, it is important to avoid the negative consequences of an extremely unbalanced intake of nutrients, not by reducing intake, but by supplying highly nutritious food where successive helpings have declining (but never negative) palatability. This, one may hypothesize, would make a first helping highly desirable and so induce the eating behavior but avoid true binging by terminating the binge prematurely due to successively less palatable helpings. This may mimick the natural case where food becomes less palatable in proportion to the amount consumed in a single sitting, but be artificially construed such as to terminate eating earlier than would otherwise occur.

Regarding the purge stage, it appears that neutralizing the feelings of shame and regret may be helpful to avoid the resumption of the early pre-binge stage. It is not clear that avoiding the purge would do any good, rather, one should avoid the extremes of binging.

Looking at the disorder as a whole, an issue of importance that should receive some attention is that of the progression of the disease. In other words, is there a gradual increase in the strength of eating-inhibitive cognitive processes or do these emerge full-blown? If they are gradual, are there early warning signs that could be of use? The reader is encouraged to consider these questions with the aid of the model and the foregoing material.

Some issues that we cannot address adequately with the model also relate to its progression: it seems that individuals with this disorder may experience a chronic state of poor nutrition despite (or because of?) bingeing. Since dieting itself appears to cause changes in serotonin functioning (see Fairburn and Harrison, 2003 and their references), chronic malnutrition may cause even more problems, hence one should not necessarily expect the early stages of the fully-developed disorder to resemble its later stages. One may have to take recourse to other models or data to understand the effects of malnourishment on the mental states that may emerge later in the progression of the disorder.

The homeostatic model demonstrated here, now provides a basis for a complex explanation of an "abnormal" condition. Although the explanations here are basic working applications of the model to understanding complex behaviors, the reader may realize that there are many other questions and issues that will be raised. There are different aspects of the model that can be analyzed for failure in structure or function. The analysis presented here with *bulimia nervosa* demonstrates a general functional analysis of how the system could fail and produce "abnormal" eating behavior. However, at any area within the model, there can be a significant structural or functional failure. For instance, there may be an abnormality in the functioning of one or more brain centers (i.e. the cortex and VTA) that lead to extreme hedonic state processes. As well, signals between various systems may be excessive or deficient (i.e. abnormal dopamine and serotonin transmissions). The reader is also encouraged to perform an analysis of the model in order to make predictions about how systems can fail or lead to certain conditions/behaviors. For instance, what will occur when: the signals from physiological homeostatic systems related to eating are deficient? Can this condition still lead to binge behavior? As well, the analysis here is without the consideration of set point alterations that may be occurring due to the extreme binge-purge behaviors. It is likely that set points do fluctuate as a result of these behaviors, especially given the large physiological conditions that are created during dieting. What are the specific consequences for lowered or increased set points for bulimic behavior? Such applications of the model may prove to be invaluable for understanding the complex nature of human behaviors.

References

American Psychiatric Association. Diagnostic and statistical manual of mental disorders, Third Edition Revised (DSM-IIIR). Washington: American Psychiatric Association, 1987.

Cervera, S.; Lahortiga, F.; Martýnez-Gonzalez, M. A.; Gual, P.; de Irala-Estevez, J.; Alonso1, Y. 2003. Neuroticism and low self-esteem as risk factors for incident eating disorders in a prospective cohort study. International Journal of Eating Disorders 33: 271-280.

Fairburn, C. G.; Harrison, P. J. 2003. Eating disorders. The Lancet 361: 407-416.

Fairburn, C. G.; Cooper, Z.; Shafran, R. 2003. Cognitive behaviour therapy for eating disorders: a "transdiagnostic" theory and treatment. Behaviour Research and Therapy 41: 509–528.

Keesey, R. E.; Powley, T. L. 1986. The regulation of body weight. Annual Review of Psychology 37: 411-420.

Mrosovsky, N.; Powley, T. L. 1977. Set points for body weight and fat. Behavioral Biology 20: 205-223.

Tuschen-Caffier, B.; Vogele, C.; Bracht, S.; Hilbert, A. 2003. Psychological responses to body shape exposure in patients with bulimia nervosa. Behaviour Research and Therapy 41: 573–586.

Index

Mechanisms of Motivation

Student's Manual

Part I: Overview

INTRODUCTION

> *"I really appreciated the problem-based learning and group work format of the course, as well as the interesting course material. This course has contributed considerably to my understanding of psychology..." Anonymous (1999)*

Problem-based learning approaches have gained wide interest in a number of fields ranging from medical and allied health sciences, computer engineering, and chemistry to psychology (e.g. Dahlgren and Dahlgren, 2002; Johnson et al; 2002; Michel et al., 2002; Srinivasan et al., 2002; Wright et al., 1998). These approaches typically facilitate self-directed learning allowing the student to explore, struggle, and discover as an autonomous agent in the learning process.

> *"I found it excellent the way we were encouraged to analyse and think independently in this course..." Anonymous (2001)*

The student's role is that of active agent: without taking risks, no effective learning occurs. However, taking risks can also result in a poor outcome on an assignment. How then, does one deal with this sort of situation wherever it crops up in life? Invariably the risks associated with independent thinking cause anxiety and the difficulty in finding an answer to the problems posed as part of the course work generate frustration and anger. However, if you know what to expect and are prepared to make an effort, you would have made a very good start to completing this course successfully.

> *"This is the end of my fourth year, and I have never spent so much effort on one course; nor have I enjoyed one more." Anonymous*

We therefore recommend the following approach, but do not wish that you follow it blindly: amend and adjust the approach as you develop your own particular style of learning. You require the following: perseverance (valuable things don't come cheap); knowledge about what to expect emotionally; perseverance; knowledge about what to expect in group dynamics; perseverance; initiative; perseverance; skills for exploration and discovery; perseverance. That's it. We'll discuss these in a bit more detail below.

Part II: Skills

PERSEVERANCE

> *"I found the initial introduction to this course rather frightening, and seriously considered transferring out, as many of my friends did. I am, however, glad I stayed as the course and the style of teaching ended up quite interesting and worthwhile." Anonymous (2000)*

Fools and freeloaders believe in free lunches. Since an effective learning process requires exploration and takes time, plenty of perseverance is called for. Don't give up!

EMOTIONS

> *"This class still has no relevance to motivation as it has been taught before. I even bought the old motivation texts and they simply do not relate. What are we trying to learn?!" Anonymous (1997)*

We strongly recommend that instructors NOT help you, other than providing encouragement, so you can learn how to help yourself. Being left to fight for yourself, you are likely to go through a number of successive emotional stages. There are approximately a dozen of them: (i) confusion; (ii) bewilderment; (iii) panic; (iv) anger and resentment; (v) abandonment of original expectations; (vi) refocusing; (vii) exploration; (viii) trial-and-error; (ix) discovery and insight; (x) increased mastery and satisfaction; (xi) and finally confidence *in your own abilities*. Knowing the sequence in which these stage are likely to occur will help you to determine where you are on the path of intellectual development. It will also make the process less unnerving.

GROUP DYNAMICS

> *"In general, I think the class was well instructed and the class discussions gave us an opportunity to brainstorm the ideas related to lecture topics." Anonymous (1998)*

If you are working in a group, now or somewhere at your future job, keep in mind the following.
(i)   everyone has the potential to make a valuable contribution, but only if you keep listening to them without dismissing their opinions outright and only if you encourage them to share their views;
(ii)   when things go round in circles….stop - it is usually a symptom of a problem, term, or concept that is not well-defined; unless you identify and carefully (re)define the item at fault, you'll be going round and round, but every time less merrily so;
(iii)   if nothing happens, nothing will continue to happen until someone shows enough leadership to get started; with many problems, especially with highly complex ones, it is *more important to get started somewhere, rather than to get started right.*

UNFAMILIAR WORDS/CONCEPTS

> *"Also, I found that he was reluctant to answer questions, but preferred for us to figure it out..." Anonymous (2000)*

It will happen that once in a while you will come across a word or a concept that you are not familiar with. Rather that provide you with everything in the form of a glossary, we recommend that you consult a dictionary, an encyclopedia, or the web to find such information. Many dictionaries and encyclopedias are freely available on-line or can be accessed electronically through your educational institution's library.

PROBLEMS

> *"Assigning homework every lecture was important in allowing me to keep up in class (even when I didn't enjoy doing it sometimes)." Anonymous (1998)*

Here are some general rules to follow when tackling any problem:
(i)   start with known information;
(ii)   explain as many aspects of the phenomenon as possible except when the question indicates otherwise;
(iii)   review your answer to ensure that you are not contradicting yourself anywhere directly or by implication;
(iv)   ensure proper internal functioning -check that the answer accomplishes its task;
(v)   ensure proper external performance - check that your answer is generally consistent with known information outside of the context of the question;
(vi)   use modifications and new elements only where absolutely necessary and flag them;
(vii)   use as high a level of detail as possible given (vi) above;
(viii) use these rules as a checklist before considering the problem 'solved'. (You may want to consider attaching them to assignments that you have to submit as part of your course work.)

AMBIGUITIES

> *"... - he encourages his students to guide their own thinking rather than just rote memorization." Anonymous (1997)*

Ambiguities and uncertainties are common in life. Moreover, they can have considerable risk associated with them. The place to learn how to deal with ambiguities and their associated risks is *here*, where at most the outcome of a course grade may be at stake and not the life of a patient or the livelihood of a family. If you think that you simply cannot afford the risk of an unsatisfactory course outcome now, ask yourself when in your future you will be in a better position to learn about risk. *Our* answer to that question is: "*never*"!

Nevertheless, some people are naturally risk-aversive and cannot proceed to discover on their own. If such is the case for you, this course may not be suitable for you. Others crave the opportunity to discover how to deal with risk and uncertainties in a rational manner and you will receive several chances here to discover how to resolve these problems on your own.

In general, if one is confronted with the problem of ambiguity, one may wish to proceed as follows (if you have a better way of going about it, we want to hear from you!):

(i)   get clarification;
(ii)   get assistance from either verbal or written expert sources;
(iii)   resolve the ambiguities yourself.

When you are confronted with ambiguities *in this course*, YOU **must** resolve the ambiguities. An ambiguity means, by its very nature, that there are at least 2 possible ways of interpretation. For example, if a question appears to have 2 or more possible meanings, say meanings A and B, you must do the following:

(i)   assume that A is correct and answer the question accordingly; when done
(ii)   assume that B is correct and answer the question accordingly; when done
(iii)   work through the remaining possibilities of interpretation, if any, in the same way; finally
(iv)   compare all of the answers, select the most reasonable one, and indicate why you view that as the preferred answer to the original (ambiguous) question. (Do not forget your checklist in the process!)

MAPPINGS

> *"It was challenging to be in a psyc course where critical thinking, integration of topics and understanding, as opposed to rote memorization, were emphasized." Anonymous (1997)*

Mappings are extremely useful methods of uncovering and recording information about unknown things. Therefore they are widely used in a variety of guises called analogies, similes, metaphors, comparisons, charting, and so on. To gain the greatest advantage from a mapping, it has to be applied somewhat rigorously rather than haphazardly.

We consider mappings as being of 2 types: functional mappings and structural mappings. Functional mappings map components of the unknown system onto components of the known system *irrespective of position* if they perform the same function. Structural mappings map adjacent components to adjacent components *irrespective of function*. Quite often functional and structural mappings yield the same result, but not always. Consider the building plans of the 2 dwellings below.

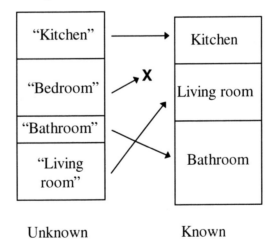

Functional mapping: rooms of the unknown structure are mapped onto the rooms of the known structure based on their similarity of function.

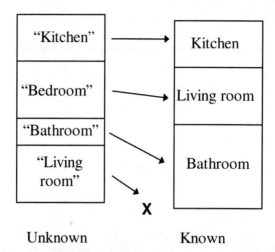

Structural mapping: rooms of the unknown structure are mapped onto the rooms of the known structure based on their similarity of position.

Although we don't want to press the point, we'd argue that functional mappings are the more important. Either way, we suggest that you always do, as far as possible, a functional mapping first and then use a structural mapping to identify those components that you cannot identify functionally. It is strongly recommended that, in the mapping process, you always draw 2 diagrams as visual aids.

Anything can be mapped onto *anything* else, the only difference being in the degree of correspondence observed as a result of the mapping. Since the very point of a mapping is to establish the extent to which different entities correspond, deciding ahead of time that "this" cannot be mapped onto "that" begs the question. Do not hesitate to use mappings oft and don't be discouraged by anyone from developing a mapping habit!

MODELING

"So while I learned very few 'facts', I did learn a different way of looking at psych. and for as difficultthe class was, this is invaluable." Anonymous (2000)

These are guidelines for the construction of a model where you are given information from some source, e.g. one or more articles, research data, a monograph, and so on. If you are confident about your own method of model construction, you are welcome to use it. These guidelines are for those completely unfamiliar with model-building. Instructors, if they want to know what information is contained in the information source(s), can read it themselves. Unless requested, they do not typically want to know what the author(s) think, but what you think. You have to extract the relevant pieces of information from your sources (e.g. an article) and use them as building blocks to construct your own model. You should not construct a model of the information source or elaborate thereon - it serves only as a source of building materials for your model. The information sources are not likely to have enough facts (building materials) for you to complete your model, so you will have to make assumptions (list them) to fill in the gaps. Before you begin the process, read your sources and summarize them. Repeat the process a few times, and generate a new, independent summary every time.

Students who have done well on this type of assignment in the past typically generated several different diagrams and tried them out to see which variant worked best. For this reason you must start early, as soon as you get the assignment. This type of term project requires way more thinking than reading: *you **cannot** do it over a weekend*!

Constructing a model

1.   Enumerate the components. This means that you should take the building (information source) apart and list all the building materials now available for your new building. Do not attempt to renovate the old one! Identify and list all the relevant components.

Example:

good: 1. Fear is generated in part X of the brain.

useless: 1. John Doe at the University of Somewhere experimented on rats to see how fear was generated.

Classify the components. Some are known facts, some are speculative, and some are ideas.

Example:

fact: Rats receiving a cerebroventricular infusion of angiotensin II drank more water (10 ± 2 mL) than those receiving an infusion of isotonic saline vehicle (3 ± 1 mL).

speculation: Ventricles must therefore contain receptors for angiotensin II or permit angiotensin II to diffuse to sites where such receptors are located.

concept: We believe that the ventricles form part of a neural circuit involved in the generation of thirst.

2.   Prioritize the components. Some facts are more important than others. Rank all your facts.

3.   Concatenate the facts. Select a few (e.g. 3) of the most important facts, based on the relevant prioritized list, and connect them together as boxes (objects) and arrows (acts), starting with the highest priority facts. Boxes that are connected one-at-a-time to others are connected in series. Multiple boxes connected to other boxes simultaneously, are connected in parallel. Add the remaining modules, one at a time to complete your model. This would produce a box-model of your phenomenon. Some sets of boxes and arrows belong together - they form modules. Identify the modules.

Note: in general, boxes represent *places*; arrows represent *actions*. Create a model (i.e. a design, blueprint, plan, or map), not a flowchart (i.e. algorithm, recipe, method, or set of directions).

Example:

Model

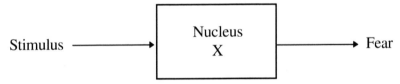

Flowchart

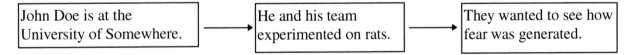

4.   Describe each module. Describe the operation of each module quantitatively (use mathematical formulae if you can) or qualitatively (in words - indicate for each module what happens if you change any attribute of your objects or acts, e.g. when you provide a stronger or weaker connection between 2 boxes, etc.).

5.   List the assumptions. Often it is necessary to make assumptions to complete step 4. You must explicitly list these assumptions at the beginning of your model, they are important. You have to do so when the model is completed and when you know how many/which assumptions were needed. Often, implicit assumptions are used. Make a separate list of the most important of these. How do you tell the difference between implicit and explicit assumptions?

6.   List the variables. Identify those components of your model that can be changed. If body weight in baboons is a function of temperature and rainfall, then temperature and rainfall are independent variables and body weight is a dependent variable. Independent variables can generally be changed by the experimenter (...neither rainfall nor temperature, come to think of it...) and dependent variables are measured (before and after changes have been made to the independent variables). In other words, independent variables are causes and dependent ones are effects.

7. List the boundary conditions. Specify the scope of your model. In other words, indicate the conditions beyond which your model is not applicable (e.g. the model is applicable to how fear is generated in children but not adults).

8. Verify the model. Your model would typically take an 'input variable(s)' of some kind (e.g. rainfall and temperature) and produce an 'output variable(s)' of another kind (e.g. body weight of baboon species). Give the input variable a specific value (e.g. a certain temperature and a certain rainfall; or qualitative values such as "high" temperature and "low" rainfall etc.) and work through the model to see what value the output variable produces (e.g. body weight). Change only one of the input variables (either up or down) and determine the outcome. Does the result make sense? More importantly, does the result accord with the known facts of this phenomenon? Can you falsify the model?

Presenting your model

1. When you write up your model, the resulting paper should contain the following sections with headings: (i) introduction; (ii) theory and model; (iii) prediction and proposed experiments; (iv) discussion; and (v) references.

2. The 'Introduction' should explain why the problem or phenomenon that you are attempting to model is important and what benefits a model would provide in dealing with this phenomenon.

3. The 'Theory and model' section should explain the important facts of the phenomenon and how they are fitted together in your model. Explain the operation of your model. Your assumptions, if you made any, should be listed and your conditions stated here. Do not include the lists of enumerated, classified, and prioritized components, their tentative concatenations, and lists of variables - these lists are only to help you with the model-building process. Provide only your model in its final form as a diagram (see below).

4. The model should include at least 1 full-page box-and-arrow diagram.

5. In the 'Prediction and proposed experiments' section:
    show how the model may be used to make a prediction; and
    describe a (hypothetical) experiment that would allow you to test the prediction.

6. In the 'Discussion' section, discuss some salient points of your model. What insights have you derived from the model?

7. Do not use more than 3 extra references. You should be able to construct the model only with the given reference(s). You should read less and think more about what you read.

8. The model should be at least qualitative.

9. Focus on quality and coherence, not on quantity (i.e. number of pages).

10. Do not ask for help from the instructor/assistant/anyone else - *it will defeat the purpose*. Struggle with the project yourself. The most important part of it is getting started (starting from 'scratch'). Use scrap paper and try out several ideas. You may discuss the model with your colleagues. If you are REALLY stuck, just follow the guidelines above as best you can. Try again a couple of weeks later and keep at it until you are satisfied or until time's up! Read the information sources and summarize them. Use the summary to start constructing your model from.

11. Observe the due date as given and other directives provided by your instructor.

Preparing an outline

        If you are required to provide an outline prior to handing in the model, and no alternative instructions are given, provide items 1 to 4 (inclusive) listed above under the heading 'Constructing a model' as your outline.

REFERENCES

Dahlgren, M. A.; Dahlgren, L. O. 2002. Portraits of PBL: students' experiences of the characteristics of problem-based learning in physiotherapy, computer engineering and psychology. Instructional Science 30: 111-127.

Johnson, E.; Herd, S.; Andrewartha, K.; Jones, S.; Malcolm, S. 2002. Introducing problem-based learning into a traditional lecture course. Biochemistry and Molecular Biology Education 30: 121-124.

Michel, M. C.; Bischoff, A.; Jakobs, K. H. 2002. Comparison of problem-and lecture-based pharmacology teaching. Trends in Pharmacological Sciences 23: 168-170.

Srinivasan, M.; Weiner, M.; Breitfeld, P. P.; Brahmi, F.; Dickerson, K. L.; Weiner, G. 2002. Early introduction of an evidence-based medicine course to preclinical medical students. Journal of General Internal Medicine 17: 58-65.

Wright, J. C.; Millar, S. B.; Kosiuk, S. A.; Penberthy, D. L.; Williams, P. H.; Wampold, B. E. 1998. A Novel Strategy for Assessing the Effects of Curriculum Reform on Student Competence. Journal of Chemical Education 75:986-992.

Woods, D. R. 1994. Problem-based learning: how to gain the most from PBL . Waterdown, ON: Donald R. Woods [Distributed via the McMaster University Bookstore].

ISBN 141201230-9

9 781412 012300